Ministering
with the
earth

Ministering
with the
earth

MARY ELIZABETH MOORE

Chalice Press
St. Louis, Missouri

All scripture quotations, unless otherwise indicated, are from the *New Revised Standard Version Bible,* copyright 1989, Division of Christian Education of the National Council of the Churches of Christ in the USA. Used by permission.

Excerpts from *The Jerusalem Bible,* copyright 1966 by Barton, Longman & Todd, Ltd., and Doubleday, a division of Bantam Doubleday Dell Publishing Group, Inc. Used by permission.

Cover design: Lynne Condellone
Art direction: Michael Domínguez
Interior design: Elizabeth Wright

This book is printed on acid-free, recycled paper.

Visit Chalice Press on the World Wide Web at
www.chalicepress.com

10 9 8 7 6 5 4 3 2 1   98 99 00 01 02 03

Library of Congress Cataloging–in–Publication Data

Moore, Mary Elizabeth, 1945–
    Ministering with the earth / by Mary Elizabeth Moore.
        p.   cm.
    Includes bibliographical references.
    ISBN 0-8272-2323-4
    1. Ecology—Religious aspects—Christianity.   2. Earth—Religious aspects.   I. Title
BT695.5.M67   1998   97–44507
261.8'362—dc21   CIP

Printed in the United States of America

Dedicated to our children—
Rebecca Mathews, Cliff Mathews,
Nan and Mike Fox, Joyce and Rob Cable,
and Glenda and David Kittinger

May they be blessed by God's creation;
May they love the earth
and be better stewards than we have been!

TABLE OF CONTENTS

PROLOGUE

Writing this book has been a journey of a lifetime. My entire life has been engaged in many different ways with the beauties and pains of the earth. With gratitude especially for early camping experiences, I came to know myself related to creation in a deep and inextricable way, and I also came to know intuitively that the relationship was far deeper than I could comprehend or articulate. This sense has only grown for me over time, alongside a gradual discovery in my college and young adult years of an urgent crisis emerging in the world. The crisis is a crying need for economic and social justice for human beings, for peace among nations and religious bodies, for the well-being of plants and animals and people, for protection of the soil and air and water. The crisis calls for no less than a vision of justice and well-being for all of God's creation.

The contrast between the more idyllic experiences of my youth and the crisis mentality of my adulthood presents a worthy tension—one that denies the adequacy of ideals without crisis awareness *or* crisis awareness without ideals. It also denies the viability of caring for the earth only for the sake of people, or posing a competition between issues of human justice and environmental integrity. Having said this, problems immediately emerge regarding our common words, concepts, metaphors, and actions.

Words cannot contain the wholeness and relatedness of the universe. Eco-justice, a term emerging in the early 1970s, was intended to hold together human justice and ecological well-being, but alas, justice is still predominantly associated with *human* justice, and "eco" is still a modifier, thus implying service to human justice. Even worse, the term is often used conversely, to refer only to the well-being of the non-human world, while economic and social justice are not really encompassed at all. Consider also such words as "the integrity of creation" and "dominion over the earth"—words that have been critiqued, formulated, and interpreted, but which can easily be ignored, romanticized, or focused only toward human welfare. Such words, and the problems that arise from them, have motivated some important theological investigation, as well as the introduction of significant new words, such as "environmental racism."[1] Unfortunately, the analyses can also reinforce self-satisfaction, confusion, or exasperation. How slippery are our efforts with words to hold everything together!

This leads to the problem of *concepts*. Much work has been done in philosophical and theological analysis of the dominant conceptualizations in Western societies, Christian churches, and other religious communities, recognizing that these conceptualizations actually support the abuse of the earth and all who dwell thereon. Some of the leading twentieth-century philosophers, theologians, and ethicists have turned themselves to this task, and many of these people are quoted in the pages of this book. People like Thomas Berry, Leonardo Boff, Susan Griffin, John B. Cobb, Jr., Larry Rasmussen, George E. Tinker, Rosemary Radford Ruether, David Ray Griffin, Jurgen Moltmann, and Delores Williams have identified conceptual biases that impede people from a healthy and responsible relationship with the earth. One of the fundamental conceptual problems is Western dualistic thinking, which sets up either-or choices and hierarchies of mind over body, culture over nature, history over cosmology, and so forth. Another major problem is the denial of organic relationships in the universe. When people focus their attention on parts of reality in isolation from other parts, they can very easily respond to issues of concern by categorizing and prioritizing, thus missing the integral connections. Still another problem is the Newtonian emphasis on cause and effect, and the mechanistic worldview in which people focus on external relationships and respond to problems by seeking causes and fixing them. Such conceptual impairments are only intensified by other conceptual inheritances from the Enlightenment—individualism, the priority of thinking over feeling, and the educational values of acquiring information and perfecting skills in analysis and logic. How heavy is the challenge if we are to analyze and reform these conceptual frames, for they have anchored human beings in clear worldviews, even when everything else in the world—technologies, values, ways of life— were changing with overwhelming rapidity!

This leads to the problem of *images and metaphors*. Perhaps we can escape the dread problems of words and concepts if we focus instead on images and root metaphors. No one has attended to this possibility more fully than Sallie McFague, for whom this has been a lifework. Others, such as Catherine Keller, have moved in extraordinarily creative and challenging directions with the analysis of metaphors as well. In McFague's work, we are confronted with some of the dominant God and world metaphors—such as Father and child— and, then, we are offered alternative metaphors—such as God as Friend, or the world as the Body of God.[2] In Keller's work, the web is a central metaphor to communicate the interrelatedness and mutual responsibility of all beings and all reality.[3] Still other scholars analyze and propose other alternatives; this work has disrupted customary patterns of thinking and contributed primal and secondary images for further meditation and conceptualization. The actual roots and sources of those images are not always clear, as in McFague's work, nor is the relationship they bear to the texts, theories, practices, and religious experiences of the past. At the same time, the images are rich in promise for offering new conceptualizations and practices, perhaps even inspiring transformative religious experience. This is all yet to be seen because the dialogue among those who deal with words, concepts, and metaphors is often fairly limited. How profound are the metaphors and models that guide us, and how limited are we in seeing their connections with words, concepts and, even more difficult, actions!

This leads, then, to the question of *action*, the most neglected and trivialized root of justice, peace, and integrity of creation. Most action by churches, judicatories and ecumenical bodies has taken three forms: (1) offering proposals for focused actions in justice-building, peacemaking, or caring for the earth; (2) engaging in strategic work on particular issues; and (3) formulating resolutions, confessional or interreligious pronouncements, and ecumenical or denominational purpose statements.

The first of these actions is obviously significant and obviously limited. By *engaging in a list of particular actions*, people shape a way of life, make some difference in the world, and open themselves to greater understanding and transformed action. The dangers of self-satisfaction, misdirected or insignificant efforts, or avoiding larger issues and more systemic responses are obvious. Fortunately, these dangers are often starkly obvious to those who participate in such actions, for people make themselves vulnerable to critique simply by stepping out and doing something (critique from themselves as well as from others). Ironically, this "list of actions" approach is the easiest place to begin, and even those who critique it also advocate it. For example, although Rosemary Radford Ruether has critiqued the dangers of placing responsibilities on the private sphere of home and family (traditionally the sphere of women), she herself practices and recommends particular actions for individuals and communities.[4] Likewise, Dieter Hessel, who introduces his *After Nature's Revolt* by recognizing the importance of complex human responses and by questioning the real effects of contemporary environmental consciousness, actually closes his introduction with a list of proposed actions.[5] Though the closing proposals are broad in sweep, they still represent a list of particular actions.

The second form of action, *engaging in strategic work on particular issues*, has been very effectively done, and examples abound in movements for peace, civil rights, community organizing, labor organizing, and so forth. In this work, large systems are usually taken more seriously, but the interaction of systems is often ignored, such as the interaction of labor systems with the cultural systems of diverse racial and cultural communities. Womanist scholars have been particularly insightful in calling attention to these anomolies.[6] Likewise, the actions taken are often incongruous with the goals, exemplified by militant actions for making peace or the practice of demonizing particular groups in order to bring harmony to a threatened ecosystem.

Finally, the third kind of action—*formulating resolutions, pronouncements and purpose statements*—has uncovered the slippery slopes of words and concepts, at the same time identifying new ways of imagining, conceptualizing, and expressing concerns by introducing new words into the dialogue. Such work stirs thinking, challenges destructive modes of thought, recreates language and theological formulations, and raises consciousness. Like the action lists, this work can yield self-satisfaction or can have little or no concrete effect. On the other hand, the very practice of creating such statements challenges those who compose, vote, or study the words to think deeply and reshape their responses to God and the world. They also provide opportunity to form alliances for further action.

We are left with three common patterns of action, and they are significant indeed. I propose that one ingredient is still largely missing, and that is the analysis of action itself. Just as words, concepts and metaphors deserve attention when we reflect on the relationship of people and the earth, so, in fact, do actions. *The purpose of this book is to reflect on action for the sake of action, particularly to reflect on acts of ministry for the sake of projecting a new vision of ministering with the earth.* Alongside biblical and historical texts, and alongside philosophical and theological formulations, numerous stories of action will be told and analyzed.

This book is infused with stories. Some are drawn from one passing moment in time; some, from encounters which shaped my personal journey; and others, from ethnographic research in congregations. In all cases, the stories are taken seriously, however, interpreted as texts, or sources of wisdom. They are intended neither as ornamentation or illustration, though they *will* often embellish and illustrate. The reader, of course, is welcome to engage the stories in whatever way he/she is inspired.

The book is intended to edify and inspire, to raise questions and evoke imagination. If I have done my work well, you will discover a theological framework of sacrality and a challenge to many long-held theological assumptions and biblical interpretations in Christianity. You will also be engaged in your own ways in analyzing the actions of individuals and communities— living and dead—and looking to them for positive guidance as well as for evidence of distorted theological interpretation and ministerial actions. In short, I have told and reflected on many stories in these pages, but as narratives are never contained in neat boxes, these narratives are now yours for dancing, singing, wrestling, and wondering. This book will live only insofar as your engagement stirs your own stories and ideas. This book will be worthy only insofar as your work, joined with mine, contributes genuinely to ministering with the earth. May it be so!

With that invitation, I add my words of gratitude to people who have already joined with me in the dialogue and action that shaped this book. Thank you to friends in El Paso, Texas, with whom this consciousness first emerged, and to administrators at Claremont School of Theology—Robert Edgar, Allen Moore, and Marjorie Suchocki—who have encouraged action projects, pedagogical experiments, conferences, and writing. Thank you to students who have influenced me in more ways than even I know. I have acknowledged many of them in notations throughout the book. Two in particular—Beverly Jones and Tisa Wenger—have commented on portions of this manuscript, for which I am most grateful.

One can hardly be aware of the power in an institution's ethos. Certainly, Claremont School of Theology's long commitment to eco-justice and its continuing work as a lead institution of the Center for Respect of Life and the Environment (CRLE) have shaped an ethos that challenges me. Special gratitude goes to Claremont colleagues and former colleagues—Karen Baker-Fletcher, Kasimu (Garth) Baker-Fletcher, Howard Clinebell, John Cobb, Dean Freudenberger, David Griffin, Joseph Hough, John Lyle, and Carolyn Stahl-Bohler—whose speaking and writing have inspired and deepened my resolve. Thanks to Richard Clugston, whose leadership of CRLE has been important to me as well as to Claremont. I am also grateful to Anita Cabrera, who created a Food Service that served the spirit of our community, and to Chip Johnson and all who have worked endlessly to create a more ecologically sustainable campus—Roberto Cifuentes, Eduardo Iligan, Amilcar Argueta, Guillermo Hernandez, and Joe Jimenez.

Several others have supported the actual writing of this book. First, I thank the trees, birds, and floating clouds outside my window, without which I would have given up this quest. Thank you to faculty secretaries Olga Morales and Sharon Thompson, who supported me in countless ways during the writing of this book, and to reference librarian, Betty Clements, who was avid in finding hard-to-find books on interlibrary loan, always mellow and always smiling. Thanks to Merle Edgar, quilter extraordinaire, who read the Appendix and gave invaluable guidance regarding the quilting metaphor. And thank you to treasured colleagues—Kathleen Greider, Bill Clements, Marvin Sweeney, Pamela Couture, and Frank Rogers. Indeed, I owe a huge thanks to Frank Rogers, my colleague in religious education and eco-justice action in Claremont—a partner in every sense and a constant inspiration for going one step further.

Two people have far surpassed my ability to express gratitude. Gabriele Mayer has read and commented on every word of this book, offering critique, support, and meticulous searching for missing sources and commas. Allen Moore has been more than a husband; he has also read and commented on every word and has given much of himself so that I could adjust life to write, revise, and edit again and again.

Finally, this book is dedicated to our children—Rebecca Mathews, Cliff Mathews, Nan and Mike Fox, Joyce and Rob Cable, and Glenda and David Kittinger. These are the people who inherit the earth and the stewardship of our generation; these are the people who prepare the next generation to love the earth even more than we do. I wish them Godspeed. May they do better than we have done!

A NOTE ON TERMINOLOGY

The central term used in this book for ministering with the earth is *God-centered, earthbound ministry*. Such a ministry is focused on God, directed to God, and serving God's purposes as best understood. It is, at the same time, grounded in a particular time and place, responsive to the realities of that place, and responsible to the interconnected web of the whole earth. In short, the phrase signifies that we are standing on holy ground.

Earthbound is also a play on words. The recovery of religious sensitivities will surely involve binding ourselves again and again to God and all that God loves. After all, the word *religion* comes from the root *religio,* meaning "to bind again," thus referring to the binding of people with God, with one another, and with the whole of the natural world. The term *earth* is used in this book to represent all of God's creation, recalling the concreteness of rocks and soil, sea and sky, plants and animals and humans. The term *cosmos* is less often used, simply for the sake of focus; however, it is introduced from time to time as a recognition that all of the cosmos is included in God's creation.

ONE

Sacred Hopes:
Gathering Hopes for Ministering
with the Earth

Imagine people gathered in the breezeway of their church for Sunday services in Hawaii. The people are Samoan, Filipino, and European in descent, and they gather in the warm breeze of a hot summer day. Their eyes face toward a small lake and the church garden, and their voices sing traditional hymns from their three cultures.

※

Imagine a child—abused by her parents at home—who travels with some close friends to their church's weekend retreat. A young woman catches the sadness in the child's eye and befriends her. She asks her about school, favorite sports, and family; mostly she listens to whatever the child wants to say. She invites the little girl to sit with her at the evening campfire and to join in singing with a small group of folks who linger over the embers after others go to their cabins. Soon the little girl snuggles close to this young woman and sits in her lap; she feels safe, and she is safe in this moment in time.

※

Imagine a summer camp bustling with adults with varying physical abilities. These people often receive pity from others, but not often do they receive opportunities to play, develop new skills, meet and pray with others in a mountainous camp setting. Inspired, they begin plans to communicate their concerns and hopes to the larger church.

※

Imagine a church that has become biracial in the past ten years as the neighborhood around the church changed.[1] Many in the congregation say that the most binding

1

event in their life as a community is the annual homecoming in which the men barbe-
cue on an open pit most of the night and the women prepare other foods in the kitchen.
Working together for this yearly event and welcoming former members to the home-
coming bind the people with one another and with the congregation's past.

Imagine a church camp for people who are diagnosed as HIV positive or with
AIDS—people whose family and friends and local churches have often rejected or
ignored them, not knowing how to respond. Imagine the opportunity of these people to
express themselves in artistic forms, to talk with people who share and understand
their journey in living with AIDS, to exercise their bodies and sense of humor, and to
nourish their spiritual depths.

Across the world Christian churches seek to minister with the earth; these
stories bear witness to that! But the stories, real as they are, seem a bit romantic in a world where confusion reigns regarding the earth and the church's
responsibility to it. Even in such a world confusion is not the last word, however. Churches, overwhelmed as they are, express their concern for the earth
by holding an annual event, an Earth Day celebration, or a special camping
activity. But herein lies a fundamental problem; these activities cannot be the
last word either.

What is the problem that gives urgency to a book called *Ministering with*
the Earth? What is the problem of ministry when the scenarios described above
take place every day? What is the problem when churches already issue public decrees and take actions in local communities far and wide? The problem
is that questions of justice and ecological sustainability are often seen as a list
of urgent issues, but the relationship among these issues and the significance
of ministering with the earth as a way of life is often lost.

More specifically, issues of the earth are frequently trivialized or left to
the work of a few ecological enthusiasts. They are often disembodied from
issues of justice and peace. Or people establish a congenial combat zone within
their churches, creating a friendly (or not-so-friendly) competition among
concerns for justice, peace, sustainability, evangelism, and nurture. In such an
atmosphere, people expect to choose which concerns they value most and to
lift those concerns above others. In such an atmosphere, people assume that
issues are like flags to be waved, rather than signals of pain and possibility in
a complex web of life. Meanwhile, possibilities of ministering with the earth
pass by, almost unnoticed. And the possibility that God-centered, earthbound
ministry could be a paradigm for the church's life never reaches the horizons
of consciousness.[2]

All the while, Christian churches sponsor outdoor ministries in many
forms. Sometimes these are called revivals, camp meetings, picnics, or church
anniversaries; sometimes they are called retreats, camping trips, or church
camps for persons of differing ages, interests, or abilities; sometimes they are
simply normal Sunday services. Whatever the form, these are important

opportunities to minister with the earth and to build up the community of faith. Whatever the form, the church has often taken these ministries for granted or seen them as specialized activities that supplement the central ministry of the church, certainly not contributing significantly to Christian witness in the larger society.

The most urgent purpose of this book is *to inspire the church to minister with the earth in all of its coming and going, its doing and being.* To minister with the earth is to serve God in such a way that we care *for* the earth, receive *from* the earth, and join *with* the earth in praise of our Maker and in healing our planet. This is a ministry of covenantal living with God and the human community and the earth. For this reason, priority is given to action. The more precise purpose of this book, then, is the one given in the Prologue—*to reflect on acts of ministry for the sake of projecting a new vision of ministering with the earth.* Specific actions, such as those described in the stories of this book or others labeled as outdoor ministries, have potential to awaken the church to this larger vision by stirring appreciation for God's sacred creation and lifting possibilities for the wider ministry of worship, sacramental celebration, preaching, teaching, and serving. All of ministry, finally, has potential for reminding people of the holy ground on which we stand, the unprecedented crises facing our planet, and the opportunities in ordinary Christian life to minister with the earth.

Ministry with the earth is present in the stories with which we began. It is present in our own lives. It is present in stories of the earth. *The specific purpose of this chapter is to gather sacred hopes for ministering with the earth by studying stories of hope.* Ministries close to the earth are already significant for some ethnic and cultural groups, such as Native American and Native Canadian communities. Thus, much can be learned about ministering with the earth from peoples in diverse cultures and regions of the world. In many parts of Africa and the Pacific Islands, Christian liturgy and teaching are infused with a sense of God's presence in creation, and ministry regularly takes place out-of-doors. In other parts of the world, as in Central Europe, camp meetings are considered important ways to introduce young people to the fullness of the gospel within a close living community. In many parts of Latin America and Africa, outdoor festivals are an important complement to religious observances within the church's sanctuary.

With this variety in mind, I invite you to consider God-centered, earth-bound ministries as having a potential fullness that is of great importance in building up the body of Christ, equipping people for ministry, and restoring the relationship between human beings and the rest of creation. Although such ministries are often ignored or pushed to the side, they are vital for re-pairing an embattled world in which the ravages of war, religious dissension, increasing gaps between rich and poor, abuse of children, and destruction of the earth leave a bleak landscape. People and lands cry out for justice and compassion. In such a world, ministering with the earth is an effort to partici-pate in the sacred circle of God's creation—to participate with God and with the earth in repairing the world. In so doing, we seek to embody the Hebrew concept of *tikkun olam* (repair of the world)—a vision of social, political, and religious transformation. *Tikkun olam* is grounded in hope for the restoration of the world, or the restoration of justice and righteousness. This hope emanates from God, but it also requires human action.[3]

Recognizing the urgency of ministering with the earth and the diversity of communities engaging in ministry, I offer this book in the hope that it will relate differently in different communities. I also hope that it will be received as an invitation to all communities to participate more fully in ministering with the earth. Particular communities will find the ways that are most natural and meaningful to them to engage with the earth in ministry, and hopefully we will continue to learn from one another.

A Personal Story

This book was born in me when I was ten years old—a camper at a two-week Girl Scout camp that I had begged my parents to let me attend. Within the first two days, I realized that this camp was going to be more of a challenge than I had realized. On the third day, I developed a strange disease that caused me great stomach pains but no symptoms that anyone else could see. I wrote miserable letters home and finally became so ill that I was moved to the infirmary. After two days of pink medicine I was no better, and I was begging to be sent home. I spent the entire first week in and out of the infirmary. Finally, I waited for the director to return from church on Sunday, and I asked her if I could go home. Her answer was a firm and uncompromising no.

At my wits' end, I returned to my cabin and told my counselor, Thorny, that I did not feel like participating in the evening program. For the first time, she called me into her cabin (separate from ours), and she explained to me that *she* was at her wits' end. She said, "I have done everything I can think of to help you enter into camp and enjoy yourself; I have finally given up on you because I realize that nothing I do will make any difference; you are the only one who can make the adjustment." With that, I left, totally dejected, but I *did* participate in the evening program. To my surprise, I found it delightful, and to my surprise again, the sun seemed a little brighter the next day, and the camp more fun. The second week of camp was one of the best experiences of my life. I entered every activity with zest and with the fullest possible effort, and I enjoyed every minute. When my parents arrived to get me at the end of that second week, my first words to them were, "Next year I want to go to camp for a month."

I did, in fact, attend camp for the next five summers (two months most years), and I was a camp counselor through college. My faith and my love of life were nourished and transformed through those years, thanks to the mountains, counselors, and campers who shared their lives with me, and thanks to God who revealed the holy so clearly to us among the trees. To the counselor whom I knew only as "Thorny," the counselor who forced me to look into myself for an attitude overhaul, I shall always be grateful.

I share this story in part because it was one of my first intensive experiences of living close to the earth. I share it also because it was one of the more dramatic conversion experiences of my life—one that opened me to many conversions yet to come. I share it, however, for one more reason; it set for me a way of looking at life that has influenced me ever since. I came to see myself as responsible for my own response to life—not always for the particular circumstances of my life, but for the attitudes and actions that I choose in responding to those circumstances.

The legacy of that first camping experience was to live with me for years to come. When I was fourteen or fifteen years old, my aunt lived with us for about six months while my uncle (her husband) lived in a sanitarium undergoing treatment for tuberculosis. This was a trying time for my aunt, to whom I was very close. Daily, she drove the several miles to visit my uncle, whose healing was uncertain. As time moved on, my aunt became more depressed and more cross; every evening she worried about my uncle's condition and grumbled about her horrible life. After several weeks of listening to this, I reached my youthful wits' end. I said to my aunt: "I give up on you, Shush, because I have done everything I can think of to make you happy, and nothing works; you are going to have to do something yourself to accept your situation and to deal with it." A week or so later, my aunt—about four times my age—said to me, "You know, you were right, Mary Elizabeth; I need to change my attitude and my way of living with these problems."

Several years later, my aunt was to refer again to that moment of truth between us. The last time I visited her before she died, she was in the hospital, much weakened by cancer. She reminded me once again of that moment so many years earlier. She said, "I have always been grateful to you for what you told me that time when your Uncle Clinton was so ill; you helped me turn my life around." My memory of that moment was not nearly so vivid as my aunt's; I suspect that I had simply reacted as an upstart kid, repeating actions and words that had reached me when I was in a similar desperate situation a few years earlier at camp. Thorny's gift to me had not been pleasant, but I had received it in a low moment of my life, and I passed it on to my aunt in a momentous moment of her life.

Such is the power of camping, or any experience of living closely with the natural world, with other people, and with one's own emotions. In such moments, people experience the beauties and strains of relationships and the realities of community life in which the actions of each person affect the life of the entire community. These moments inspire what Gregory Cajete calls "thinking the highest thought," or "thinking of one's self, one's community, and one's environment richly."[4] Such thinking, according to Native American traditions, contributes to living "a good life"—a life of respect, compassion, and spiritual wholeness.[5]

I have learned much about living from the simple camping experience of my childhood. Some of it, enlarged by other stories and research, finds its way into the pages of this book. As an initial reflection, however, I will identify some insights from this single personal story; these insights have quite a lot to do with why I have written the book:

1. *Camping is a powerful context for social and personal change.* In camping and other intensive earthbound ministries, people are vulnerable to see realities they have never seen and to try responses they have never tried.

2. *Transformation is sometimes mediated in unexpected ways through unexpected people.* Not only did I learn an enduring lesson from Thorny, but I did not even like her. I found her from the beginning of camp to be gruff and cold, and I could not admit to myself for some time what an important influence she had had on my life.

3. *Camping experiences can have an enduring influence for the whole of a person's life, and for a larger community as well; the influences spread.* I have focused here on one story, and on the counselor whose words have echoed in my voice a few times since. Other aspects of that early camping experience have also endured. I discovered in the camp that I was capable of a dramatic reversal of attitude; I was able to give myself fully to a community and its activities, actually changing my relationship with it.

4. *Giving oneself to living can nourish interpersonal relationships, physical abilities, and self-confidence.* Only later did I learn that such active living *nourishes the whole of spiritual life.* As I invested myself in camp life during the second week of that first camping experience, I grew in wisdom and in stature and in relationship with God and other people.

5. *An imperfect camp with imperfect counselors and imperfect campers can mediate grace.* I had far richer camping experiences later in my life—experiences in which spiritual and interpersonal relationships were nourished more deeply, community life was stronger, and the earth was allowed to be more fully a part of camping life. The fact remains, however, that this first camp of my experience, flawed as it was (as any camp will be), mediated grace to me and to many others.

6. *God and God's creation are present and active, even in those situations where God seems most far away.* I can remember moments in that summer camp when I turned to God for help, and no recognizable help came; yet, I remember the pure wonder of sleeping under the stars. In retrospect, I believe that God was active in my life and in this camp from beginning to end.

These initial reflections are not intended to exhaust the meaning of camping or earthbound ministries, nor to form the framework of this book. They do sow seeds for upcoming reflections, and they reveal some of my motivations for writing. These initial reflections are only a beginning, however, because much more is at stake than one person's joy, and much more wisdom is needed than one person's experience.

A Circular Story of the Earth

A generation goes, a generation comes—
They are nothing but puffs, puffs, puffs of wind!
But the earth remains forever—
Circling, circling, circling in cycles never ending!
The sun rises and falls,
The wind blows round and then it returns,
And streams flow into the sea, flowing again and again—
Circling, circling, circling in cycles never ending!
"What has been is what will be,
    and what has been done is what will be done;
    there is nothing new under the sun."
Circling, circling, circling in cycles never ending!
And the people come and go,
Come and go,
And what they did,
Nobody remembers and nobody knows.
You and I are but a puff, a puff, a puff of wind
But God's world is circling, circling, circling in cycles never ending!
And God—the Mystery of mysteries—
Lives at the beginning and at the end,
Circling in the mystery—
The eternal source of our enjoying
But always and forever beyond our knowing.[6]

Far beyond the comprehension of any individual or community is another story—the story of the earth. In the four and one-half billion years of the earth's existence, no moment has been of greater urgency than the present, for so much of the planet's life is under threat. Even as the urgency grows, however, the planet earth continues to do what it does best. Daily the earth rotates around on its axis, and yearly it circles the sun. It lives close enough to the sun to receive heat and far enough away to prevent the burning of its fragile atmosphere, its mountains and valleys, its plants and animals. And as the planet is circling, the moon is circling around the earth, glowing on the darkest nights and sometimes on the shiniest days. And as the planet is circling, the seasons of the earth are cycling from winter to spring, summer and fall, or from wet season to dry season and back again. This circling and cycling shapes the rhythms of a very large earth story. The rhythms may evoke a sense of passing moments, as in the introductory poem based on Ecclesiastes 1; it can also evoke a sense of vanity or worthlessness, as in other translations of the Hebrew word *hebel*, used twenty-eight times in Ecclesiastes.[7]

All the while, the cycling of the seasons continues, and the cycles of interdependent living also continue. Plants draw in sunlight and, through a process of photosynthesis, convert the sunlight to energy, then breathe out oxygen, which is breathed in by animals and transformed into energy within their bodies. Animals then breathe out carbon dioxide and water, which is received by the plants as raw materials for making carbohydrates to sustain themselves. But these carbohydrates also sustain the animals who eat the plants and breathe the oxygen that the plants have released as a byproduct of their "plantly" work. Thus, the natural process is an interdependent cycle; every part of the creation needs, and is needed by, others. Further, the various parts make their unique contributions by being themselves—by being and doing what they are created to be and do.

To complexify the picture still further, the tiniest bacteria and fungi also participate in the cycle; they break down those animals and plants that die and fall into decay, releasing carbon into the atmosphere. The disintegrating process of limestone releases carbon into the atmosphere as well. Thus the earth is created and sustained by the work of bacteria and fungi on rotting matter and by the work of the wind and rain on limestone; even the processes of decay and erosion are contributing to the renewal of the earth. Scientifically, the complementary processes described here are called the carbon cycle. In everyday language, they are simply nature's program of recycling. In spiritual language, they represent the circle of Life—a circle in which we meet the Spirit of Life. This is a circle in which every creature of the earth receives from, and shares with, other creatures for the well-being of the whole.

The carbon cycle is paralleled by other cycles, such as the natural food chain in which plants produce food, which is eaten by animals. Then, both the plants and animals die, only to be decomposed by the natural processes in which small organisms, such as bacteria and insects, feed on the dead and thereby enrich the soil, which can then sustain the growth of more plants and animals.

On this circling earth with its circling seasons and its interdependent circles of relationship, we also find mountains and valleys—old and new—and mountains that are still forming through the awesome movement of volcanoes and earthquakes. The mountains and valleys are themselves interrelated, most often arising from the movement of the twelve tectonic plates that form the outer crust of the earth like the cracked shell of an egg. These plates are like a crust surrounding the whirl of energy inside the earth, and they form the base that undergirds the visible formations of planet earth—the mountains, valleys, rivers, and seas.

Not only do the plates undergird the earth's formations, but they also help create them, for the plates continually move against each other and release pressure from deep inside the earth's surface. Volcanic activity arises between the tectonic plates, as on the Island of Hawaii, where volcanoes are still active. As the plates shift, however, volcanoes of earlier times become dormant or extinct. Thus, long ago, when the plates of the earth were in different positions, volcanoes were quite active in forming Kauai, Oahu, Maui, and other Hawaiian islands; now those are quiet, while Hawaii (the youngest island) is still growing. In addition to volcanoes, earthquake activity is also greatest at the edge of the tectonic plates where one plate rubs against another.

The movements on the surface of the earth are rooted in movements deep within the crust of the earth—another circle!

Why would we introduce such a story as this within a book focused on Christian ministry? The answer is very simple. The early Hebrews probably developed their creation stories *after* they experienced deliverance from slavery in Egypt, and after they came to see themselves as a people of Yahweh (God). Their sense of shared history with Yahweh led them eventually to seek their relationship with the whole of human and cosmic history. To do so, they drew upon the cosmologies of their day. Similarly, when Christians focus on their shared Christian history and Hebrew origins, they naturally yearn to understand their relationship with the larger cosmic story. We can do this by engaging with the cosmologies and cosmological questions of our day.

Stories of the Cosmos: A Question of Language

Although I have been focusing on a story of the earth within the solar system of this galaxy, the circles do not end here. The birth of the earth itself took place in relation to the many galaxies of the cosmos. Some 18 billion years ago, as the scientific story goes, the forces of the cosmos were born— forces like gravity and electromagnetic and nuclear energy. So how do we tell such a story? What language do we use?

According to Thomas Berry, this is a very important question, especially in light of the dominant industrial myth that explains the earth in technological, human-centered language. For Berry:

> It's all a question of story. We are in trouble just now because we do not have a good story. We are in-between stories. The Old Story, the account of how the world came to be and how we fit into it, is not functioning properly. We have not learned the New Story.[8]

Berry is not concerned with disputing creation stories of the world's religions. He disputes the story of the industrial age, which has carried power as if it were a religion. He wants people to learn from the earth and to speak a language informed by movements of the earth. He wants Christians to restore their interest in cosmology. According to Berry, the story of the cosmos is essential for human life; thus, "We cannot discover ourselves without first discovering the universe, the earth and the imperatives of our own being."[9]

So what kind of language do we need in this new story? As many scientists tell the story, the birth began in a big explosion from a single nucleus— what many call the "Big Bang."[10] Others, like Rosemary Radford Ruether, prefer to bring theological sensitivities to bear and to describe this scientific story of beginnings with words such as "cosmic egg" or "superabundant nucleus."[11] Ruether wants to move away from mechanistic thinking and to recover a sense of mystery and interrelationality; thus, she offers alternatives:

> Mechanistic thought is reductionist...Its language prefers nonliving parts to living and dynamic wholes. This bias disposes scientists to

describe the extraordinary mystery of life's origins as the Big Bang, a term that suggests a loud explosion, rather than choosing a term, such as the "cosmic egg" or the "superabundant nucleus," that might put us in touch with the wonder of the very story that they themselves have uncovered. The masculinist bias undoubtedly also operates here in the choice of a metaphor of destructive violence, rather than of gestation and birth.[12]

So what is the earth's story? Was it also born from a cosmic egg? Our planet probably emerged late in the birth of the cosmos, as did our entire solar system. As stars exploded, new elements were formed, and more stars exploded, bringing still more stars into being until, eventually, the star that we know as the sun came to be. Along with the sun, the planets of our solar system emerged as well, and with them, the planet earth. This probably took place more than 4.5 billion years ago.

As Thomas Berry retells this scientific story, the galactic drama unfolds in the Story of the Universe:

> The Story of the Universe is the story of the emergence of a galactic system in which each new level of being emerges through the urgency of self-transcendence. Hydrogen in the presence of some millions of degrees of heat emerges into helium. After the stars take shape as oceans of fire in the heavens they go through a sequence of transformations. Some eventually explode into the stardust out of which the solar system and the earth take shape.[13]

This story according to Berry draws upon an expansive language that connects the earth with the whole cosmos. Rosemary Radford Ruether also uses the language of stars and stardust. Drawing from astrophysics, she points out that elements of the earth, including our human bodies, were formed from "the alchemy of exploding stars and came to us from the galaxies as stardust."[14] Further, earth scientists have demonstrated that "all the elements that make up our present bodies have been circulated billions of times through other biotic and abiotic beings throughout the 4.5 billion-year history of earth's evolution."[15] To give poetic depth to her point, Ruether explains what this means:

> The elements of our bodies were once part bacteria that floated in the primal seas, rocks that were crumbled by wind, rain, and plants to make soil, insects that ate the algae of primal coastal pools, reptiles and birds that ate the algae, giant ferns nibbled by dinosaurs, as well as the bodies of those dinosaurs themselves, myriad plants, animals, and their decaying bodies that found their way back to the earth and waters as nutrients, or were cycled through the air to descend as life-giving rain.[16]

So the stories of the earth and our human ancestors link us with the whole cosmos—with movements of energy; with movements that break some entities apart and give birth to new ones; with awesome changes that have taken place over billions of years. We are connected elementally with everything that exists in the cosmos.

The story presented here is not a complete version of the scientific story. It is certainly not told as a scientific story to be debated against a biblical story of creation; the biblical stories form a major focus of chapter 2 and succeeding chapters. What we do have here is a story that bursts the confines of ordinary language and evokes words such as Big Bang, cosmic egg and stardust. Thus, I share this description of whirling energy and matter as a not-so-simple story— one that is based on scientific evidence to be sure, but one that is nothing more than the best story that scientists can tell. Scientists have drawn what they do know and what they do not know into a narrative describing the origins of the cosmos and the earth.

Ecological Stories: A Question of Destruction

One more element of this story requires further attention, and that is the best story that ecologists can tell about the destructive forces at work in the cosmos and, more specifically, in the earth. The earth is presently facing challenges of unfathomable proportions. The earth is being stripped of resources, even renewable resources that cannot be renewed as fast as they are being used. The earth is filled with more and more people with larger and larger appetites for consumption. Resources are used and waste is tossed away. The encroachment of technology, population explosion, and over-consumption wears the earth and its atmosphere away. Consequently, the ozone layer is diminishing, the globe is warming, rain forests are disappearing, vast tracts of land are becoming deserts, and nations and factions within nations are embroiled in conflicts regarding who should do what in resolving environmental crises.

In reporting on the ecological crisis, James Nash observes that the term "environmental problem" is "a monumental understatement, comparable to calling a nuclear conflagration a fire."[17] He adds, "The ecological crisis is not a single, discrete problem, but rather a massive mosaic of intertwined problems that adversely affect humans and 'every creeping thing.'"[18] And so we are greeted by another circle, a circle of destruction in which relationships within the earth, and between the earth and the rest of the cosmos, have potential for diminishing or destroying the planet and all who live on it.

Here we meet an ugly part of our story—one in which people worldwide seem to have little doubt that a crisis exists but cannot agree on diagnoses and prescriptions for change. Diagnosis is difficult when scientists are still studying and have not fully resolved such questions as global warming. But diagnosis is even more difficult when people, caught in their own social interests and values, seek to understand the problem by casting blame or responsibility on others—people in other parts of the world, in other vocations, with other values.

Diagnosis has moved in many significant directions. Consider a few. Some people attribute ecological problems to a Western ethical system based on individualism and profit-seeking; this diagnosis suggests an alternative in the form of a more communitarian ethic.[19] Other people identify the ecological culprit as the lack of a land ethic grounded in human stewardship, or trusteeship, of God's creation; these people often pose an alternative in the form of regenerative agriculture and resource management.[20] Still others argue that the global crisis results from a complex interplay of forces, including the use and abuse of technologies from the Industrial and post-Industrial Age, the heavy use of energy reserves and dumping of wastes, and inadequate economic and developmental practices.[21] For these the best solutions lie in developing an earth system science in which people seek to understand the world as a whole and to study the various parts of the world in interaction; another critical solution is to reform economic and political structures so as to support sustainable development.[22] Still other concerned people diagnose the crises in eco-justice as arising from spiritual deficiency, or the failure of human beings to attune to the Creator of life, and the consequent failure to attune with rocks and trees, rivers and seas, animals and other human beings.[23] For these, the most hopeful alternatives lie in developing a relational worldview and in deepening human relationships with God and the world, encouraging a relationship of awe, appreciation, justice, and care.

The major purpose of this book is not to present an ecological diagnosis. This work has been done well elsewhere. The purpose here is to recognize how serious is our crisis, how great are both the destruction and sacred power of our universe, and how large is the challenge of working together in responding to God's movements to repair the world (*tikkun olam*). We live in a world where people know better how to cast blame on others than how to join hands and seek communal answers for common concerns.

People in upper and lower latitudes of the earth find it easy, for example, to expect people who live in tropical regions to protect the rain forests. They do not recognize the survival issues faced by tribes indigenous to the forests, nor do they heed the economic interests owned by individuals and companies in wealthier parts of the world. Those who live near the rain forests are asked to avoid clearing the land for timber and agriculture, thus, to jeopardize the lives of their families. At the same time, they are cut off from other means of support (such as pharmaceutical formulas) that could be derived from the protected forests. In diagnosing the declining rain forests, blame is often placed on the people who live in them; in prescribing solutions, responsibility is also laid at their feet. All the while, indigenous peoples are often threatened with total displacement as rain forests (in Malaysia and Brazil, for example) are destroyed; these are the very forests in which their tribes have found home and nurture for centuries, living in relative balance with the dense, tropical ecosystem.

Likewise, people in countries of slow-growth population, like the United States, pass advice to other countries where population continues to grow at alarming rates, all the while ignoring their own over-consumption; this debilitates the environment at a rate comparable to over-population elsewhere. In short, we tend to oversimplify ecological analysis into isolated problems with isolated solutions, often placing the burden of responsibility on people other than ourselves.

Learning from the Earth's Story

So what can we learn from the story of this earth? As in the personal story told earlier, the story of the earth communicates insights that promise to guide a ministry with the earth. Brief attention will be given to these insights here, and they will be developed further in the book.

1. Most striking, *the earth lives by circles*. The earth circles, as do all planets in the solar system, and the earth circles in relation to the grandeur of the cosmos. The relation is so intimate that one can say the creatures of this planet are made of cosmic stardust. The seasons of the earth also circle, and the earth itself is a circle of energy, marked by mild and explosive cycles on its surface and below. These include cycles of electromagnetic exchange, cycles of volcanic eruption and erosion, and cycles that form and decompose organic matter. Animals who live on the earth are made of the water and oxygen waste of plants who live beside them, and of decomposed matter from plants and animals who have gone before. And in their living, they too discard waste, which feeds the plants who live beside them, and they eventually return to dust, feeding the soil for generations yet to come.

2. More traumatically, *the cycles of the earth are not always painless or smooth*. Even when the cycles are allowed to move with little obstruction, they comprise birth, struggle, and death. Birth often takes place by eruption or pain; struggle is often a treacherous grasping for survival in a threatening social or physical world; and death can be violent, untimely, and filled with suffering.

3. *The cycles of the earth are often ignored, and this is done to the detriment of the earth and her creatures.* The cycling seasons are often manipulated; cycles of death are denied; and cycles of relationship among animals, plants, and soil are ignored and destroyed (usually for the short-term benefit of humans). Also, cycles of production, consumption, and decomposition are distorted so that production and consumption are maximized and decomposition (nature's mode of recycling) is ignored.

4. *Ministering with the earth begins with attunement with the earth and its cycles.* Attunement to the cycles themselves, attunement to the awesome energy of the earth's forces, and attunement to the wonders of creation are ways of relating with the Creator who is the source and spirit of creation. Although the natural world can easily become a source of enjoyment or usefulness, to be tossed aside when the enjoyment and use are complete, the very fullness of the earth cries out for more compassion. Although the natural world can easily become a backdrop to the drama of human relationships, the largesse of the earth cries out for more appreciation. Although the natural world can

easily become a victim to be mourned over—a victim of human waste and abuse—its very persistence and its continuing ministry to its creatures cry out for more than sympathy. The cry of the earth is for attunement— attunement that includes compassion, appreciation, sympathy; and attunement that is deeply grounded in the wonder of creation and in the benevolence of our Creator.

5. *Neglect of the earth's relationality will destroy the well-being of relationships and the very fabric of life.* At the heart of ministering with the earth is the recognition that all of life is interrelated; ministry takes place in a web of relationship that includes the whole cosmos. To be in ministry is to participate with God's creation for the well-being of the whole.

This book has come to life with a sense of awe before the wonders of the universe, a sense of shame before human abuses of the planet on which we live, and a sense of hope that we might attune ourselves to the earth and minister with the earth in a way that renews life. The complex relationships of human beings with the rest of the earth can be a source of strength for ministry—a strength that derives from God, who has created the whole. At the same time, the complex relationships are sobering reminders that everything we do in ministry has effects on the planet and will be judged, in part, by the consequences of our actions.

Affirmations Born of Intersecting Stories

This chapter began with stories of ministry, and the flow has led through a personal story and a story of the earth. These are all starting points for ministry with the earth because they represent human experiences of God, alive in creation. These are not stories that stand in isolation; the stories intersect and lead us more deeply into relationship with God and the earth. Further, the stories give birth to basic affirmations, and I have already identified some of these in the process of sharing and interpreting stories. I will identify other affirmations in the remaining pages of this chapter in order to prepare readers for passions and commitments that fill the book, and to interpret some of the intersecting stories that influenced me as I pondered ideas and wrote these pages.

In the following chapters, many stories will be drawn from the Bible, the historical tradition, and peoples around the world. In this introduction, however, some of the stories come from my experience. To choose such an approach is not to value my experience over others' but to recognize the sacredness of all experience and the urgency of attending to ordinary moments of experience in knowing God and God's creation. Thus, I conclude this introduction with affirmations drawn from stories in this chapter and from significant encounters and ideas that have jolted me to care about ministering with the earth.

The first affirmation is that *God is revealed to human communities as they live closely with the earth.* This is implicit in many of the stories with which I began this chapter, but particularly in the first story of the congregation gathered in a breezeway for Sunday services. The people of this congregation expect that such a setting will inspire their reverence and enhance their worship. This first affirmation is also supported in my personal experience of the summer camp in which the work of God, not particularly apparent at the time, seemed to be sustaining and challenging me through some hard days.

The second affirmation is that *human life is broken, and relating deeply with creation contributes to human healing.* Both brokenness and possibilities for healing are evident in the opening story of the abused child who travels to a weekend retreat with family friends and discovers a young woman with whom she can find trust and closeness around a campfire. The retreat setting and aura of a campfire cleared the way for a healing moment—a moment that seemed to change the little girl's spirit through the rest of the weekend, although it could not wipe away the realities of her home life. In fact, most of the opening stories focus on the power of creation and earthbound ministries to heal human hurts. These include the hurts of people whose disabilities often cut them off from outdoor, active, and communal activities; the hurts of a biracial church that seeks to be unified and whole amidst racist attitudes in the larger community; the hurts of people who test positively for HIV or AIDS and who are rejected and restricted in their daily lives. Even my personal story, and that of my aunt, were stories of brokenness; healing emerged for us in contexts of communal living. In these various stories, healing touched physical and emotional pains, inner attitudes, and personal relationships.

One of the people who first inspired me to see the role of the earth in human healing was Linda Filippi, a pastoral counselor who understands pastoral counseling as the art of healing broken persons, broken communities, and the broken earth as they relate with one another. She believes that human healing and earth healing are interconnected, and in practical terms for counseling, she affirms that working with the soil is as important to human healing as talking. She says:

> Our long-term healing and the long-term healing of the earth will come as we awaken to the realities of our continuity with nonhuman nature, welcome the vulnerabilities of flesh, learn to use power in the service of liberation not oppression, live simply and lightly on the earth, and find courage to embrace diversity and the full personhood of all people...Deep healing will come as we open to the experience of the holy in our midst and work together to create a peaceful, just, sustainable, and flowering earth.[24]

In such an affirmation, Filippi adds texture to my assertions that human life is broken and that relating deeply with creation contributes to human healing. Such an affirmation suggests that working with the soil and air, and working with the pain of broken communities and unjust economic and political systems, are essential to human healing. Both lead us more deeply into relationship with the beauty and pain of creation.

The third affirmation is that *healing is urgently needed for the whole cosmos.* This affirmation is implied by the last one, but the very fact that human attention focuses more easily on *human* healing suggests that the need for *cosmic* healing is often neglected in Christian affirmations of ministry. The church has been relatively slow, as compared with the United Nations, to address environmental degradation. John Cobb argues that the very description of human justice by the western Christian Church has often been grounded in a dualistic view of history and nature; thus, many people have feared that attending to cosmic healing will distract attention from human justice, having pictured them as competing interests.[25] Certainly, stories of the earth and the cosmos reveal a different picture. They reveal the miracle of creation, the cycles of life, the relatedness of all things, the pain that comes from neglect and destruction, and the inextricable relation between human history and movements of the natural world.

Stories of the earth need to be revisited and supplemented. Biblical stories have been interpreted through the eyes of a highly rationalistic, individualistic, and human-centered culture, and scientific stories are often presented as debates over data, or a random collection of brute facts, rather than as narratives of the universe. The popular argument between biblical creation stories and the story of evolution reveals a bankruptcy in our ability to hear and interpret the stories of our heritage. The biblical stories are multiple (with four quite obvious ones), and they lend themselves to multiple interpretations. Likewise, scientific stories are multiple (including but not limited to evolutionary stories), and they also lend themselves to multiple interpretations. By limiting discussions to creationism vs. evolution, we close off many stories, many languages of wonder, and many interpretations that could open our eyes to the cosmos.

We can be especially enriched by encountering worldviews and stories from various parts of the world. Peter Mwiti Rukungah, for example, has found inspiration from the traditional Bantu worldview of his native Kenya and other countries in Africa. Because he is particularly concerned with the anthropocentricism and individualism of contemporary psychotherapy, he offers an alternative, which he calls a cosmocentric model of pastoral psychotherapy.[26] In this cosmocentric model, Rukungah suggests a paradigm in which the cosmos is taken to be the center of therapeutic interactions, and therapy takes place in relation to the ecological community, which includes the whole of human community in relation to the cosmos. This view of healing expands far beyond human concerns. Healing is sought for the whole of creation. What shape might our ministry take if we sought healing for the whole?

A fourth affirmation is that *small actions can carry great significance in ministering with the earth.* The stories shared in the opening pages of this chapter are all very particular and small in the great scheme of things, but each has import for the people involved and for the land and air most directly affected. They also have import for wider communities. For example, the camp for

HIV- and AIDS-diagnosed campers is one that has inspired others across the United States to do similar camps, and it has inspired other initiatives in local churches and judicatory bodies. The camaraderie built within the biracial congregation has enabled the congregation to exert biracial leadership with young people in the local high school.

Another example of significant small actions can be seen in the work of my former colleague, C. Dean Freudenberger—a published author on the care of the earth.[27] Although he advocates many dramatic actions on the part of churches and other institutions, he has possibly influenced communities most radically by encouraging them to build small action upon small action. Over a period of ten years, he engaged the whole community of Claremont School of Theology in renewing our campus with trees and other plants to give shade in summer, light in winter, and oxygen year-round. The legacy of Dean Freudenberger grows with those robust plants, but also with our graduates who return to campus to see "their" trees ten years later, and with the school's constituency who remember the excitement of those years of planning, planting, and caring for our shared corner of the earth. Now a whole new movement of earth-care has emerged in our community, growing in part from the seeds planted by Dean Freudenberger and his eager band of students, staff, and faculty. Such is the power of small actions!

A fifth affirmation is often neglected or denied, but without this, the other affirmations are inevitably undermined: *Concerns for the well-being of the earth are inextricably bound with economic and political justice in human communities.* One of the inescapable affirmations of the 1992 Earth Summit in Rio de Janeiro was that socioeconomic and environmental issues are not only interwoven, but are resolvable if the human family is willing to work together and to analyze and address issues in relation to one another. For example, the pharmaceutical formulas held and produced by companies in the United States prevent rain forests from being economically valuable to the countries in which they exist; thus, people who live near the rain forests are often tempted to destroy the forests for the livelihood of their families. Further, the near silence of the church and other religious bodies at the Summit was particularly discouraging, considering the potential role of religion in contributing to justice and the healing of the earth.[28]

Even the brief stories of ministry in this chapter are connected with major justice issues in our world—justice for people of diverse races and cultures, for children abused in their families, for people suffering from AIDS, for gay and lesbian persons, and for people with varying abilities. Concerns for justice and for healing are always intertwined, and both are also bound to concerns for the integrity and regeneration of the earth. Competition among racial and ethnic groups often leads to destruction or competition over the resources of the earth; likewise, destruction of the earth makes human communities more vulnerable and more contentious over limited resources. Such is the reality, and such is the challenge for ministry.

A sixth affirmation is that *transformed communities can contribute to the transformation of the world*. Certainly the communities described in the brief vignettes of this chapter have contributed to a larger transformation. I also think of a class shared twice with my colleague Frank Rogers and several students, a course entitled "Learning in Community and Caring for the Earth." Frank and I designed the course in the rhythmic way of a monastic community, meeting for several hours a week. The purpose of the class was to live in community with one another and with the earth as we learned simultaneously how to support community life and the care of the earth. We began each class with prayers, followed by work in the earth, eucharist, formal presentations on focused topics, a common meal, reflection on texts and class assignments, and closing prayers. We learned a great deal in the process. The inspiration that grew from the first class led to a grand celebration of the first Earth Day, the establishment of a recycling system on campus (which has continued), the renewal of our community garden, and the distribution of information on conserving water and electricity. Inspiration from the second class led to designing and beginning work on a biblical meditation garden, refurbishing the visitors' rooms and children's playground on campus, establishing a new vegetable garden, and sponsoring a community festival in the school "cafe."

Another community that is continually transformed and transforming is the Native American United Methodist Church in Southern California. There people practice a familial sense of community that includes the members of the congregation, the Native American people of the Los Angeles basin, and the whole earth. On a typical Sunday, the pastor, Marvin Abrams, may tell a story of creation from his Iroquois Nation, drawing parallels with a biblical creation story. Later, a Sunday school teacher may walk with children around the church grounds to see "the beautiful flowers and grass that the Creator has made," or people may study and organize a legal debate over land rights. Every Sunday, church members prepare a meal for people who come from a distance or have minimal money with which to buy food. Unlike many communities, the whole congregation sits down to the meal; it is not a meal for the needy, but for everyone.

Yet another transforming community is the Seminari Theoloji Sabah (S.T.S.) in Kinabalu, Malaysia, where the students live closely with one another and the land. The students here live by translation, learning in Bahasa Malaysian or Chinese, but speaking many tribal languages as well. People share their ethnic customs, share their lives closely with one another, work together on common projects, and work out reconciliation when problems emerge. The school offers courses in agriculture, and all students contribute to the care of the soil and plants on campus. They have planted the hillside to protect the soil from erosion, and they gather and enjoy the fruit from surrounding trees in season. This institution has moved toward intentional community with one another and the earth, and in a country of many cultures and religious groups, the quality of this one community promises to contribute to reconciliation in the entire nation.

In these stories from California and Malaysia, one glimpses ways that transformed communities contribute to transformation of the world. Certainly these communities are not beyond reproach, but their very courage in engaging in transformational action and celebration opens them to self-critique and critique by others, thus contributing to further transformation of their perspectives and actions. The process never ends.

The seventh and eighth affirmations are developed much more in the rest of the book, so I will only mention them here. Seventh, *human beings are called to receive from, and participate with, the earth in the redemptive work of God.* The relationship between people and the rest of creation is a mutual one, a theme more present in Christian tradition than has often been recognized. In fact, most religious traditions carry strong teachings about the human relationship to creation.[29]

The theme of mutuality between people and the earth is particularly strong in many Native American traditions; human beings are expected to receive from and contribute to creation and to divine work. Alfonso Ortiz of San Juan Pueblo recalls the words of a wise Tewa elder who counseled him as he prepared for the relay races which his people run in order "to give strength to the sun father as he journeys across the sky."[30] The elder said, "Young one, as you run, look to the mountain top. . . Keep your gaze fixed on that mountain, and you will feel the miles melt beneath your feet."[31] In this brief interchange, we see the strong Tewa affirmation that human beings, in their running, can give strength to the sun father, and the mountains can give strength to the runners. The story points to a potent relationship of reciprocity and mutual responsibility.

The final affirmation is that *outdoor ministries are a primary avenue for ministering with the earth and a paradigm for ministry in all of its many forms.* My earliest writing on this subject was done for an ecumenical meeting with leaders in camping and outdoor ministries.[32] We met near the sea in South Georgia, under spreading branches of ancient trees and near salt water marshes teeming with life. The people formed one of the most whole communities with whom I have ever lived. They played with gusto, related with one another, engaged in the diverse sessions of the conference, interacted sensitively with the earth, and worshiped with a sense that their community's relationship with God was significant. I learned something about wholeness from these leaders in camping and outdoor ministries; I also learned something about their marginalization in various denominations. To many of the leaders, the church communicates that their work is frivolous when compared with the "real ministry" of the church. I began to wonder why outdoor ministries could be so inspiring, yet not be considered vital.

Sacred Hopes for Ministry

The most obvious purpose of this book is to reflect on the potential beyond what any of us have yet imagined for ministering with the earth. In the journey toward that purpose, we will explore biblical and historical texts, studies of eco-justice, and also ministries of people who care about God's creation and who have given themselves to receiving from and caring for the earth. We will focus on several major concerns: the challenge to discern God's presence and movements in creation; the urgency to minister with the earth; the challenge to understand issues of human justice and ecological well-being as interdependent; and the need to inform philosophical and theological reflection on justice and sustainability with the actions of living communities. The challenge in writing the book is to address such concerns with an eye to the future.

As I have studied texts, gathered case studies, reflected, and written this book, I am aware that we live on the brink of the twenty-first century. Much has happened in the world since I began my research ten years ago. Central European countries are immersed in a struggle for new life; the struggle for a lasting peace goes on in Israel and Palestine and in Britain and Ireland; divisions in Somalia persist; Rwanda and the region of Bosnia and Serbia are torn by political war and now by hunger and disease; cities around the world are faced with needs that push the limits of their economic, political, and human capacities; and the worldwide desertion of rural lands and rural peoples continues. These changes underscore more boldly than ever the urgency of ministering with the earth and the potential of earthbound ministries to guide the church in ministering with the natural world. The call of the future is for Christian communities to minister in ways that will contribute to repairing the world—to repairing human relationships with one another and with the earth.

The concerns are serious. The calling is urgent. But ministering with the earth is grounded in more than urgency; it is grounded in the Spirit of God. Central to this book are the sacredness of God's world and the responsibility that comes with standing on holy ground. The book is thus formed around themes of sacredness—sacred hopes, sacred creation, sacred meetings, sacred confrontation, sacred journeys, sacred partners, and sacred vocation. My hope in writing is to illuminate the presence of God, who always precedes and exceeds our awareness and who draws us toward fullness of life.

One can compare the book design with the act of making a quilt. Six basic actions are involved in quilt-making, and the book describes actions fitting to that metaphor. The Appendix is actually a retreat design, formed around the metaphor of quilting in relation to spiritual life; here we will look at the whole book in relation to quilting.

- The first action—gathering fabric—is represented in chapter 1 by gathering sacred hopes. These hopes are the fabric out of which ministering with the earth can be made a reality.
- The second action—imaging a design for a new quilt—is an act of imagination that is usually grounded in the creation, frequently in flowers, trees, ocean waves, and experiences in people's lives. In chapter 2, we will imagine

a new way of being in the world, which is grounded in the sacred creation where God is always present.

- The third action in quilt-making is cutting patches (squares, strips, and triangles); this action prepares the basic materials from which the quilt will be made. The third action in the quilt-making metaphor (chapter 3) is to prepare the basic materials for ministering with the earth, shaping the elements of a relational worldview and covenantal theology.

- The fourth action—stitching the patches—is sewing basic materials into a colorful whole of rich diversity and texture. Chapter 4 focuses on the sacred confrontation that takes place when people meet diversity and meet God. The particular focus is on diverse traditions of ministering with the earth and diverse manifestations of God in history.

- The fifth quilting action is basting on a backing; this is the work of putting everything together for warmth and strength. In chapter 5, the task is to strengthen ministry by binding it to critical forms of our sacred journey—wondering, wandering, retreating, deciding.

- Finally, in quilting, one stitches everything together with designs that will add strength and beauty to the patchwork. Chapter 6 stitches designs of ministry that are drawn from many sacred partners, giving special heed to suppressed voices and forgotten partners.

- The completion of the quilt then is to sign it and use it. Chapter 7 focuses on the sacred vocation of ministering with the earth; thus the quilt is complete, ready for service.

The hope for ministering with the earth is a hope that we will come to see the earth as more than a source of beauty and a deposit of resources for human benefit, but rather as a creation of God. Such a view suggests a ministry that receives from and gives to the rest of creation, a ministry carried out in partnership with the whole creation. Lest that sound overly abstract and idealistic, consider the simple acts of taking a walk when you need to calm yourself or looking out a window when you need to think. In these simple acts, the natural world is participating in your renewal, ministering to and with you. However much we take such moments for granted, I propose that the spirit behind them can be a vision for understanding ministry—ministry that invites us into deeper relationship with God and God's world.

TWO

Sacred Creation:
God in our Midst

At the very center of this book is the sacredness of God's world. Even in a swirling, hurting world, God is present—living with creation in intimate relationship. The theme of sacred creation is like deep groundwater in the Jewish and Christian traditions. It flows to the surface in psalms and stories of creation, in Jesus stories, and in stories quilted into the long history of Jewish and Christian communities. It evokes praise and responsibility. It stirs a desire to know the depths of creation, the agony of destruction, and the reinterpretations that will be necessary to face the future.

The purpose of this chapter is *to seek God's presence and imagine God's design for a new creation.* This is the second action of quilt-making—*imaging a design for the quilt to come.* To this end, we will explore five themes: praise (singing to God), creation (pondering stories of God in creation), destruction (facing dilemmas that threaten life), reinterpretation (rethinking the work of God), and responsibility (meeting challenges). The chapter begins and ends with the human search to comprehend and respond to God's movements in creation, and the three middle sections explore what is revealed of God in the tradition and in the natural world. Some of the chapter is old; some is new; some is old with new interpretation; and some is subversive, reversing dominant traditions. All is written with a desire to understand and respect God's mysterious presence in creation.

Singing to God

Nowhere is singing to God more joyful and mournful—more real—than in the psalms. The psalms echo with songs and prayers of sacred time, sacred place, sacred journeys, sacred people, sacred leaders, and sacred creation.[1] Because these themes are more vivid in the poetry and rituals of a people than in philosophical discourse, a study of Psalms can illuminate sacred themes particularly well.[2] *Sacred time*, for example, is marked by psalms of praise and thanksgiving (as Ps. 112—118 and 136), which often recall particular times in Israel's history. Some recall deliverance from slavery in Egypt and are sung during Passover. Other psalms mark other moments of God's action in history (Ps. 78; 105; 106).

Sacred place is marked by the Israelites' joy in entering Jerusalem and the temple, echoed in Psalm 122: "I was glad when they said to me, 'let us go to the house of the LORD!' Our feet are standing within your gates, O Jerusalem." (Ps. 122:1–2) This is followed soon after with prayers for peace:

> Pray for the peace of Jerusalem: "May they prosper who love you. Peace be within your walls, and security within your towers." For the sake of my relatives and friends I will say, "Peace be within you." For the sake of the house of the LORD our God, I will seek your good (Ps. 122:6–9).

Note in this psalm the awareness of Jerusalem and the temple as sacred space.[3] Note also the people's joy to be there, as well as their prayer for peace and their promise to seek good for Jerusalem. In these words, one sees the powerful Jewish yearning to live in, or journey to, Jerusalem. If one is able to cross an enormous gap in time and culture, one can also imagine the powerful grief of the Jewish people when they were torn from that place and sent to Babylon as captives. Hear their cry in another psalm:

> By the rivers of Babylon—there we sat down and there we wept when we remembered Zion... How could we sing the LORD's song in a foreign land? If I forget you, O Jerusalem, let my right hand wither! Let my tongue cling to the roof of my mouth, if I do not remember you, if I do not set Jerusalem above my highest joy. (Ps. 137:1, 4–6)

After the reforms of 621 B.C.E., King Josiah had destroyed places of worship across the land; separation from Jerusalem, thus, marked a serious separation from the Jewish faith and people.

The themes of sacred place are intensified when one considers the related theme of *sacred journey*. The most sacred journey for the Hebrew people was ascending to Jerusalem and the temple. The Psalms of the Steps, or Ascents (120—134), were sung along the way as people approached the temple of Jerusalem on their sacred journey. John Day particularly identifies Psalms 84 and 122 as pilgrim hymns.[4]

As for *sacred people*, several psalms celebrate God's relationship with the people (Ps. 47; 93; 95—100), referring at times to the children of Abraham and, at other times, to all peoples. In addition, the Royal Psalms celebrate the particular relationship of the King with God (Ps. 2; 18; 20—21; 45; 72; 89; 101; 110; 132; 144:1–11).[5] Many of these people- or leader-oriented psalms are songs of joy, but many are laments. They include communal laments (Ps. 12; 44; 60; 74; 79; 80; 83; 85; 94:1–11; 126; and 137) and personal laments (Ps. 3—7; 9—10; 13; 17; 22; 25—28; 31; 35; 38—39; 40:11–17; 42–43; 51—52; 54—57; 59; 61; 64; 69—71; 77; 86; 88; 94:16–23; 102; 109; 120; 130; 139–143).[6] Clearly, the sacred relationship between God and God's people encompasses both joy and pain.

Of particular note in The Psalms are the ways in which the psalms celebrate *sacred creation*, calling forth images of the natural world. Psalm 104 carries very explicit creation themes, as do Psalms 19a and 29. Certainly, a repeated chord in the music of the Psalms is that all creation should praise God, including Israel, other nations, angels, and the whole of the natural world.[7] Some argue that this is the only psalm that deals with creation and not with the redemptive history of Israel, but this can be misleading. Close reading of the people-oriented psalms described above reveals that God's closeness with people is often linked with God's closeness with the earth. Consider, for example, the continuing recollection that God is the creator in Psalm 95:3–5:

> For the LORD is a great God, and a great King above all gods. In his hand are the depths of the earth; the heights of the mountains are his also. The sea is his, for he made it, and the dry land, which his hands have formed. (cf: Exodus 15)

We also find that the heavens and earth are active—called to praise, as in Psalm 96:11–13a:

> Let the heavens be glad, and let the earth rejoice; let the sea roar, and all that fills it; let the field exult, and everything in it. Then shall all the trees of the forest sing for joy before the LORD; for he is coming, for he is coming to judge the earth.

In addition to the celebratory tone of these psalms, we also find a relationship between what God reveals in the natural world and in the Torah. This is especially vivid in the joining of Psalm 19a (vv. 1–6) with 19b (vv. 7–14); the former focuses on God in the natural world and the latter, on God in the law.[8] What is communicated in this particular psalm is that people are actually instructed about life by the natural world as well as by the law.[9] Further, the cosmos itself praises God, and its lavish praise is not just for human benefit because humans often do not even hear it (vv. 1–4).

What is evident in these psalms and comments is that God is Creator, and all of creation is called to give thanks to God. This praise is important to people's lives. Walter Brueggemann explains that, according to the psalms, the human vocation is to praise, and the act of praise is both a response to God's work and a constitutive act.[10] Human praise gives credit to God, but it also allows people to respond actively to God and to form themselves as a people.

These themes echo throughout Hebrew spirituality. According to Rolf Knierim, Hebrew spirituality is related to the totality of the world, where God is everywhere present. The Hebrew "reverence for the hidden presence of

God in this world" is exemplified in Psalm 139.[11] In its "wisdom spirituality," this psalm describes how a person is confronted through the world with fundamental questions of existence.[12] In short, God is in all creation, and God faces us with ourselves as we experience the world.

The actions of the Jewish people, both in creating and singing the Psalter, are echoed through Christian history as well, both through the Psalms and through particular actions of particular people. Consider Saint Francis of Assisi, who preached to the birds and implored that they praise God:

> My sisters the birds, you have much from God and should always praise him [*sic*] for the free flight you have, for your double and triple plumage, coloured and decorated vesture, for your nourishment set out for you without care, for your song accorded you by your Creator...So take care, sisters mine, the birds, not to be ungrateful but be zealous always to praise God.[13]

Francis was, in some sense, perpetuating a Christian emphasis on humanity and the God-human relationship because *he* was preaching to the birds. On the other hand, he was praising the wonder of the birds and calling them to active praise of their Creator. He was not only appreciating them but also calling them to be active agents in God's creation.

Such actions of Jewish and Christian people, represented by the psalms and the story of Saint Francis, illumine the theme of this chapter—the sacredness of God's creation. Singing to God also leads people to wonder about God's role in creation.

Pondering Stories of God in Creation

What is sacred creation? The idea does not fit easily into words, for even the most fitting words seem superficial or abstract. We begin, therefore, with stories because most experiences of God's sacred creation happen within the context of living and reflecting on ordinary life events. The first story is biblical—a familiar story often used as a basic text for ecological sensitivity and action. This story grew out of the life of Hebrew people as they related with God and the world, and as they tried to celebrate and comprehend the earth where they lived.

> In the beginning when God created the heavens and the earth, the earth was a formless void and darkness covered the face of the deep, while a wind from God swept over the face of the waters. Then God said, "Let there be light"; and there was light. And God saw that the light was good; and God separated the light from the darkness. God called the light Day, and the darkness he called Night. And there was evening and there was morning, the first day.
>
> ...And on the seventh day God finished the work that he had done, and he rested on the seventh day from all the work that he had done. So God blessed the seventh day and hallowed it, because on it God

rested from all the work that he had done in creation.

These are the generations of the heavens and the earth when they were created. (Selections from Gen. 1:1—2:4)

This creation story was told by the Hebrew people, long before it was ever written, and even longer before it became known as Genesis 1. We will return to the story later in the chapter, but for now, note the rhythm of the story. Again and again, the story announces the words of God, the acts of God, the accomplishments ("And it was so"), the affirmation ("And it was good"), and the conclusion of another day ("And there was evening, and there was morning, the first day"). The compelling movement and rhythm of the story is an invitation to feel the cycles of the earth's story, and the repetitive rhythm of the story suggests circles within circles.

Further, the actual words of the story recall the familiar cycles of the earth—the day and night, land and sea, plants and seeds, signs and seasons and days and years, sun and moon, sea creatures and air creatures, domesticated creatures and wild creatures, males and females. Even more subtly, but also powerfully, the word for human (*adam*) refers simultaneously to earth (*adamah*), a word play paralleled in other languages such as the English words humus (for soil) and human (for people), both derived from the Greek. In these pairings, we see interrelations in the natural world and the cycling of days, seasons, years, and birth and death.

In the cycle of birth and death, birth (or generativity) is directly communicated; all plant and animal life are called into being and prepared to be fruitful and multiply. Death is more subtly communicated. Certainly, days come and go, and plants are given to animals and humans for food, but the text is strangely silent about death. Even in this romantic story of God and creation, however, the hearer or reader knows that death is part of life. And when one reads further in Genesis, one encounters another story that deals explicitly with death: "You are dust, and to dust you shall return" (Gen. 3:19b).[14] Interestingly, the explication of *death* comes after the explanation of *life*. The ancients selected Genesis 1 to open scriptures, thus facing people first with a drama of life—a drama of circles and interrelatedness.[15] The drama points to the awe-filled earth story, but it does one thing more: It points to God—the One who creates and delights in the whole of creation.

The stories of God's active presence in the midst of creation did not end with Genesis, however, so we turn now to contemporary stories of people who experience God and the sacredness of God's world. In Australia, Boniface Perdjert writes his experience of the stories of Jesus. As a deacon of the Uniting Church of Australia and as an Aboriginal person, he finds in the Christian Gospels a picture of Jesus that is inspiring to him and compatible with the traditions of his people. He says:

When I read the Gospels, I read them as an Aboriginal. There are many things in the gospel that make me happy to be an Aboriginal because I think we have a good start.

So many things that Christ said and did, and the way he lived, makes me think of the good things in our way of life.

[Christ] loved the little things like the mustard seed and the grain of wheat and the corn drops of cold water and the little sparrows. We have similar things like seeds and berries and yams, small water holes and we like the quietness of the hills and the bush. Like him we have a deep sense of God in nature. We like the way He used the things of nature to teach and the important part nature plays in the Sacraments.[16]

In these reflections, Boniface Perdjert reveals awareness of the relation of Jesus Christ with himself and his people. Further, he expresses awareness of Jesus' relationship with the earth. We find no debate here between a Christ-centered and a creation-centered theology, for Perdjert sees in Jesus Christ a reverence for creation and Creator. Further, he sees in creation the presence of God, and he delights that the "little things" were of value to Christ as they have always been to his people.

Such an appreciation for the little things is also revealed in the story of Sani Vaeluaga—a Samoan-New Zealander. Our meeting in Auckland is told in my words:

Sani and I talked one Sunday morning after worship in Auckland. He was a student at Trinity Theological College where we were living for a few weeks, and in our first meeting, he shared something of his past and his experience of coming to theological college. Sani, originally from Samoa, had lived in New Zealand for some years, holding an important position in business. He and his family had then moved to Australia, where they lived quite comfortably on his good salary. During this time, some of Sani's colleagues at work invited him to come with them every day at lunch and sit under a tree. During those lunchtime meetings, they ate and prayed together before returning to work for the afternoon. Sani said to me, "I had never eaten my lunch under a tree before, but that daily lunch changed my life."

Sani described how he grew to value these lunches under the tree, how he learned to pray with the others, and how he and his family decided to give up their security and good income and return to Auckland so he could prepare for ordained ministry. Sani said, "You know, we are very poor now compared to before, but we have managed well; God seems to open possibilities."[17]

In this story of Sani's lunching under a tree with friends and colleagues, I was struck that he mentioned the tree. Then, when I asked him later if I could tell his story in this book, he readily agreed and said again how strange the experience was for him, sitting under that tree and having these moving moments take place that had so transformed his life. All of this began under a tree. God's Spirit somehow moved through that tree and through Sani's family and colleagues, and his life was changed.

The next story was also life-changing, but in a different way:

My daughter and I went on a snorkeling trip with the Pacific Whale Foundation. We had chosen this particular trip because the proceeds of the boat excursion would be given to marine research and the care of whales. Also, we had been told that the guides were researchers who knew a great deal about animal life in waters around Hawaii. We had chosen our day for travel, carefully avoiding the weekend days when storms were predicted. Of course, weather predictions are not always accurate, and the week-end days proved to be sunny and calm, whereas the day we went on our big excursion was "as rough as it ever gets off of Molokini."

Undaunted, we jumped off the boat into the rolling water, snorkels and fins in place. Having snorkeled only a few times before, we thought we were very rusty in-deed when the saltwater kept rolling into our snorkel tubes. This did not prevent us from rolling with the waves and enjoying the beautiful sight of the tropical fish and colorful coral. We had been well taught on the boat as we rode to the coral reef off Molokini. We had been told about the various kinds of fish, as well as the delicate ecosystem of the coral reef. The living coral exists in symbiotic relationship with other fish, and the Pacific Whale Foundation tries to upset that system as little as possible. We were told not to feed the fish because this attracts more fish into the area than the ecosystem can support. We were also told not to touch the coral because that destroys the immune system and lays the coral open to disease and predation. We took our lessons seriously and vowed that we would respect and appreciate the animals.

After a time, our leaders decided to look for calmer waters; we boarded the boat and headed for Turtle Bay. There we found the waters much calmer, though rougher than normal for that bay. Since we, along with others were suffering from rolling stomachs by this time, we jumped into the water to combat seasickness. We swam vigorously and, again, watched and enjoyed the fish. We neared one coral reef with particular admiration, and realizing that the water above it was shallow, we turned to retreat. At this moment, strong waves swept us directly onto the reef, only to retreat and leave us just above it. My daughter cried out, and one of the crew swam quickly to her rescue, motioning me to swim out. Rebecca was rescued, but only after more waves swept her farther onto the coral and she was cut by sharp edges of the living organism.

Back safely and headed homeward on the still-bumpy boat, we were all told lightheartedly that, having experienced snorkeling on the rough seas, we would find any other snorkeling a breeze. I asked Rebecca if she had been frightened by her experience on the reef. She responded, "No, I wasn't afraid; I just panicked because I knew I was not supposed to touch the coral." In her effort not to touch the coral, she had been washed further into it. She had felt a tremendous surge of remorse that she was destroying life that had built up over hundreds of years. In the days that followed, she treated her scratches and cuts, but every time I asked her how the places were healing, she re-sponded, "I'll be all right; I just feel bad for the coral." Two days later she completed the form to adopt a whale through the Pacific Whale Foundation.

This story is a sobering reminder that human beings cannot interact with the rest of the natural world without causing damage. Whether by mistakes of judgment, by natural consequences of natural phenomena (like waves), or by the temptation to venture into parts of the earth that are better left alone, damage follows in the wake of human activity. Some of this damage is even intentional, as revealed in coral reefs ravaged for souvenirs.

This chapter began with the affirmation that the earth is sacred—that God is always and everywhere in our midst. That simple affirmation is not so simple, however; tensions inevitably emerge. To affirm the sacredness of the earth is to face the inescapable tension between God's holy presence and the reality of destruction in which we also participate.

To affirm the sacredness of the earth is to recognize the sacramentality of creation. It is to take seriously the Genesis 1 affirmations of the good creation. It is to recognize the inspiration Jesus received from the natural world, and the tender care he extended to the smallest beings (as expressed by Boniface Perdjert). It is to feel the power and guidance of God's Spirit in creation (as experienced by Sani Vaeluaga under a tree with some lunchtime friends). To affirm the sacredness of the earth is also to recognize the fragility of creation, as experienced by my daughter in the coral. To interact with the world is to have an effect on it and to know oneself and the world as vulnerable.

This realization faces us with the reality of ecological issues facing the planet. Any honest discussion of the sacredness of creation must address these issues. We stand on holy ground, but we face major dilemmas. We turn now to explore some of these dilemmas, and then to move, in the last sections of the chapter, to Jewish-Christian affirmations of God and challenges for ministering with the earth.

Facing Dilemmas of Destruction

We live in a time when dilemmas facing the earth are escalating, pressing people to find their way toward common action. The dilemmas are of such urgency that differences in nationality, social class, race, theological orientation, denomination, and religious tradition cannot be allowed to divide and divert us from the earth. Such urgency was recognized by the Parliament of the World's Religions that met in Chicago in September 1993. They produced this declaration:

> The world is in agony…
> Peace eludes us…the planet is being destroyed…neighbors live in fear…women and men are estranged from each other…children die!
> **This is abhorrent!**
> We condemn the abuses of Earth's ecosystems…
> We condemn the poverty that stifles life's potential…
> We condemn the social disarray of the nations; the disregard for justice which pushes citizens to the margin…and the insane death of children from violence. In particular we condemn aggression and hatred in the name of religion.
> **But this agony need not be.**[18]

With that collective agony ringing in our ears, we turn now to ecological problems that face the earth. Facing dilemmas of destruction is part of the mission of God-centered, creation-based ministries; these dilemmas are, in actuality, spiritual failures. As people interact with the earth, they are often awakened to new possibilities of ministering with the earth but also to the failures embedded in our efforts to do so. These failures, or dilemmas, are accessible through stories of people living with the earth.

Dilemma #1: *A few years ago, I participated with a group of adults in planning a youth backpack trip for our church's annual conference. At our first planning session one counselor asked whether this trip, sponsored by the church, would be different from other youth backpack trips. Another said he hoped we would help the youth and ourselves grow in respect and responsibility for the creation. He added that another organization in our state sponsored backpack trips, but their emphasis was on mastering the environment. The young people developed a lot of skills, but they tore up the trails and ecological balance in the process.*

This story names the first dilemma: *thinking of the creation as something to use, play with, or master for human benefit.*

This little story is not the story of a small dilemma; we can see on a grand scale how this dilemma takes shape if we look at coral reefs, rain forests and other natural habitats that are being destroyed daily by human use. Not only habitats are destroyed, but all of the species that live in them. Even when small patches of natural habitats are preserved, the ability of animals to move freely with changing conditions is hampered. This limits animals' ability to move for self-preservation through safe corridors to new habitats; thus, they are endangered further.

The dilemma of thinking of creation as something to use or play with for human benefit is a large dilemma indeed. Consider the rate at which human beings have proceeded in disintegrating the ozone layer and destroying the topsoil inch by inch, even after the thousands of years nature took to build up each layer of topsoil. Consider, also, the evidence of a greenhouse effect in warming the earth and shifting ecological balance. This issue has been much debated, even in international treaty negotiations in Kyoto, Japan, at the end of 1997. The causes of global warming are debated (whether high emissions or solar intensity), as are the solutions (whether economic, technological, or political).[19] The threat of warming is sufficiently real, however, to evoke debate across nations, institutions, and disciplines of study. James Nash explains:

> Since the peak of the last Ice Age, perhaps 18,000 years ago, the earth's average temperature has warmed only about 5 degrees centigrade. Thus, an average increase of 1.5–4.5 degrees centigrade...in less than a century is a drastic shift.[20]

Nash further points out that, even if such a change is part of the natural process, the rate and radicality may be "too swift and massive for gradual cultural adaptations by humans and biological adaptations by many other species of plants and animals."[21]

So how do we respond? In light of the evidence and growing consensus among climatologists regarding global warming and its likely consequences,

Nash concludes, "A go-slow policy, waiting for conclusive evidence that may not appear until it is too late to act, is therefore a high-risk strategy."[22] If we made some changes in our industrial practices (through economic or political sanctions), we would likely reduce the warming trend dramatically. We could counter the greenhouse effect by preserving the earth's forests, by shifting from coal to natural gas for industrial energy, and also by using more energy-efficient methods of burning fossil fuels, thereby reducing our consumption of resources and release of wastes. Nash adds further that conservation is critical, requiring a move toward more frugal lifestyles, the use of mass transportation, and other means of reducing the use of fossil fuels.[23] In any case, this is not a problem for a few ecologically minded people; it is a problem that affects the whole earth and requires the whole human community to resolve.[24]

We will not really seek solutions to such problems with significant investment of time or money if we continue to think of the creation as something to use or play with for human benefit. Certainly we will use and enjoy the natural world in all kinds of practical and recreational ways, but if our sights of the natural world are limited to this, we will continue in our spiritual self-centeredness, and we will continue to destroy the earth at an alarming rate. Likewise, we will perpetuate a devastating legacy of the Enlightenment, an emphasis on the ability and desirability for human beings to master the earth.[25] In the backpacking story, someone at least questioned another group's emphasis on mastering the environment. The ideal of mastery is not only self-delusion; it reinforces a theology of human domination and encourages practices of using the creation for human benefit.

Dilemma # 2: *A few years ago, a young family moved to the mountains. They loved the rural area where they could raise animals and roam the mountain regions. The first few weeks they took many pictures and shared them with their family and friends. Half of the pictures were sunsets and mountain landscapes. This family knew that they were standing on holy ground, and they loved it. But the family had to drive a hundred miles each day into the valley for work. They complained about the smog when they reached the valley, and they expressed how terrible it was. One said, "I am glad that we moved so that we don't have to put that smog in our lungs twenty-four hours a day." They did not seem to realize that they were adding to the smog that others were breathing as they made their 100-mile commute.*

This family is not alone, because all of us in one way or another participate in the problems of the earth. This story introduces dilemma two: *thinking that we can create islands of sacred ground for ourselves and continue to desecrate land and air in our daily living.*

To show how complex the problem is, consider the complex questions raised by attempts to preserve endangered habitats—islands of sacred ground. Ecotourism is an attempt to preserve the earth and encourage people to grow in appreciation of the natural world. The purpose is for people to enjoy the creation to the maximum while affecting it to the minimum. This is particularly important for fragile habitats such as rainforests. In Malaysia, for example, the Endau-Rompin National Park has been set aside as a protected area. According to Jake Statham, the park "is like a modern day Noah's Ark afloat on an inhospitable sea."[26] He decries "the rolling waves of development that have swept down the Malaysian peninsula in the past decades, washing away great tracts of rain forest and leaving in its place stark urban developments or manicured plantations of palm and rubber trees."[27] The preservation of the park is important for the forest itself and for creatures that live in it.

The plan for the Endau-Rompin Park is to guarantee its survival, but the problems are immense. Statham says, "If there are any mistakes at all, there will be no second chances to save Endau-Rompin—and one of the biggest problems is to identify all the threats to the survival of the area."[28] Here is where the real work begins. The obvious threats of development can be addressed more directly than the subtle threats that environmentalists are now raising—threats such as "tourism, recreational development and poor management policies—that have wreaked havoc in other 'protected' areas."[29] At stake for Endau-Rompin is the habitat itself, as well as endangered animals such as the Sumatran rhinoceros; this forest is the last refuge for their dwindling wild population of 20 rhinos. Also at stake is the life of the native people, the *orang asli*, who fear that logging and ecotourism will demolish the last of their natural home.[30]

The plan for Endau-Rompin is to focus efforts on preservation, conservation, research, education, and recreation, and the plan is being implemented by creating three zones distinct from each other. The visitors' zone will be the locus of all exploring activity; the conservation zone will be the locus of activities to conserve and repair the damaged ecology by scientists and park rangers; and the core zone, which is half the park, is to be left untouched.[31] The plan seems well-conceived, but the dilemma in setting aside an island of sacred ground looms large, this time in the form of eco-tourism. In fact, some people reflecting on the future of Endau-Rompin worry that the new visitors cannot be sufficiently controlled. According to Statham: "Some cynics even go so far as to say the moment Endau-Rompin was identified as an especially rich rain forest area, its chances of survival began to diminish even further...It's ironic that the new legions of eco-tourists could be destroying the very thing they seek to protect."[32]

In a similar vein, explorers have recently discovered a remote forest area on the border of Laos and Vietnam, and new species of animals have been identified. John MacKinnon discovered a new genus distantly related to cows and variously called Vu Quang ox, pseudoryx, or Sao-la. In addition, two new species of deerlike animals—the giant muntjac and quang khem—were discovered, and a new species of fish.[33] This news seems worthy of celebration, but it reveals an encroaching danger. The very fact that these animals still exist suggests that the region of Vu Quang has been stable for millions of years, supporting a diversity of plant and animal life and providing a refuge when other regions were being transformed radically by climate shifts and human encroachment. The problem now facing the region is that its discovery may invite more encroachment and further destruction of species. According to Eugene Linden:

> It is quite likely…that all the new species once roamed over larger areas than they do today. Human activities have transformed Southeast Asia far more significantly than climate shifts in recent centuries, and these changes have accelerated. As recently as 40 years ago, Vietnam had at least 50% of its original forests. Today less than 10% of those forests are still pristine.[34]

This scenario reveals an almost impossible dilemma—a conflict between the value of humans' caring for endangered habitats and the need for humans to stay away from these habitats altogether.

This emphasizes the danger in Christian theologies of dominion and stewardship. Perhaps Paul Santmire is correct in warning that stewardship theology has been used so long to justify domination and is so easily distorted that it should be allowed to rest.[35] On the other hand, Dieter Hessel proposes to reform theologies of stewardship. He argues that stewardship should be shaped by views from below, from abroad, and from nature.[36] If we listen seriously to Hessel's advice, our future decisions about stewardship of endangered habitats will be shaped by the habitats themselves and by other realities all over the natural world.

People clearly need to reflect from diverse perspectives, give particular attention to neglected parts of the creation, and make the most responsible decisions possible. If not, environmental safe zones and protected exploration will be delusions, even excuses, to avoid other necessary action. The simple story of Rebecca and the coral reef suggests that the dangers of eco-tourism are sometimes paired with the possibility of converting and empowering people into significant action, both in their private worlds and in more far-reaching political action. Can preserving islands of sacred ground contribute to the preservation of the whole earth—a sacred planet in a sacred cosmos? The question has no simple answer, only simple urgency.

Dilemma #3: *Once upon a time (in the 1700s) a community in North India practiced nonviolence in their religion.[37] The Bishnois people had a religious precept against cutting down trees or killing animals. Now, when the Maharaja of Jodhpur decided to build a palace, he needed bricks. To make bricks, he needed kilns and firewood. In the desert province firewood was scarce, so the Maharaja's lieutenant sent woodcutters to the land of the Bishnois people, where they had long protected their trees. The Bishnois people protested; they pleaded for the cutters to leave the sacred trees alone. The woodcutters ignored their pleas and began to cut. The villagers finally rushed into the grove, where every person—adults, children, and elderly—hugged a tree. On that day in 1730, 353 villagers and 353 trees were slaughtered. The rage in the region was so great and the Maharaja was so penitent that he passed laws that no* *tree or animal could be killed by anyone in or near the Bishnois settlements. Still today, the Bishnois people protect the lives of trees and animals.*

This story raises the third dilemma: *The desire to own and accumulate possessions leads to destruction of the earth, and consumerist cultures drain the resources of their own lands and many others.* Many of these cultures are Christian.

A listing of ecological problems in the world is always a bit overwhelming and sometimes misleading because people are tempted to choose their favorite ecological disaster and address that one while ignoring others. Underneath most ecological disasters, however, is an underlying spiritual failure—the desire to own and accumulate possessions even at the expense of destroying the earth. The denial of this dilemma is evidenced when people in the so-called First and Second World countries become avid enthusiasts for population control, while their *per capita* use of resources far outweighs the resource depletion of more populated countries.

James Nash recognizes that overpopulation and overconsumption actually have similar effects. Regarding population, he points out that humankind took "thousands of centuries to produce one billion people living simultaneously on the planet, but that number can now be reproduced in little more than a decade."[38] Such figures suggest that overpopulation is indeed a problem to be addressed, and with considerable urgency. On the other hand, Nash and other environmentalists refuse to pretend that population problems stand alone. Nash points out that overpopulation is not the main cause of poverty or environmental destruction; the major cause is maldistribution, "accompanied by the grandiose consumption of the affluent."[39] He concludes, therefore, that reducing population growth is "an urgent moral demand on *all* nations" (emphasis his), but that affluent nations also have a moral demand to reduce consumption and equalize distribution.[40]

In making this link, Nash undercuts one of the most dangerous threats to ecological integrity, debating priorities for economic justice against ecological preservation. He argues that the maldistribution of economic resources is, in fact, one of the more significant threats to ecological well-being; thus, "a preferential option for the poor entails a preferential option for ecological integrity—and vice versa."[41] This point cannot be underscored enough. As I co-chair the Eco-Justice Task Force in my community and teach courses focused on ecological sustainability and social justice, I discover how easily ecological concerns and concerns for economic and social justice slip away from one another. To say that they are related is one thing, but to be conscious of the full and complex interaction is quite another.[42]

Unfortunately, ecological care can easily reinforce economic disparity and support environmental racism. In fact, many responses to protect the natural environment have placed the heaviest burden on the poor, and on some racial groups more than others (toxic waste dumps, plant closures, and loss of jobs, etc.). At the same time, the bulk of rewards are enjoyed primarily by wealthier folks (toxic waste removal, clean air, environmentally sensitive products). One poignant example is the story of logging and ranching practices in the

Philippines and Brazil that have been supported by the national governments, large businesses, and international economics and politics. These practices have denuded rain forests while slash-and-burn farmers are given the blame.[43] Such tragic outcomes are inevitable if ecological and economic concerns are not held together in all of our efforts.

What would happen if the phenomenon of blaming were transposed into a phenomenon of naming, and if the naming of problems and proposed solutions in different communities of the world were taken to be the first step on the road ahead? What would happen if we engaged in extensive analysis of economic systems in an attempt "to create and maintain a healthier system," rather than bouncing from crisis to crisis and pouring all of our energy into combative debates about the best responses to crises?[44] We might begin to develop curriculum resources, liturgies, and festivals to "touch people's hearts and raise their consciousness about what is happening to the world around them."[45] Could we possibly see a bigger picture if we could hear the diagnoses and prescriptions of people from diverse social situations, races, cultures, and regions of the world? Would we experience conversion if we allowed full expression to diverse peoples around the globe?

Dilemma # 4: *Once upon a time, a woman visited the Canadian Rockies. Seeing a glacier for the first time, she was ecstatic. She chipped off a bit of the glacier and put it in a baggy. As she was leaving, someone asked, "Why are you taking that home? It is going to melt." She replied, "It has been up there frozen for 10,000 years; it is not going to melt now."*

Once upon a time, a man was traveling on a bus tour. The bus stopped for people to get off to walk and look at a dramatic mountain. The man turned to the tour director and asked, "How much does that mountain weigh?" The tour director, stunned, paused first and then responded, "Do you mean with or without trees?"

These two stories, taken together, raise the fourth dilemma: *thinking of the universe as if it were autonomous pieces that could be separated from each other without ecological disruption.* The woman in the first story seemed to think that the ice was autonomous from the glacier so that it could be removed and would remain frozen. The man in the second story seemed to think of the mountain as so disconnected from the earth that you could lift it up and weigh it. In both stories, naive as they are, we can see the "commonsense" tendency to think in terms of separate bits of reality rather than in terms of interdependent wholes.

These stories are so naive that they may seem safe, easy to deny; however, the prevalence of single-issue politics testifies to the ease with which people engage in autonomous thinking. People argue for "family values" on the one hand and for cutting support for environmental protection on the other, thus assuming that families can be healthy in a poisonous environment, or that families are autonomous from one another and from the earth. Likewise, people engage with their favorite ecological or justice issues with little regard for how these are connected with other issues. Population control is set in opposition with consumption control, rural concerns for the protection and use of land are set in opposition with urban concerns for goods and services, northern hemisphere concerns are set in opposition with southern hemisphere concerns, and so forth.

In all of this discussion of environmental dilemmas, one can easily enter into statistics and abstractions. Debates in international, church, and business bodies often take this form and have minimal effect on participants. The issues can be vivid and real, however. A particular family or tribe in the Philippines can be affected simultaneously by the pressures of international debt, agri-business takeovers, logging policies, increasing population, destruction of habitats and species, the declining sustainability of their bio-region, the pressures of immediate survival, and religious sanctions against most forms of birth control.[46] The people, animals, and plants are interwoven from beginning to end.

Disconnected, autonomous thinking denies complex interconnections among issues facing our planet. Consider how many issues are then hidden: toxic dumping; exploitative labor practices in the clothing industry; economic practices that destroy indigenous economic structures, reinforce poverty, and support child prostitution; the export of pesticides; acid rain; pollution of waterways; destruction of natural aquifers; animal maltreatment; and overconsumption. Such problems are connected in ways that shock common sensibilities about autonomous entities.[47] They remind us of an interconnected world, countermanding the dominant individualistic and growth-oriented worldview.

When local consumers are unwilling to investigate conditions under which their clothes are made, or when local churches are unwilling to investigate local food sources and conditions of farmers and farmland, they are contributing to wanton destruction of God's creation. The same is true when local businesses are not willing to cooperate in just and ecologically responsible practices. We think we are autonomous individuals and institutions, and what we do does not make much difference. But it does!

Reinterpreting the Work of God

Faced with such environmental dilemmas, what can Christians say about sacred creation, about God in our midst? The Christian tradition can certainly offer wisdom for facing environmental issues, but patterns of destruction also raise difficult questions. In looking at the global ecological agenda, we can see that Christian theology has often supported environmental destruction; now we must ask how the tradition can support environmental life.

Here we will explore three Christian affirmations regarding God in creation. Biblical interpretation in the last decade has uncovered the possibility for scripture to illumine themes and raise issues related to ecological integrity, social justice, human greed and oppression, and God's call to live in covenant with God and creation.[48] The affirmations below represent strands in that rich tapestry of biblical interpretation. The first two affirmations highlight themes that are commonly acknowledged but not always related to ecological destruction. The third affirmation introduces a reversal in common interpretations.

In the Beginning God Created

The biblical witness offers three creation stories and fragments of another. The three more complete ones are Genesis 1:1—2:3, Genesis 2:4–25, and Proverbs 8:22–31. These stories are all different, but together they communicate the wonder of creation. They all communicate that God created, but the technological details vary. The effect is that the mystery of creation is not resolved, but the relationship between God and creation is clearly affirmed.

We began this chapter with the first creation story, but the message of the story is not altogether simple and noncontroversial. James Nash finds within the story a vital source for ecological care, and Rosemary Radford Ruether finds within it many enduring problems, such as anthropocentricism and misogyny. Nash, for example, emphasizes that relationality is affirmed by the story in Genesis 1, represented by the creation of human beings and other land animals on the same day—a mark of affinity.[49] He further emphasizes that God pronounces the goodness of creation before human beings are even created.[50] God declares goodness that is cosmocentric and biocentric; creation is home for all life. God declares goodness in a world pervaded with birth and death, joy and pain. God's declarations are seemingly guided by divine purposes; humanity is reminded that creation is not designed solely for human benefit and happiness. Thus, Nash sees the story as offering hope by pointing to the goodness of God, the value of every aspect of creation, and the humble relationship of human beings to the whole.

On the other hand, Ruether calls attention to some ambiguous aspects of the story. She recognizes an unfortunate elimination of the primal Mother from earlier Babylonian stories of creation; the positive shift away from a "king-warrior" image of God to a "priestly" image of God, who calls things into being by the ritual naming of "Let there be"; a partially realized shift from dichotomizing rulers and workers, work and leisure; an inclusiveness in the creation of male and female in the image of God and, yet, an exclusiveness in the use of male pronouns for human beings and God; and, finally, an ambiguity associated with the word *dominion*.[51]

In a sense, both Ruether and Nash recognize the power and ambiguity of the first creation story, and both are concerned with how the story and its interpretations shape human societies and their relations with the earth. Both bring this story into dialogue with many other stories—other biblical stories, Babylonian and scientific stories for Ruether, and stories of people and movements in Christian tradition for Nash. In short, both recognize the first creation story as actively involved with what preceded and succeeded it. The story has participated actively in the lives of Jews and Christians, and it has contributed to larger movements that are unintentionally or indirectly affected by the story.

Clearly, creation stories are neither passive nor benign in their effects. They shape our attitudes to the world, to ourselves and to God. They are far less important as technical descriptions of how creation came to be, and far more important as conveyors of meaning. Even in the case of the scientific story told in chapter 1, drawn largely from scientific data, the power lies in the majesty and mystery of the story. In the case of biblical stories of creation, the intent of storytellers seems to have little to do with *how* the creation came into being, and everything to do with the movements and intentions of God. The story is carried by oral rhythms—appropriate to an oral culture; thus, the accent is on communication. God's speaking does not reveal the primacy of word over deed; word is simply a central deed for communicating in an oral culture. The story is also carried by visual images—appropriate to a storytelling culture—and, thus, God's actions in creation may have little to do with technological details and more to do with images of wonder—wonder upon wonder in an interconnected whole. We are met in the biblical stories with God's actions, God's communication, and wonder!

Emerging from the first two creation stories in Genesis is the vivid image that *God's relationship with creation is covenantal.* God is the giver of life. God creates each part for its own purposes, and the parts need each other. For example, God gives the plants and trees to people and animals for food (Gen. 1:29–30), and a river flows through Eden to water the garden (v. 2:10). Human beings are placed in the garden to tend it (v. 2:15). Also, God sets limits, such as the command to the first people not to eat the fruit of one tree in the garden (v. 17). Both of these creation stories attest to the creative power and presence of God.

These two Genesis stories also attest that *God's interaction with the creation is responsive.* In the first creation story, God delights in creation, and when God looks over it on the sixth day, God says that it is very good (Gen. 1:31). In the second creation story, God responds to Adam's need for a partner and creates Woman (2:20–23). When Adam and Eve do eat the forbidden fruit, God again responds, this time with a reprimand and punishment (3:8–19). God is a responsive God. In the covenant stories we find God enjoying, being angry, and feeling sadness, but God is always responsive.

The covenant grounded in the creation stories affirms that God creates and transcends creation, and is also present in it. God's spirit moves through the natural world, and every part is connected with every other part. Therefore, *the relationship between human beings and the rest of nature is also covenantal.* As described above, the plants and trees provide food for animals and humans, the river waters the garden, and the people tend the garden. All are related and interdependent. We are called to care for nature for the sake of the whole, and not simply for human benefit.

God Will Be with You

Another recurring affirmation in the biblical witness is that *God is a continuing presence and guide with the people, though sometimes hidden.* One of the most vivid stories of God's presence is the promise God gave to Moses when Moses expressed reluctance to lead the Hebrew people out of Egypt. God said, "I will be with you" (Ex. 3:12; compare 4:12). This promise is a recurring one. God also promised the Hebrews to go before them as a cloud by day and a fiery pillar by night (Ex. 13:21–22; 14:19–25).

Indeed, *God persists with the people through the most desperate of times.* When the Hebrew people were wandering in the wilderness after leaving Egypt, they turned away from God, but God, with some persuasion from Moses, was still with them. When Job struggled with God, God was present (Job 38—42). And when Jonah tried to run away from God and avoid the command to go to Ninevah, he discovered that he could not escape from the presence of God. God continued to call him, even in the belly of the fish (Jon. 1:17—3:3).

This theme persists throughout Christian history, particularly illumined by the mystics, but also carried by such theo-political activists as Martin Luther. Consider Luther's affirmation that God is present in every single grain: "That the Divine majesty is so small that it can be substantially present in a grain, on a grain, over a grain, through a grain, within and without."[52] In quoting this phrase, Larry Rasmussen argues that Luther was making "a massive protest against a Christian world with Greek philosophical genes and against the kind of idolatry this Christianity fostered, an idolatry that took the form of the speculative theology of glory."[53] He argues that Luther's theology was pan*en*theistic, recognizing the presence of God *in* all of creation. He further believes that Dietrich Bonhoeffer's insistence on the proximity of God is more like Luther's earthbound theology than is Karl Barth's theology of God at an awesome distance.[54]

The issue here is suffering. Martin Luther in the sixteenth century, and Bonhoeffer in the twentieth, were both concerned with the social and ecclesial abuses of their day—abuses that were harming and bringing death to humble people. Their views of God—present in the grains and realities of this world— were not romantic naiveté. In their theologies, God's presence leads to God's awareness, suffering, and redemptive activity in the world, thus echoing the compassionate God of Exodus, who says to Moses:

> I have observed the misery of my people who are in Egypt; I have heard their cry...and I have come down to deliver them from the Egyptians, and to bring them up out of that land to a good and broad land. (Ex. 3:7–8a)

God will be with you, according to these accounts. Suffering is indeed real, but God comes again and again.

God Multiplies the Gifts of Creation

God's presence is affirmed yet again in the life of Jesus. Central to Christian teaching is that God was incarnate in Jesus—revealed in his life, death, and resurrection. Further, Jesus continually pointed to God in his teaching. Less visible in Christian teaching is attention to what Jesus revealed about

God's relationship with the creation. We will pursue this question in more detail here, reflecting particularly on one set of revealing stories—*stories that reveal God's presence in the midst of creation and God's multiplication of the gifts of creation.*

We turn to Mark's Gospel to examine three stories that appear close together, just before the middle of the Gospel. The stories are the feeding of the five thousand, Jesus' walking on water, and the feeding of the four thousand. These stories raise striking questions about God in our midst.

In Mark 6:30–44, we find Jesus and the disciples seeking after quietness. Instead of quietness, they found throngs. Rather than send the people away, Jesus had compassion, and he taught them. After some time, the disciples came and whispered to Jesus that he probably should send these people into the villages to eat. Jesus had a better idea; they would feed them. The disciples asked Jesus if he really intended them to go buy bread for all of these people; they were probably thinking that this would settle the matter. But Jesus came back with another idea. He sent the disciples into the crowd to see how much food people had. They came back to report they had found five loaves of bread and two fish. Jesus' response was to ask everyone in the crowd to sit. He took the five loaves and two fish and blessed and broke them, probably with the traditional Hebrew blessing. Everyone ate their fill, and the disciples collected twelve baskets of leftovers. Five thousand people ate that day.

Immediately following this incident, Jesus and the disciples were again seeking after quietness (vv. 45–52). This time Jesus had gone off alone to pray, and the disciples had gone fishing. A storm arose while the disciples were in the middle of the sea, and their boat was tossed by the winds until they were straining at the oars. As they stood in the boat, they saw a figure moving across the water. They were terrified. When Jesus saw their fear he told them to relax, letting them know that he was there. When Jesus entered the ship the winds faded and the storm ceased.

In both of the stories, Jesus and the disciples were seeking solitude—*a spirituality of silence.* In both stories, they found instead a need and responded— *a spirituality of response.* John Paul Heil points out that Jesus' seeing is important to the stories. In the feeding story, Jesus saw the need of the crowd, and in the sea-walking story, he saw the distress of his disciples.[55] In both stories, he responded to the needs he saw. What is often overlooked is that *Jesus responded in both stories through the ordinary gifts of creation*—bread and fish in the first story, and water in the second. This view of God as working through the ordinary gifts of nature is not unusual in biblical accounts. In the Song of Deborah (Judg. 5:21–22), the Kishon River and stars helped the Jewish people in battle. What we discover is that miracles come from the natural elements of creation, emanating from a spirituality of response.

With these reflections we move to the next story, from Mark 8:1–9. *Again, the story begins with a crowd gathered. Jesus was concerned that the people had been there a long time without food, and he said to the disciples that he did not want to send them away hungry for fear that they would faint along the way. The disciples asked how they could possibly provide bread in this wilderness, and Jesus asked his familiar question about how many loaves they could find. They reported seven loaves and a few small fish, and Jesus responded by asking the crowd to sit down. He gave God thanks for the food and broke it, giving it to the disciples to distribute. Again the people ate their fill, all four thousand of them, and seven baskets of leftovers were collected.*

These three stories are often put together in Markan studies, and certain common interpretations emerge. These interpretations correspond with major themes in Christian theology. We will look at each of these interpretations briefly, and then I will propose an alternative. Existing interpretations are not mutually exclusive, nor is the purpose here to replace these with a new one. The purpose is to add another alternative—one which addresses a gap in Christian theology and which is also true to the texts.

One common interpretation of these stories is that the miracles reveal who Jesus was as Messiah. I will call this the *glory of God* interpretation. Certainly in Mark, the unfolding of the Messianic secret (the gradual revealing of Jesus' identity) is a clear theme. Also, the miracle stories in early chapters of Mark's Gospel accent the glory of God, even suggesting associations between the feeding stories and God's gift of manna in the wilderness to Moses and the wandering Israelites.[56]

Another common interpretation is that these stories foreshadow Jesus' passion and death. I call this the *sacrifice of God* interpretation. The passion was central to Mark, and he devoted the second half of his Gospel to the passion narrative. The feeding stories serve as reminders of what is to come in the breaking of the bread and the breaking of the body, foreshadowing the Last Supper, the crucifixion, and the church's eucharistic celebrations. The miraculous nature of the stories themselves tends to bring together the glory of God and sacrifice of God interpretations, one intensifying the other.[57]

A third common interpretation is that the stories reveal the disciples' slowness to grasp what is going on around them. I call this the *human fallibility* interpretation. The disciples seem to have comprehended almost nothing; their expectations were certainly more limited than what they had seen from Jesus. They had been with Jesus from the beginning, and they had witnessed his miracles and teachings continuously. Even in the second feeding story, soon after the first one, they were perplexed. Robert Fowler places particular emphasis on this "obtuseness" and "stupidity" of the disciples, who would finally betray and abandon Jesus altogether in the last eating story of Mark, the last meal Jesus shares with his disciples (Mk. 14:12–25).[58] When we read these stories, the natural inclination is to think that if we had been there we would have done better. Likely, however, Mark expected his readers to identify with the disciples. Today, we are they.

You will notice that these three views fit nicely together. The human fallibility interpretation calls forth the glory of God or sacrifice of God interpretation in order to resolve the human predicament. John Paul Heil, for example, identifies two major functions of Mark's sea-walking epiphany. The story is: (1) a high point in the disciples' inability to comprehend fully the significance of Jesus, and (2) a revelation of Jesus' identity and character, thus building toward the acknowledgment of Jesus' significance in Peter's confession (Mk. 8:29) and the centurion's confession (15:39).[59] The first function corresponds to a human fallibility interpretation, and the latter, to a glory of God interpretation. Others make a similar argument, with the idea that the fallible disciples are better able to grasp what is going on in Mark's story as the glory of the Messianic secret is unfolded.[60]

What is at stake in these various interpretations? At stake is no less than the dominant Christian metaphor of God's redemption of flawed humanity. Dominant interpretations preserve a redemption emphasis by highlighting the glory and power of God, the fallenness or failings of humanity, and the sacrificial acts of God for the sake of humanity. Such interpretations fit naturally with the "the-anthropocentric" emphases that Santmire bemoans in Christian theology, focusing on God, humanity, and the God-human relationship.[61]

Another kind of interpretation may also be drawn from the texts, namely a *sacredness of creation* interpretation. This interpretation is based on the recognition that creation contains the material for miracles—bread and fish, wind and water. Jesus actually did thank God or bless the food before breaking and distributing it; thus the connection between the ordinary food and the miracle is affirmed. The sacredness of creation interpretation is also based on the recognition that Jesus acted to *multiply* the gifts, acting in harmony with creation rather than over or outside of it. He also acted in harmony with his own Jewish tradition, which affirmed the importance of food for all.[62]

This interpretation stands in harmony with reflections on these stories as epiphanies, revealing the character of Jesus and Jesus' response to problematic situations; it also challenges these interpretations, however, for they ignore what is revealed of the character of creation.[63] In the communities of first-century gospel writers, the focal issues may well have been to establish the divinity and power of Jesus, thus anchoring faith in Jesus and responding simultaneously to people's fears of storms, floods, and other natural phenomena. Even so, the gifts of creation are characters in their gospel stories. What of our day when the over-control of nature has become a destructive force? Perhaps we need to rediscover and reinterpret these unseen characters of the Jesus stories—the bread and fish, wind and water.

What we see further in this trilogy of stories is a spirituality of response—Jesus' response to the immediate needs around him. The response was not one that came as a consequence of silent time with God (though Jesus often sought and practiced such silence). Instead, the response took place in the midst of the world's activities, and God was there in the midst of creation.

Such an interpretation is fitting to later action stories in Christian history as well. Consider the action of Archbishop Eberhard of Salzburg in 1237 to forbid the use of cleared forestland so that the forest could grow again; consider the pledge of the Bishop of Bamberg in 1328 to grant the protection of the Christian church both to people and to forests threatened by deforestation.[64] Such pledges, mixed as they were with political and economic motives, proclaimed that God's response is intended for land as well as for people. Consider, also, legends of Saint Clare (1194–1253). Once a sister told Clare that they had only one piece of bread in the whole house, and no further food for the sisters or the two beggars at the door. Clare's response was to break the bread, give half to the beggars, and ask half to be divided among the sisters. The sister did so while Clare prayed, "and the food increased, becoming enough to feed the whole convent."[65] The story of the loaves was thus repeated.

Consider further the response of Saint Francis (1181/2–1226) to a disillusioned, angry man suffering with leprosy. Francis offered to be at the man's service and to do for him whatever he wished. The leper replied that he wanted a bath, which Francis did with warm water, fragrant herbs, and gentle hands. The story climaxes:

> And as the water washed him on the outside, so he was totally cleansed of the leprosy, and inside his spirit was cleansed and healed. And just as his body was washed and cleansed of leprosy, so his soul was baptised in tears and cleansed from sin.[66]

This story reveals a spirituality of response, embodied in Francis' ministry to the physical and psychic needs of the hurting man, and interpreted by a storyteller. In the story, Francis draws upon the ordinary gifts of creation. As he does so, the gifts are multiplied, thus yielding physical healing and spiritual blessings, suggestive of baptism. The Christian faith carries with it many such stories of responsive spirituality and multiplied gifts of creation. Which parts of these stories actually happened is not the critical issue. The stories themselves have helped shape an ethos and interpretive framework within Christianity, and these now face us with many challenges in the postmodern era.

Meeting Challenges

We are now faced with a set of dilemmas on the one hand and, on the other hand, affirmations that God is in our midst—as Creator, as Presence, as One who multiplies the gifts of creation. By placing an accent on the sacredness of creation interpretation of God's work, we are faced with new challenges for ministry in the midst of environmental crisis. I will pose five challenges, and readers will think of others.

The first challenge is *to focus less on God beyond the world and more on God within the world.* We need, for example, to draw on images of God that communicate God's presence in our midst. One such biblical image is the presence of God's angel in the burning bush that was not consumed (Ex. 3:2). Another image comes from a Chinese monk, who served for a time as spiritual director for a woman who had many questions about God. The woman asked him how she could tell what parts of herself were of God and what parts of herself were other than God. The monk responded by taking her up on a hill and showing her two small rivers that flowed together into one big river. He asked her to tell him which part of the big river came from the right fork and which came from the left. She said that she could not tell because the waters flowed and mingled together. He replied, "It is the same with you and God."

To affirm God's presence is to embark on a second challenge: *to recognize God's presence in sacred places as well as in sacred time and human history.* Jace Weaver writes of his people, the Cherokees, who were forcibly removed from the southeast United States to Oklahoma, being robbed of even more than land:

> Stolen from them was a numinous landscape where every mountain and lake held meaning for their lives and their faith. Yet, in one sense, they were lucky. When they arrived in Oklahoma, they found, like the Israelites of the Exile, that their God had gone with them.[67]

Recognizing the spatial dimension of indigenous worldviews, Weaver argues that Western humanity has been preoccupied with human history, connected to a "fall/redemption" theology. He adds: "Creation never 'fell' in Native spirituality and so is not in need of redemption. It may be that the true nature of the fall of humanity is to be condemned to live only in history."[68]

Sacred space, or place, is a critical focus if we are to honor the sacredness of God's creation. More will be said in chapters 4 and 5, but for now, the challenge of recognizing and tending sacred places is highlighted as ministry with the earth. Echoing this sentiment, Jay McDaniel calls people to "a sense of place" and the opportunity it offers to experience "green grace."[69] For him, this is no glib notion; he is calling people to know their bioregions—the movements of people, animals, and land; the native species; the phases of the moon; the patterns of water distribution and garbage treatment; and so forth.

The third challenge is *to focus not only on the mediation of God through Jesus Christ, but also on the mediation of God through all of creation.* Much of Western spirituality has centered almost entirely on Jesus Christ. Spiritual practices have included meditation on the cross, praying to Christ, singing hymns of Jesus, and maintaining the centrality of baptism and the Eucharist, both of which are grounded in the life of Christ. The proposals here are not to eliminate those spiritual practices, but to include others.

Furthermore, even spiritual practices focused on the Christ can point to the presence of God in the world, as Jesus pointed to God throughout his ministry. The sacraments—grounded in the life, death and resurrection of Jesus—point to the sacramentality of the whole earth, which itself nourished Jesus. The gifts of creation—water, bread and wine—are actually mediators of God's grace in the sacraments, powerfully real as the connections are enacted and named. The celebration of Eucharist may include naming the relationship between Jesus' body and the ordinary bread of life, and naming the link between those who partake in the Eucharistic meal and the hunger of people across the world.[70] For Orthodox Christians, this meaning of Eucharist, associated with the life of the world and the food of creation, is understood as intimately connected with the work of Christ and the eschatological journey of the Church.[71]

The church has rich liturgical traditions for ritualizing the sacredness of creation. In Orthodox Christian Churches, the Feast of Bread is such a liturgy, and it has traditionally played an important part in the ritual life of the people. It is not the same as the eucharist, however; in this service, the bread represents creation, and the liturgy highlights the presence of God in creation. The agape meal has carried similar symbolism in Western Christian tradition, representing the sharing of God's creation—through the basic elements of bread and water—within the gathered covenantal community.

In addition to rituals, the mediation of God through creation can also be accentuated through spiritual practices such as inviting people to meditate on a tree or leaf or rock. Such a meditation may be focused first on the physical features of the subject, and then on the act of receiving what God may be trying to communicate through that tree or leaf or rock. Spiritual practices such as these are grounded in the expectation that the natural world *will* teach people about God and will allow people to commune with God. In one Native American educational practice, a child was taken to a place of solitude every day and left among the boulders and plants and sun. At the end of the day, the parent or mentor returned for the child. The school was the world of nature, and the teachers were everything in the natural world. Recent attention to Native American educational theory emphasizes just such an educational process, including the full cultural, communal, and geographic context.[72] Theologically, one can say that God is mediated through the culture and life patterns of a people and also through the land, air, animals, and plants.

A fourth challenge is *to focus not only on human fallenness and God's salvation, but also on human giftedness and God's multiplication of the gifts.* If you have a deep sense of God's presence in the midst of creation, then you know God is present in every human being and in every other being. All entities in God's creation have intrinsic worth and are to be respected accordingly. As for people, the gifts of each human being can be a guide to that person's calling or responsibility in the world.[73]

Such belief is quite different from focusing on fallenness, and it leads to different emphases in practice. The practice of encouragement is particularly important—encouraging people to identify their gifts, discern God's distinctive call, and multiply their gifts. These practices are distinct from asking people to identify their flaws, name ways they will work to improve themselves, pray their confessions, and listen for words of assurance. Such fall/redemption practices are not being condemned here, but they are not sufficient in themselves if we are to take seriously God's presence in our midst. To identify and build on human gifts is not to deny that people have flaws they need to confess; it is simply to accent human gifts and the multiplication of them. In such a view, a mentor is less a confessor and more a vocational guide. A mentor is one who helps people discern what God is doing in their lives and respond to the pulses of God's Spirit.

The fifth challenge is *to focus less on prayers of petition and more on prayers of participation.* Thomas Merton critiqued the practice of prayer as pure petition.

He urged that, in prayer, persons seek first a sense of union with God, and then they will know for what they need to pray.[74] Such a practice is an act of attuning yourself to God's presence in your midst. Prayer, then, is seen not simply as imploring God to act, but as participating in God's power, even mediating or channeling God's power to those in need.

To these challenges could be added others: the need to balance appreciation for oneself with walking gently on the earth; the importance of living with paradox; the need to respect the human body and the earth, recognizing their deep interconnection; the need to relate with painful realities as well as joy; and the need to seek illumination from the worldviews and spiritual practices of many peoples—East and West, North and South, past and present, many races and many faiths.

In conclusion, the most fundamental challenge is *to live as if all in creation are our brothers and sisters*. In the words attributed to Chief Seattle:

> Teach your children what we have taught our children—that the earth is our mother. Whatever befalls the earth, befalls the children of the earth. All things are connected like the blood which unites one human family.[75]

The challenge that we all carry is to teach one another what none of us fully understand, that we live together in one community with this earth. God has created us to be in covenant with God and one another, and the covenant community includes the earth itself and everything on it. God bless this sacred creation!

THREE

Sacred Meetings:
Meeting as Covenant People

A few years ago, my two grandsons (aged 8 and 10) participated in the opening retreat of my seminary community. As we drove through the mountains and approached the campground, they asked, "What are we going to do? Are we going to have a campfire like last year?" One said, "That was my favorite thing!" The other agreed.

✖

A cluster of small-membership churches in the rural Midwest became alarmed about the problems of hunger and homelessness that existed all around them. As people from the various churches talked among themselves, they realized that they could work with the farmers in their congregations and respond. They established a gleaning program. The farmers covenanted with one another and their churches to leave some produce on their land at harvest time; then, people who needed food could come glean food for themselves and their families and friends.

✖

A group of people planning a camp for younger youth was eager for the camp to be a grand experience, but they worried about the "problem of the last campfire." Problems had emerged in previous camps when youth had had dramatic religious experiences and returned home without integrating their experiences. Sometimes youth left camp with much confusion or emotion and no one at home with whom to discuss these matters.

During one stage of planning, one of the team—a recent seminary graduate— pulled out a book describing common developmental features of young adolescents. Among the features listed in the book were excitability, self-doubts, the desire for emotional or dramatic experiences, and the need for adult mentors or guides. The

49

planning team began to reflect on those characteristics; the list resonated with the youth they knew. The conversation suddenly turned from the "problem of the last campfire" to a discussion of possibilities for being with the youth as they entered into the closing experiences of the camp. Plans were made for a closing campfire on the second to last night, with plenty of time for group and personal interaction the next day, and a ritual of sending on the last night. Recognizing that God's Spirit does move and that youth are often eager for significant religious experiences, the counseling team made plans that left the doors wide open for movements of the Spirit, providing also for companionship in the community and preparation for leaving the mountaintop. And so it was!

In the midst of a large city, a local church debated what to do with the space around their building. Some of it was cemented, and some grew in weeds (unwanted plants) that were dutifully pulled from time to time by people of the church. The people felt that the space was wasted, especially in the midst of a city that needed green plants for better air quality and food for people who lived on the streets.

In the meantime, the people gathered in small groups to study the challenges of urban ministry and some of the unique problems and strengths of their own city. One group emerged with the idea of converting their land into a green space, with trees to breathe oxygen into the air and cool the church building in summer and with a large vegetable garden to produce vegetables that would be available through their food distribution center. After months of digging and planting and tending, so it was!

What do these stories have in common, and what do they have to do with God-centered, earthbound ministries? All of the stories in some way *point to a circle of relationship.* The very symbol of a campfire is rich with the imagery of people meeting in a circle around one of the most elemental and mysterious acts of nature. We should not be surprised that people often feel the movement of God's Spirit in campfire moments and are often moved in these moments to see themselves and their world in a new light. But circles of relationship go far beyond the obvious. In some of these circles, people relate and respond to needs in their community, as in the youth camp described above. In some, they relate and respond to needs in the larger community, as the rural Midwestern community did in the second story, and the urban community in the last one. Circles of relationship can be small and intimate, or large and ever-expanding, but they are critical to understanding and nurturing the sacred creation described in chapter 2.

The stories are similar in another way; they *point to a sense of joy and expectation for themselves and the world around them.* The joy of the first campfire story is the most obvious; our grandchildren could not wait for what was to come. But joy and expectation are evident in the other stories as well—joy in discovering new possibilities for ministry and expectation that churches can make a difference in the world. Such expectation propelled the churches of the rural Midwest to discuss what they could do; it propelled the counselors of the youth camp to wrestle with a problem from years past. Expectation also propelled the church of the large city to form small groups to study and pray for guidance. Expectation in these congregations is complex, but the communities also share the freshness of my grandchildren who simply could not wait for the campfire because it was their favorite thing.

This leads to a third common feature in the stories; they all *point to a sense of responsibility*. These people feel compelled by their experiences to respond to God and to the world around them, and they have a sense of their ability to respond, even if the response seems small in the context of pressing needs. Thus, the people of these stories have a sense of response-ability. In the story of the church's garden, the people felt responsibility not only for church property and for hungry people on the streets, but also for the air of their city. In the rural Midwest, the churches felt responsibility to work with local farmers in developing a program to serve immediate needs. In the youth camp story, the counselors felt responsibility for youth, and also for their families, friends, and churches back home. Even for my grandchildren a sense of responsibility was called forth as they prepared to meet new people and enter an unfamiliar world. The campfire represented the promise of community in the midst of these challenges.

The purposes of this chapter are to reflect upon *the nature of relationships* in an interconnected, interdependent world; *the meaning of covenant relationship* for the Christian community; and *the possibility of supporting covenantal living through sacred meetings*. This is the action of *cutting patches for quilt-making*—preparing the basic materials from which ministry with the earth is made. The remainder of the chapter is organized around the three themes. And in the spirit of covenant—imaged as a circle—the chapter is a circular dance through meditative reflection and theological analysis.

An Interconnected, Interdependent World

On the cliffs of Hawaii grows a plant called Brighamia Insignis. *When the plant began to disappear, people wondered why. Scientists studied the problem and discovered that the birds responsible for pollinating the* Brighamia *had become extinct, so the plants, without a means of reproduction, were slowly becoming extinct too.*

Much has been written in recent years about the reality of an interconnected, interdependent world. The language of relationality, however, has not fully penetrated the psyche, particularly in those Western cultures where autonomous individualism is applauded as a virtue or taken for granted as a commonsense description of the world.

Some of the most extensive analysis of interconnectedness has been done by ecofeminists. They argue that the universe is not composed of autonomous beings, but of interconnected beings and social systems; thus, actions in one part of the world affect people and ecosystems in another.[1] Such thinking has been questioned and enlarged by African and African American womanist scholars who demonstrate that white feminists have largely ignored the reality of racist and classist social structures, thus limiting their own perspectives on interconnections and interdependence.[2] Likewise, *mujerista* and Asian feminist theologians have argued that feminists have attended too little to the voices and meanings of ordinary women, especially the *mujeristas*, or women from the Latin Americas, and the women of the Philippines, Korea, China, Japan, and elsewhere.[3] Increasingly, women around the world are acting and speaking for ever-larger understandings of the circles of relationship.

Realities of Interconnectedness

The realities of interconnectedness are easy to deny, leading to fragmentation on the one hand (discussed in chapter 2) and a push for uniformity on the other. When governor of California, Ronald Reagan was quoted as responding to conservationists who sought to preserve the coastal forests, "If you have seen one tree, you have seen them all."[4] This offhand comment sounds small enough, but it represents an attitude that all trees are alike, that one tree can represent them all, and that coastal forests that are hundreds of years old are not terribly important in the scheme of things. If the earth is understood as more than a site for human sightseeing, however, those trees (each one and all together) are vital to the vitality of the creation.

While the work of feminist, womanist, *mujerista*, and Asian feminist scholars has opened new doors for understanding interconnectedness, the conflicts that have emerged among diverse liberation theorists have also shaken any possibility for narrow, separatist understandings of urgent issues. We have experienced the radical shaking of oppressive worldviews and social systems as issues of gender, race, class, and nature have been debated against one another.[5] However competitive those debates have been, they have forced a recognition that issues are interwoven in such intricate and tightly woven patterns that one cannot possibly do justice to one complex of issues without considering others. Single-issue politics is a luxury that neither human society nor the planet can afford.

Two particular forms of relationality are important to consider here. One is the *relationality of human beings with the rest of creation*. Process theologians, such as Jay McDaniel, Carol Johnston, John Cobb, and David Griffin, commonly argue for a relational view of creation. Within such a view, human beings are understood to be unique, as all creatures are unique; the uniqueness, similarity, and relationship among creatures are a motivation for respect and responsibility.[6] A relational view is also argued by ecologists, such as David Suzuki, who believe that recognizing human beings as animals is a key to understanding human dependence on the biosphere.[7] On the other hand, some ecologists express nervousness about any kind of holistic worldview, especially when connectedness is so emphasized that difference is ignored.[8] More will be said of this in the next chapter.

I would argue that both difference and continuity are important to understanding relationships between human beings and the rest of nature.[9] We need to recognize the uniqueness of each individual being and every part of creation (rock soil, sandy soil, saltwater, freshwater, and so forth). We also need to recognize the ways in which we share qualities, concerns, and needs. On these grounds, our relationships can be respectful and mutual, rather than alienating or dominating. We are quite different beings from the *Brighamia Insignis* (the plant whose story opens this section), but like the *Brighamia*, we depend on the actions of other beings; without them, we would become extinct.

A second form of relationality is *across time*—generation to generation. All of creation is related with what has gone before and what will come after. Peoples in many parts of the world honor their ancestors and thus maintain intimate ties with peoples and realities of the past. In some Native American traditions, people seek to live for the benefit of the seventh generation of people yet to come, thus honoring the close link between lifestyles of today and the quality of life for future generations. Perhaps most human beings long for a more life-giving relationship with the past and future.[10] Perhaps the considerable attention to death and life in the world's religions is grounded in this longing, whether the religion focuses on eternal life, reincarnation, the passing of heritage from one generation to another, or some other form of generativity and connection.

Denials of Interconnection

However real relationships are, they are also denied. Much denial of interconnection is communicated in physical actions more than in word actions—acts of racial discrimination by people who claim they have no prejudice, or acts of ignoring toxic waste disposal near residential and recreational areas by people who claim to value children. The failure to see such inconsistencies is sometimes a conscious choice, but at other times it is a more pernicious, unconscious action.

To understand the conscious and semi-conscious choices for denial, the work of liberation theologians is particularly fruitful. When Cornel West tells the story of African American men and boys who are stopped repeatedly by police for a disproportionate number of investigations, he is trying to disrupt the practice of denial and convince readers that race really does matter.[11] When James Cone argues that God is black, he is trying to help people see how dominant white images of God have reinforced white dominance, and how black images of God can transform the way African American peoples understand and value themselves.[12] In short, the way people image God and the way people image human beings are intimately connected. Likewise, language plays a crucial role that cannot be denied. Elizabeth Johnson argues that language about God affects the way people relate with God and the world; she says:

> The way in which a faith community shapes language about God implicitly represents what it takes to be the highest good, the profoundest truth, the most appealing beauty. Such speaking, in turn, powerfully molds the corporate identity of the community and directs its praxis.[13]

In light of these critiques, one can hardly deny the interconnections within social systems, and between social values and theological discourse. The critique goes further, however. Liberation theologians paint a picture of the economic and social relationships that keep some countries wealthy and other countries in their debt. Scholars such as Elsa Tamez uncover the oft-ignored biblical critique of such contemporary socioeconomic realities, especially realities of poverty and systems that perpetuate economic oppression.[14]

But denial is sometimes unconscious as well. To understand the unconscious choice to deny interconnectedness and interdependence, the idea of psychic numbing is important to consider. In the early 1980s, Robert Jay Lifton and Richard Falk described psychic numbing in relation to nuclearism, recognizing that the brain functions to eliminate stimuli as well as to receive and sort them; thus, people cease to perceive and react to certain hideous realities. The brain is able to numb people to massive death, distracting influences, and stimulus overload.[15] Such brain actions are functional (as in helping people to concentrate), but psychic numbing can, over time, allow people to hide from issues and mask their feelings. The problem is accentuated when image overload combines with a loss of traditional symbols and forms, and with a loss of historical rootedness.[16]

Envisioning More Nourishing Relationships

If everything and everyone are connected and interdependent, then the quality of those relationships is very important. To say that a young boy is connected and interdependent with his father who has sexually molested him is not to give a beautiful testimony for relationality. Relationships can be physically, psychologically, or economically abusive. The toxic wastes of the Midwest United States destroy trees with acid rain 500 miles away in New England. The desire for national security in Europe or North America leads to nuclear testing in the Pacific. The desire of people in wealthy countries to possess more clothes, machines, and technological products for lower costs leads to underpaid and overworked employees in parts of Asia. The efforts of agribusiness and large corporations to control more land and resources leads to the destruction of small family-owned, self-sustaining plots of land, and it contributes to the destruction of family livelihood, stability, and survival, even leading to such radical survival efforts as selling children into prostitution. This is the nature of our interconnected, interdependent world.

Attending to the quality of relationships becomes a matter of urgency in such a world, and people in many philosophical and religious traditions have addressed this concern. Philosophically, some have argued that the existentialist and humanistic schools of thought have left at least one destructive mark in isolating humanity from the rest of nature, thus elevating humanity and demeaning or demonizing the rest of nature. Erazim Kohák argues that we need, instead, a philosophy of personalism, in which the porcupines, the people, the trees in the forest and the cosmos itself are understood as persons, existing in social relationships with others.[17] From Kohák's point of view, this suggests the moral necessity of I-Thou relationships among all beings. This neither elevates humans above the rest of the natural world nor romanticizes a world without humans, but rather calls forth relationships of respect.[18]

This view of the world represents a radicalized version of the personalist philosophy that influenced Martin Luther King, Jr.'s, moral view of the world when he studied at Boston University.[19] It represents an extension of Martin Buber's I-Thou relationships, which Buber himself extended beyond humans. Consider Buber's reflections on a tree:

> I contemplate a tree...I can feel it as movement: the flowing veins around the sturdy, striving core, the sucking of the roots, the breathing of the leaves...I can assign to it a species and observe it as an instance, with an eye to its construction and its way of life...But it can also happen, if will and grace are joined, that as I contemplate the tree I am drawn into a relation, and the tree ceases to be an It.[20]

Such a personal view of creation also converges with a theological emphasis on covenant, which is fundamental in Jewish and Christian traditions.

Covenantal Meeting

When people gather as Christians, as when people gather in any religious community, they are gathering as a people bound together by shared history, views of the world, and ethical convictions. Within Jewish and Christian traditions, this sense of being connected as a people is expressed by the idea of covenant. Jews and Christians understand themselves to be a covenant people who are bound by the natural delights of the creation and by human needs for relationship, but more important, by a relationship with God. God calls the people to be bound together, not simply by mutual enjoyment (however welcome such mutuality can be), but by a sense of connectedness and responsibility with God and the earth and one another. The covenant is a bonding between God and God's people that is initiated and made possible by the gracious acts of God. As such, the covenant is a gift and that gift from God with expectations for the righteousness of the people stands at the center of both the First Testament (Hebrew Bible or Old Testament) and New Testament traditions. The word *testament* itself means "covenant." It is also embodied in some small way in the stories with which this chapter began—stories that reveal a circle of relationship, a sense of joy and expectation, and a sense of responsibility.

Covenant: A Circle of Relationship

To say that covenant is a gift of God is to say that God has chosen to create the cosmos and breathe life into it; thus, God initiates the covenant relationship. To say that covenant is a circle of relationship is to recognize that God and human beings and the whole of creation are in continuing interaction with one another—dancing in a circle of life. God initiates the relationship, but all are interwoven and have responsibility to the covenant. The idea of covenant is richly textured in Jewish and Christian traditions, and many debates have yet to be resolved. Our approach here will be quite simple, however, analyzing content and discerning major threads in the literature on covenant.

Gift: A Circle of Relationship with God and God's Creation

The binding thread of covenant is a relationship initiated by God; that thread joins people with God, one another, and all of creation. Covenant is sometimes misunderstood as a relationship between God and people, or between God and Christian people. As we will see below, however, covenantal relationships are much larger and more complex than that, especially if one explores the riches of biblical tradition.

Covenantal theology centers on a few widely shared convictions, even in the midst of diverse texts, interpretations, and debates. Thus, we begin with a concise summary of covenant from Thomas Parker. Although his description is anthropocentric, it is helpful in identifying four complementary ideas that are generally signified by covenant:

> As an arrangement created by God who makes covenant, *it is a gracious gift*. As it stipulates a form of life based on the gift, *it is realized in a response of faith and obedience*. Because it is based on consent rather than coercion, *it establishes a responsible moral relation between people and God*; sociality becomes solidarity. And as it envisions a way of life pressing beyond the limits of any particular culture, *it establishes a history of seeking a universal community of justice and friendship*, 'a blessing in the midst of the earth'.[21]

Although these themes are stated differently and debated by various scholars, they form a broad framework for understanding the bonding God has initiated with people and the earth. And though Parker has stopped short of naming the earth as a full covenant partner, the biblical witness does not stop there, and we will not stop there either.

Enlarging upon themes identified above, one is quickly aware that covenant is too significant to be exhausted by one interpretation. In the Bible itself, covenant is central in importance, but diverse in interpretation. For example, the four sources of the Pentateuch (the first five books of the Bible) are very different from one another, but they reveal shared convictions among the Jewish people. The sources "are united in their conviction that what happened to Moses must be seen as definitive or paradigmatic for understanding their own age's standing in relation to God."[22] David Brown points out that all four sources of the Pentateuch—commonly identified as Yahwist (J), Elohist (E), Deuteronomist (D), and Priestly (P)—appeal to the covenant as God's special relationship with Israel, grounded in God's liberation of their ancestors from slavery in Egypt.

Differences emerge because the four sources address their communities during different periods of time in relation to diverse experiences and needs;

thus, the covenant can be variously understood as: intimacy to be celebrated, protection against assimilation, a source for religious renewal, and a preserver of national identity.[23] Such interpretive variation exists within the canon, and it continues throughout Jewish and Christian history. The circles of relationship do not fit one simple pattern, but they are real.

RESPONSIBILITY: JUSTICE AND COMPASSION FOR ALL PEOPLES AND CREATURES

One covenantal theme that persists through the varieties of interpretation is God's concern for justice; no individual or nation should be marginalized or dealt with unjustly (cf: Isa. 2:2–4; Mic. 4:1–5).[24] In fact, to be the people of God is to live in honest relationship with both wretchedness and hope, to be "a people living and on the move" toward dignity and liberation.[25] Aracely de Rocchietti argues that the Gospels portray Jesus as one who sought to call an eschatological people, not to found an institution.[26] The human calling, then, is to practice communal disciplines that foster love toward neighbor and faithfulness to God. The call to follow Jesus is the call to identify with the marginalized.

> This idea of a new people, a people open to the action of God—a people inclusive enough to be for the poor, for women, children, the disabled, Jews, and Gentiles—did not make itself apparent in any great expansion of this new people...The demands of the call left many by the roadside.[27]

We see in this imagery of the people of God a calling into radical forms of ministry, but not ministries based on the superiority of Christianity or the closeness of Christian fellowship. Rather, the emphasis is on ministries that send people more fully into defending life and the dignity of every person.

The association of covenant with justice and compassion can be understood in terms of blessing. God blesses people—enters covenant—not because they deserve blessing, nor to make them happy, but so they can bless others. Consider Genesis 12:1–3; 18:17–18; 22:15ff; 26:2–5; and 28:14. For David Napier, the threefold message of these texts is clear: You are blessed by God, you are called to bless the unblessed, and through you, others will be able to bless themselves.[28] The unblessed are the victims of a destructive society. Blessing is directed both to the causes of their non-blessing (Isa. 58:3ff) and to the possibility of blessing the unblessed.

Although Napier focuses more on the human non-blessed, we find many creatures in the biblical tradition for whom God asks the people to show compassion or preservation. God commanded Noah to take two of all living things aboard the ark "to keep them alive with you" (Gen. 6:19). Further, God gave the Sabbath for *all* beings—for the land itself and for slaves, servants, sojourners, cattle, and other beasts. God even gave special instructions to the early Hebrews regarding birds found in a nest, giving permission for people to take the eggs or the young but asking that the mother be set free (Deut. 22:6–7), thus protecting the birds and their future. Regarding trees, these are not to be destroyed even when people are besieging a city[29] (Deut. 20:19).

The covenantal responsibility is, thus, to practice justice and offer compassion to all peoples and all of creation. We need not even distinguish between *human justice* and *ecological integrity*, for we are simultaneously to concern ourselves with *human integrity* and *ecological justice*. In short, the distinctions among creatures and the various parts of the cosmos are not obliterated by these interpretations, but all are part of the circle of covenantal responsibility. The last word of covenant is not responsibility, however, but hope—the subject to which we now turn.

HOPE: GOODNESS AND MERCY FOR THE WHOLE OF CREATION

The circle of covenant contributes to the future of God's creation; thus, covenant is grounded in hope. The hope is frequently expressed anthropomorphically—as hope for human life. Lewis Mudge, for example, expresses a vision that Christians will bring the fullness of their traditions to bear for the good of all humanity.

> I want to see a vision of the people of God grasped by the churches and then lived out. The essential point is that the churches and other religious communities should go deeply into their resources for ways of living distinctively *traditioned* lives for the sake of the *whole* of human life.[30]

Mudge's words, like the earlier words of Rocchietti, bear much hope and much responsibility for the people of God. For Rocchietti, in particular, the hope is for those who are most downtrodden, and ultimately for all peoples of the earth.

God's covenant is not only with people, however; it is with the whole earth. Thus, covenantal theology needs to be enlarged to include the life and dignity of all creation. Indeed, the covenantal relationship with all of creation is emphasized in recent writing on ecological theology.[31] And even among ecological theologians, the concern is with those who are oppressed and abused. In the midst of his plea for a hurting natural world, James Nash writes on behalf of hurting people:

> Faithfulness to covenant relationships demands a justice that gives special consideration or a "preferential option" to widows, orphans, aliens, and the poor—in other words, the politically marginalized and excluded, the economically vulnerable and powerless, the communally bruised and bullied (Ex. 23:6–9; Deut. 15:4–11; 24:14–22; Jer. 22:16; Am. 2:6–7; 5:10–12).[32]

This pervasive concern for justice is echoed in biblical appeals for a Jubilee Year (Lev. 25) and a Year of Release (Deut. 15:1–18), a theme which will be discussed further in chapter 7.[33] The biblical texts, taken together, require people to return acquired properties after fifty years, to remit debts for members of the community, and to release Hebrew servants from their servitude. The texts reveal great hopes for justice, both for humans and for the earth. The Jubilee

Year may not actually have been practiced, however, and requirements for the Year of Release were limited to debts and servitude within the community. Even if the teachings were not fully realized, however, the vision challenges people to practice covenantal living.

QUESTIONS: COVENANT AS INCLUSIVE OR EXCLUSIVE?

The most debatable aspect of covenant is whether the covenantal thinking of the Bible, and of later Jewish and Christian traditions, is limited to God's covenant with the religious community or whether it pushes toward a universal relationship between God and all of humankind. That is an important question, and the answers are filled with ambiguity and complexity. The thrust of this discussion is to accent the way that the covenant at least *pushes* toward inclusiveness by including all of the earth and, at some points, all peoples of the world. At the most basic level, the covenant texts carry a message of inclusiveness to the communities who are addressed, calling them to be faithful to God and one another. This is evident whether the concern is for Hebrews wandering in the wilderness (Ex. 20), disciples of Jesus facing his impending death (Mk. 14 and Lk. 22), or Corinthians torn by dissension within their church (1 Cor. 11).

We see some indications of a push toward broader inclusiveness in the covenant with Noah in Genesis 9:8–17. In early verses, we see the discussion focused on Noah and his descendants and the living creatures *with* him. God says, "I am establishing my covenant with you and your descendants after you, and with every living creature that is with you, the birds, the domestic animals, and every animal of the earth with you, as many as came out of the ark" (Gen. 9:9–10). In later verses, the discussion expands:

> "I have set my bow in the clouds, and it shall be a sign of the covenant between me and the earth…When the bow is in the clouds, I will see it and remember the everlasting covenant between God and every living creature of all flesh that is on the earth." God said to Noah, "This is the sign of the covenant that I have established between me and all flesh that is on the earth" (Gen. 9:13, 16–17).

Some moral ambiguity remains even in this story. In the beginning, God is seen expressing fury against human wickedness by flooding the entire earth. On the other hand, the interconnection and interdependence of all creation is affirmed clearly in the story, and God is seen "making an unconditional pledge in perpetuity to all humanity, to all other creatures, and to the earth itself, to preserve all species and their environments."[34] Bernhard Anderson has identified this story as the "ecological covenant."[35]

Likewise, in the New Testament, we find texts that push toward inclusiveness, though again in complex and ambiguous ways. Words attributed to Jesus in Mark's and Luke's stories of the Last Supper associate Jesus' blood with the covenant. In Mark, Jesus says to his disciples, "This is my blood of the covenant, which is poured out for many" (14:24). In Luke's Gospel, Jesus says, "This cup that is poured out for you is the new covenant in my blood" (22:20b). Some scholars believe that the earliest form is found in Paul's letter to Corinth: "This cup is the new covenant in my blood. Do this, as often as you drink it, in remembrance of me" (1 Cor. 11:25b). Even without detailed interpretation of these texts, we can see vividly that the covenant sealed with a rainbow shown to Noah, with tablets of law at Sinai, and with the blood of Jesus' death are intertwined and centered in the relationship between God and God's people. Further, the cup of covenant is poured out for many; people are invited to drink from the cup and remember. At the very least, the invitation to drink the cup and remember is a wide invitation to participate in covenant relationship.

A covenantal focus can also be the impetus for eliminating religious intolerance and building relations of mutuality. As Padraic O'Hare seeks to build such relations between Christians and Jews, he finds himself hoping for covenantal relationship with other religions as well. He concludes "that triumphalist religion destroys the very clues to holiness that the religious community seeks to pass on to its members."[36] He thus draws a connection between the health of a religious community and its reverence for others. Consider the implications: As we set aside negative language and practices toward others, "we are doing something that adds to the health of our religious community, to its capacity to assist people to become holy."[37]

Such associations between inclusiveness and covenant, and between inclusiveness and holiness, may be very old indeed. In the catacombs outside of Rome, where early Christians gathered and buried their dead, many of the walls bear pictures of the Last Supper. The frescoes do not depict twelve disciples, but rather, five people sitting at table. The number five was known in the early centuries of the Common Era as a symbol for the whole of humanity. Perhaps these early Christians understood the covenant as inclusive of all peoples, at least in the sense that Jesus lived and died for the sake of all. Perhaps this image inspired their worship and living. Such questions regarding the inclusiveness and exclusiveness of covenant traditions will certainly remain, but the covenants of God do seemingly point to the self-confessed people of God in some times and places, and more broadly to all peoples and the whole of creation at other times.

POSSIBILITIES: EATING AND DRINKING TOGETHER

Shared eating and drinking in the Middle Eastern world of Jesus would have been understood immediately as covenantal, binding the people not only with Jesus but also with one another. Herein we see a binding feature of covenant stories. When biblical stories describe contexts in which people are torn apart, doing evil, or destroying others in combative dissension, the acts of covenant call attention to broken community; they may also function as means of grace and reconciliation. Whether we speak of the wayward human beings of the Noah story, the confused and soon-to-be-scattered disciples of the Last Supper, or the divided community of Corinth, the covenant is pronounced as a promise of new life and call to relationship. The covenantal relationship certainly exacts requirements, but it is defined less by the boundaries of who is in or out, and more by the critical reality that God is in relationship with creation and people are called to be in relationship with God and creation.

Thinking of covenant in this way, one recognizes that *meeting in covenant is meeting that is touched and empowered by God's grace*. God is there before we gather, and God's Spirit permeates our gathering. What is called out from us is response, and that *response includes hope* (as in the covenant with Noah), *faithfulness* (as in the covenant on Sinai) and *remembrance* (as in the cup of the new covenant and in all of the covenants that had gone before). This discussion is not intended to explain covenant fully, but it suggests qualities that hold communities together with God and one another—qualities of hope, faithfulness, and remembrance that are themselves generated and supported by acts of God. These are qualities that can be inspired in sacred meetings.

Covenant: Lamention for a Broken Circle

The language of covenant may sound idealistic or utopian, but we are people who live with broken covenants. Although we are born into a circle of relationship with God and the earth, we live in broken relationships. Husbands are separated from wives, parents from children, gays from straights, race from race, upper classes from lower classes, humans from animals and plants, and creatures from their dwelling places in land and water and sky. Further, the relationships that persist are sometimes more destructive than not. The actions of wealthy countries create economic hardships for poor countries, parents abuse children, women are forced into prostitution for survival, people tear resources from the earth, and so on.

Lament is a neglected form of protest in many cultural traditions, but within some cultures lament is a primary way of communicating with God regarding the broken circle of covenant. One such culture in the United States is Appalachian, where people sing their laments, as well as pray and shout them.[38] Lament is also a common expression of the prophetic ministry of women in the Hebrew Bible. According to Tereza Cavalcanti, lament arose when the people of Israel experienced "their strength choked off and their ability to resist falter."[39] In Judges, for example, the lament is more than a request for help from God; "it is also a public expression of the people's pain."[40] This echoes stories of Exodus in which God hears the groans and cries of the people (3:7–10; 2:23–24).

In these and other texts, lament serves multiple purposes. It can serve "to raise consciousness, and provoke a response from the people," as in the case of Esther (Esth. 4:1–3).[41] It can be a form of prayer, as in the pleas of Judith (Jdt. 9:1,11). It can be a reminder of the suffering of the whole people, as in the story of Naomi (Ruth 1:13, 20–21). And it can be a cry that evokes response from God, as in the case of Hagar, whose lament led to direct action from God.

Hagar, in fact, was the only woman in the Hebrew Bible to experience a theophany, and she responded by naming her son Ishmael, meaning "God listens" or "God heard" (Gen. 16:11; compare 16:1–14; 21:8–21).[42]

Lament itself arises from the realization of a covenant in which the people are bound with God and one another, and a covenant in which God stands with and for the oppressed. The lamenting women cited above are people who, in the storytelling of the Hebrew Bible, recognize the importance of solidarity with their people. Cavalcanti recognizes the collective struggles of resistance in Deborah, Judith, and Miriam, which "reach almost 'epic' proportions," but she also notes that many collective struggles are far less dramatic.[43] The struggles are not always clannish either; sometimes people of other tribes enter into the struggle, and sometimes God is complicit in the struggles of the people. Consider Jael (Judg. 4:17), the Egyptian midwives (Ex. 1:15–21), Rahab (Josh. 2), Ruth, and Hagar (Gen. 16:11; 21:17–20).[44] These and other struggles reveal people placing confidence in God as one who cares for the oppressed and who gives responsibility to the people to preserve the covenant. Cavalcanti points out that for people to be faithful to the covenant is to prepare the way for God to fulfill promises:

> God does not need to be reminded of God's promises; the people of God must make room for the realization of these promises. The contractual relationship between God and Israel is viable only when those who suffer injustice are attended to.[45]

We see in the prophetic movements of the Hebrew Bible a sense of urgency to be faithful to the covenant, and often to do so by crying out, or lamenting, when the covenant is violated.

When Christians and Jews speak of the cosmos as God's creation, and as created to be in covenant with God, we are faced simultaneously with our human responsibility to be faithful to the covenant and to lament when it is broken. The first challenge is to recognize the fullness of pain within that cosmos of God. Thus, we turn now to a lament based on Genesis 2:4b–17.

When the Lord God made the earth and the heavens, nothing was growing on the earth; that was for sure. Now there were some waters, but no one knows much about those. Our great-great-grandparents tell us that waters used to rise up from under the earth and water the whole land. That one is hard to explain, but we know for sure that nothing else was there—no plants, no animals, no people.

Now the Lord God went to work, first forming a human being—a person—from dust, mind you, so dust can't be all bad. Then, God breathed breath—Spirit—into that person, and the person lived. Surely, this was a holy person, filled with Spirit. Now our great-great-grandparents tell us God created a man person first—why, we do not know, but our ancestors often remembered more about men than about women. Later God did create a woman person. She would be the man's companion, and he would be hers, but that's another story. In this story, we have just one person, standing alone.

But the earth was still a-movin', as my grandmother used to say. The Lord God created a garden and put the person in it. You know about gardens—dirt, rocks, water, plants of every kind. Now, this garden had lots of trees—every kind of tree pleasing to the eye and good for food. It was a garden for fun and for nourishment. But God set something in the middle of the garden, the tree of life and the tree of the knowledge of good and evil. Why would God do such a thing? Mystery, mystery, all is mystery.

This garden had one thing more, a river flowing from Eden to water the garden. But the old folks say that the river divided into four and flowed around Havilah (land of gold and gum resin and cornelians), Cush, Asshur, and the land around the Euphrates. That's the whole earth—everything they knew about anyway.

Now, God got to talking with this person in the garden and asked the person to till the garden and take care of it. The garden could give fun and food, but the person would need to give care. God had one special request: "You may freely eat of every tree of the garden; but of the tree of the knowledge of good and evil your shall not eat, for in the day that you eat of it you shall die" (Gen. 2:16–17).

This is the earth the Lord has made. It is mystery, mystery, all is mystery. But the earth was made so well. The plants were crafted to delight the eye and give food; the river was crafted to water the earth—all of the earth; the person was crafted to care for the garden. Later, animals of every kind were crafted, and even a woman, to be companion with the man and he with her. Ask your great-great-grandmother to tell you that story another day. We focus now on gardens and rivers and people.

The ozone layer above us and the topsoil layer below us are being eaten away. The destruction each year above and below would require thousands of years to regenerate. We can even see some of the devastation. Acres of forest are converted to desert every year—the consequence of overgrazing, overlogging, abusing. Trees wither with the effects of acid rain. And the globe is warming. Some would debate this one, but we do know that the years are getting hotter. Oil spills remind us of how much oil we are taking from under the earth to feed our hungry cars and machines and give us ease and pleasure, only to send our refuse back into the air to pollute the breathing space of all living creatures.

Even when we want to do something responsible, we can do so little. Our recycling is less than 15 percent of what is possible. Churches that try to buy recycled paper for stationery cannot get it because the supply is so limited. And we are limited. We lament that we have done what we should not have done, and we have not done what we should have done. We have forgotten that the animals and plants are our brothers and our sisters; we have forgotten that the soil and seas are our teachers. Instead, people have eaten from the tree of the knowledge of good and evil, and have mastered the environment with knowledge. Our technology is tops for getting the most fun and food possible with the least effort in tilling and tending the garden. But knowledge and technology have yet to learn about our covenant-making God, who created the garden for the person, and the river for the garden, and the person to look after it all.

But God's own Spirit is breathed into this creation. God is bound in covenant too. Surely God must ache and cry to see the covenant torn asunder and the earth moaning in travail. Surely God cries out to see the people of the baptismal waters read this very creation story to accent human superiority and to trample the holy ground.

*But God loves this creation and keeps calling us back to covenant with the gar-
den, the river, the animals and persons everywhere. We are the people of the earth, and
to live in covenant with the earth is to live in covenant with the God who created it. As
God's Spirit blows across the earth, even today and tomorrow, we pray that the garden
and the river and the animals, and the people might love one another. Amen.*

This lamentation is a reminder that people are now faced with what it
means to meet in covenant when the gift of covenant is broken, when response to covenant is called forth but is instead denied or destroyed. This is
the challenge of ministering with the earth—to live in covenant relationship
with God and the human community and the earth. The challenge is to respect and nourish relationships so that the circle of life is repaired and enhanced rather than torn asunder. How better can we nurture communion with
God, build communion within human community, and build community with
the earth? If the broken circle is to be repaired, surely we are called to minister
to, for, and with the earth.

Earthbound Ministries as Times of Sacred Meeting

Earthbound ministries are always times of sacred meeting—times for
meeting God, the natural world, and human beings in community. Such ministries will take many forms. They may take place in ordinary church councils, planning meetings, or family meals; they may take place in committees
or special events. Whatever their specific purposes, they will bear marks of
covenantal relationship. People will seek to embody the visions described in
this chapter: to appreciate the *gift* of relationship with God and God's creation, to exercise the *responsibility* of justice and compassion for all peoples
and creatures, and to live in *hope* for goodness and mercy for the whole creation.

Consider some of the possibilities. One image is the council ring, which
has been used for centuries in many parts of the world as a place of meeting
where all can be equal and participate in decisions. Council rings usually take
place in a designated place, often outdoors where people can commune with
the natural world as they commune with one another. Many tribal people
around the world still rely on such councils for decision-making, and some
church bodies seek to function by means of circular councils (circular in process if not in seating).

Another image is the special gathering, created outside the normal routine to support the lives of people within their normal routines. Mary Hunt
describes such a gathering—the second international meeting of women associated with the Women's Alliance for Theology, Ethics, and Ritual (WA-
TER). The thirty-five women and one child came to Washington, D.C., from
fourteen countries to focus together on "Moving Beyond Violence." The very
shape of the meeting reveals something about sacred meetings:

> The child sang songs in Spanish and Portuguese, watched her mother
> and colleagues discuss and celebrate, and invited many a participant
> to go outside and play with her regardless of how pressing the agenda.

In that small way, we moved beyond violence. By creating strong links between people and countries, groups and organizations, we took a giant step forward.[46]

Certainly some of the key features of this sacred meeting are named in Hunt's brief description—singing, watching, discussing, celebrating, playing with a child, and creating linkages. Ivone Gebara summarized the intentions of WATER's meeting as utopian: "This is the utopia of women trying to build a web of love, justice and solidarity together."[47]

Another familiar image of sacred meeting is the retreat. A retreat design is offered in the Appendix, but we will reflect in the remainder of this chapter on retreats as paradigms for sacred meetings—paradigms that stir imagination for reshaping the quality of meetings throughout the church. But how do people live covenantally in sacred meetings? What is possible, and what are the risks? To consider what is possible, we will reflect on two retreat texts—the story of a theological student in Malaysia and the proposal of a theological ethicist in the United States.

The first text comes from Chieng Leh Hii, who attends Seminari Theoloji Malaysia (STM). He describes his first day of school:

> This first day of school was also the start of a 4-day retreat. Lecturers, students old and new came together at the Methodist Retreat Centre in PD [Port Dickson]. During that time, my heart was still heavy because the death of my elder sister kept coming back to my mind. I cried out from the depth of my heart to the Lord, "O Lord! Please strengthen me!" Then when I gazed across the vast sea that seemed endless, I felt a gentle breeze that drew me into nature's beauty. Suddenly, I felt a power of some sort touch my wounded heart.
>
> The theme of the retreat, "One in the body of Christ," was encouraging and challenging. For a group of theological students and lecturers who come from different cultural, denominational and family backgrounds, coupled with different personalities, to be one in the Spirit is definitely not easy. But thanks be to God, the message by Rev. Ezra Kok, the times of praise and worship, sharing in groups and the entertainment programmes were organised well. I really experienced God's overflowing grace.[48]

Hii, in telling his story, is aware of the pressures that the community faced in this opening retreat—his own loss of his older sister and the pressures on everyone to live in this newly forming, diverse human community. At STM, people speak many languages, and cultural and family differences are vast. In addition to pressures, Hii is also aware of blessings in this retreat: "the vast sea," "a gentle breeze," and well-organized worship, sharing, and entertainment. Hii's story reveals both the challenges and possibilities of earthbound ministry as a time of meeting, and he recognizes that the power of this event originated with the mystery of God. He says, "I felt a power of some sort touch my wounded heart," and he concludes that he "really experienced God's overflowing grace."

Based on Hii's story, one can identify some of what is possible in earthbound ministries. People might be more aware of their hurts and challenges; touched by the beauty of nature; comforted, challenged, or healed in their internal struggles and social relationships; and dazzled with special moments drawing near to God. These very possibilities are enhanced as we expand on the role of retreats and other set-apart times and places in supporting and empowering human communities in times of upheaval.

For a second text regarding retreats as sacred meetings, we turn to an ethicist. Larry Rasmussen has described the urgency of providing havens for people who seek to act morally and to create moral communities. He concludes his book *Moral Fragments and Moral Community* by describing four roles of the church as a servant community of moral life. These include: (1) being an inclusive community of ecumenical, egalitarian membership; (2) experimenting creatively with practices to support a new humanity in a world of interdependent strangers; (3) creating a haven or "way-station"; and (4) acting as moral critic.[49] All four of these roles are important to sacred meetings and earthbound ministries. Sacred meetings are opportunities to create inclusive communities that reveal what the larger community could be, and they are opportunities for creative experimentation with new ways of living together with others, including others very different from ourselves. Certainly, sacred meetings can offer a haven and encourage people to critique the world as it is. All of these themes will reappear in the next chapters, but in this chapter, particular attention will be given to the significance of providing haven.

Rasmussen likens the present era to that which early Christians faced at the turn of the first millenium—an era of diversity, fragmentation, and violence. Modernism has proven to be an empty shell; its progressive, utopian expectations have not been realized. Yet postmodernism is fragmented, and its proponents offer little hope. Rasmussen concludes, "We need 'sanctuaries,' sacred spaces and places of safe retreat and balm very close to home, places of prayer, consolation and the company of those who understand."[50]

As a challenge for ministry, this is no small matter. But Rasmussen is not speaking of havens as places of escape from social change; rather, he envisions havens more "in the manner of many base Christian communities on the margins."[51] Such havens are sites of resistance, places where moral conviction is sustained and fed. Rasmussen says:

> Moral conviction cannot be sustained—indeed, almost none of the dimensions of the moral life can be—without such havens and way stations. It is cruel and fruitless to call for social transformation in a long season of unavoidable experimentation without, at the same time, providing this community haven. The community of struggle should also be the community of mercy on the mountain.[52]

Such havens can be places where people protest their pain, analyze their oppression, and construct new forms of social organization and political activism. Such havens can be important to the comfortable middle class, as well as to those on the margins. For different reasons, both the poor and the middle class in the U.S. are facing major disillusionment with the progressive and utopian visions upon which their earlier hopes were built. What Rasmussen calls for are havens that offer a "counterdrama to modernity's misplaced confidence and post-modernity's empty fragmentation."[53]

In analyzing Rasmussen's proposals, the story of Hii is placed in a much larger frame. Not only is Hii's story a sweet tale of a person who found solace and inspiration during a retreat experience; it is also a revolutionary tale in the sense that Hii and others on the STM retreat were nourished and empowered by their time together. They were being prepared to live as an ecumenical, multicultural, multiethnic community within their country of Malaysia, where diversity presents a challenge to every religious community and to all communities together. This is a country in which the witness of STM and the future graduates could contribute significantly to justice and peace or they could impede that process. The haven offered by the retreat that Hii describes could be a critical building block in this educational community for moral living and building a moral society.

We can also analyze Rasmussen's proposals in relation to the stories with which this chapter began. Recall the joy of my grandchildren as they approached the weekend retreat. Recall the hopefulness of the churches that began a gleaning program, the counselors who planned for a youth camp, and the local church folk who planned a church garden. In all of these stories, we saw a circle of relationship, filled with joy and expectation and a sense of responsibility. Perhaps this is what sacred meetings can be—nourishment for the circles of relationship in our ordinary lives. Perhaps we can even hope that sacred meetings will empower ordinary communities to embody the roles described by Rasmussen. If this is the case, then the roles Rasmussen describes are turned to questions: To what extent do our sacred meetings embody ecumenical, egalitarian participation?[54] How do they experiment with practices to support a new humanity? To what extent do they provide a haven? How do they engage people as moral critics?

Meeting Challenges

When people gather for working meetings, they usually hope that the meeting will make a difference, even though they may be quite pessimistic about that possibility in light of past experience. If people are intentional, however, they can at least remember covenant and direct their efforts toward covenantal meeting. In light of the stories and reflections of this chapter, sacred meetings need to embrace the gifts, responsibilities, and hopes of covenant relationships. This is not to deny the brutality and destructiveness that often exist in relationships. The challenge is to recognize the complex circles of relationship represented in any gathered body, including the more destructive circles. The challenge is to face these relationships honestly and hopefully. The questions with which we closed the last section provide a significant guide. Within this context, we are called, then, to exercise responsibility toward God and all of creation, and to hope for goodness and mercy. This calls for seriousness about meetings, and attention to the quality of community, as well as to the distinctive purposes of particular meetings.

When people gather for retreats or special events the same challenges exist, but in this case, the people are often seeking a Sabbath—a day of rest, a time to recall the month that is past, a moment to hope for the future that is to come. People are often seeking after a quiet time in a quiet place, what was described in the last chapter as a "spirituality of silence." But whether people go away on retreat, journey to an international meeting, or simply go into the church garden to work the soil, they usually carry their worries with them. These may be worries for a hurting child, for people who need a healing touch, for someone who has been treated unjustly, for a personal struggle or conflict. These may be worries for nations at war or wreckage among the plants and animals of creation. Thus, when people gather in the haven of a retreat, as when they gather for working meetings, they do so with hope (even a dim hope) that being together will make a difference.

This is a challenge for earthbound ministries—to nourish covenant in gatherings where people come together with expectation. One can say this about the most ordinary business meetings or the most exotic travel seminars, camps, and retreats. One can also say this about more localized earthbound ministries, such as outdoor worship, church gardens, hikes, and picnics. Sacred meetings are times for sowing seeds that continue growing during the weeks and months *after* people gather. Sacred meetings can be dramatic in their influence, but the fruits of these meetings will often be invisible at the time of gathering. Harvest comes later!

FOUR

Sacred Confrontation:
Meeting Diversity—Meeting God

A group of folks stood sadly and strongly together after the memorial service of a mutual friend, a woman who had mentored everyone in that small group and who, at the same time, had kept the church stirred up for justice. Our friend had befriended hundreds of people and worked hard on behalf of people most ignored or oppressed by the dominant structures of the church and community—women and men, gay and straight, young and middle-aged and senior, people of all races and nationalities. She had served in many leadership roles; yet the outpouring at her memorial service was a reminder that she had done more than go to meetings and campaign for justice. She had always and everywhere been a friend. She had even extended friendship to those with whom she disagreed on every matter dear to her, and her friendship had been powerful; it had converted some, mellowed others, and warmed and inspired us all.

In these minutes after the memorial service, several people spoke their grief and their sense of responsibility to the memory of Lois, a responsibility to carry on her spirit and work. Then we talked about our lives. One of my friends, a pastor, confessed to being disgruntled with her congregation. Church members were pouring all of their energies into a divisive conflict, and into a general effort to prevent anything from changing in the church. She said that the church had become a place where people go to worship and attend meetings. Furthermore, the church leadership spends so much time in meetings that they have little time for the rest of ministry. She wondered if the time had come for the pastoral leaders to stop going to meetings and to give their time in other directions.

This story embodies a dilemma faced by church leaders, business leaders, people struggling with welfare systems, parents, youth, medical professionals, and people in many walks of life. People expend a lot of time in conflicts and meetings to maintain the status quo. These efforts drain energy and lead people to wonder what they are really doing and why. The temptation is to give up on meetings altogether. Sometimes that *is* the best response, but the life of Lois speaks another answer. Lois' life does not say how much energy people should invest in pursuing conflicts and formal meetings. Her life speaks, instead, to the spirit of ministry—the spirit of friendship, the unbending determination to work for justice, and the effort to welcome and embrace people who are quite different, even antagonistic, to ourselves. That spirit is the subject of this chapter.

The explorations of this chapter lead into the messy middle of diversity and the challenge to meet difference, even while seeking common purposes. In the midst of diversity, we often meet God—incarnate in the messiness and wonders of life. The contribution of this chapter to quilt-making is *stitching patches together*—bringing the materials of ministry with the earth into a colorful and textured whole. To this end, we will *explore diversity*, confronting diverse traditions of ministering with the earth. We will also *explore incarnation*, through which God confronts us with unexpected challenges and surprises. Hopefully, sacred confrontation will emerge. Although confrontation can be uncomfortable, it also nudges and empowers people with the presence of the Holy.

Visually, the primary image of chapter 3 was a circle of covenant. The visual image of this chapter is the more linear image of a road or path. Such imagery runs deep in Christian history, poetry, and art, where life is often depicted as a journey, with wide and narrow roads and eschatological hopes for the future. In fact, circular and linear images coexist in Christian tradition, and they are really more complementary than contradictory, as often assumed. Both illumine the nature of God-centered, earthbound ministry. Sacred meetings invite us back into the circle of covenant, and sacred confrontations challenge us to transform our visions as we meet God along the roads of ordinary living.

Meeting Diversity:
Diverse Traditions of Ministering with the Earth

Ecological concerns are sometimes seen as safe issues within the Christian community, less controversial than economic and political issues. Ironically, however, concerns for the earth have become increasingly controversial as the relationship between ecological and social-economic injustice comes more fully to light. Also, the Christian community is becoming more aware of its own complicity in environmental destruction via much of traditional theology and many actions of the church. These issues are all the more reason to explore streams within the larger Christian tradition and to search other traditions that can contribute to a better understanding of ministry with the earth.

One of the challenges in such exploration is to discover and draw upon the riches of diverse traditions without becoming detoured by ideological debates that lead to further neglect and victimization of the earth. A case of detour is the censure of Matthew Fox, well-known exponent of creation theology. The case initially appears to be a controversy regarding Fox's theological tenets and sources.[1] The issues are larger than formal censure by the Vatican, however; many other other church communities have also raised concerns.

The responses often go far beyond a simple expression of disagreement; they yield strong reactions of anger, fear, or disgust toward anything that sounds like the creation theology of Matthew Fox. I experienced this reaction, for example, when sharing the story of a Native American Protestant congregation with a group of Protestant educators. The response from several educators was that they could not approve of this congregation because it sounded too much like Matthew Fox. In fact, the native congregation had had no interaction with Fox or his writing, but was seeking a way to be Christian within their Native American context. When Fox's approach to creation theology is generalized and used to label other ecologically sensitive Christian communities, the concerns that Fox and other communities have for creation become lost in the midst of controversy.

Another example of controversy happened in Britain in 1989 and the ensuing years. Because of increasing ecological consciousness in Britain and the necessity for people to work together to address the crisis, the British Council of Churches and World Wide Fund for Nature (WWF) planned a conference on "Christian Faith and Ecology," part of a larger "Festival of Faith and the Environment."[2] The conference became controversial before it even took place, and the organization Action for Biblical Witness to Our Nation (ABWON) began a letter-writing and protest campaign, particularly raising questions about the plans for "interfaith worship." In the actual conference, the service of welcome and the service of eucharist took place in Canterbury Cathedral, and the biblical and liturgical texts were all drawn from the Christian tradition (including readings from Psalms and Proverbs that are shared by Jews and Christians). Eucharist followed the Church of England rite. Neither readings nor people of other faiths were involved in that particular service, but the back of the service booklet did include some reflections written by members of several faiths on the subject of nature.[3]

Despite the distinctly Christian character of both of these services, the criticisms of "multi-faith" worship escalated after the conference, and the two worship services were blamed for "leaving Jesus out" and for treating all religions as equally valid.[4] Christopher Lewis observes, "As the focus of the service was environmental it became associated in the minds of many with 'New Age' thinking and therefore with a pantheistic blurring of the distinction between the Creator and his creation."[5]

What eventuated from this furor was an Open Letter in December 1991, published in the press and addressed to the Leadership of the Church of England. Many leaders, clergy and lay, signed the letter, and the protests have continued. The letter affirms centrally that only through Jesus Christ may people be saved:

> Believing that Jesus Christ the incarnate Son of God, is both God and man, the unique revelation of God, the only Saviour and hope of mankind—we, the undersigned members of the Church of England, are concerned that his Gospel shall be clearly presented in this Decade of Evangelism.

> We desire to love and respect people of other faiths…We wholeheartedly support co-operation in appropriate community, social, moral and political issues between Christians and those of other faiths wherever this is possible. Nevertheless, we believe it to be our Lord's command that his Gospel be clearly proclaimed, openly and sensitively, to all people (including those of other faiths) with the intention that they should come to faith in him for salvation.

> In consequence we are deeply concerned about gatherings for interfaith worship and prayer involving Christian people…We believe these events, however motivated, conflict with the Christian duty to proclaim the Gospel. They imply that salvation is offered by God not only through Jesus Christ but by other means, and thus deny his uniqueness and finality as the only Saviour.[6]

I have quoted a large section of this open letter to indicate how concerns for the environment were so quickly subsumed under evangelistic concerns to proclaim Jesus Christ as the only Savior. In this particular case, as in many other cases around the world, the concerns for evangelism and care for the earth were set in opposition, whether directly or indirectly. When debates shifted to interreligious relationships, concerns for creation were lost.[7] In any such debate, people on all sides care passionately about the views they express; the challenge is to discern and respond to the Holy in the midst of confrontation.

The cases of Matthew Fox and the Open Letter lead to questions about what churches can do to meet diversity and minister with the earth. When John Cobb wrote *Is It Too Late?* in 1970, he hoped that his book would stir the church to awareness, action, and theological transformation. When the book was reprinted in 1995, he added in the Afterword that awareness has indeed grown, some things have changed, and some signs indicate that Christians are rethinking their theology.[8] He said, however, that the declining health of churches has meant that changes have had only modest effects on local churches and most church members.[9] In the context of 1995, Cobb still wonders if it is too late.

An irony rides on the pages of Cobb's book, especially in light of the avid debate that erupted in Britain in late 1991. Whereas the conference that stirred the debate does reveal a growing ecological awareness, the furor that arose exemplifies the allegory told by John Cobb in his book, first penned in 1970.[10]

Cobb tells the story of a ship (the world) which is filled with conflict between first-class and steerage passengers, mostly of cultures and races different from the first-class people. When news arrives that a leak has been found, the people hardly listen; all the while the conflict on board rises to enormous proportions, leading to physical fights and even the shooting of some children. More leaks are found, some ship supplies are ruined, and the ship is listing. The story ends with the question of what should happen next. Cobb offers three possibilities: (1) continued fragmentation of disgruntled minorities, leaving little time for leaders to repair leaks; (2) an action to preserve the ship for a few (the first-class passengers and crew); or (3) persuasion by the captain that an immediate, corporate and massive action is needed.

I believe that the Open Letter case in Britain, and much environmental action and theorizing in the United States, have furthered Cobb's first two options. Fragmentation has grown, as has the elitism of groups who think themselves to be wiser or more significant than others, whether they be Christians, deep ecologists, eco-feminists, or other.[11] What is needed, instead, is a way of joining hands. This would represent a radical alternative in our world where people seek to be prophetic or critical only by tearing others down. What would be truly countercultural, and serving of justice and ecological integrity, is the act of coming together. Thus, the central issue is no longer awareness, isolated action, and modified theologies, though all of these will continue to be important.

The central question now is how to *be* together with one another and the earth in mutual care for the well-being of all. This view echoes a basic principle embodied in the earth itself, namely that biodiversity enhances the well-being and stability of an ecosystem. I join with others in suggesting that we need diversity in actions, methods, worldviews, and religious traditions.[12] I emphasize in addition that we need to work avidly together, even when we do not agree. Integrity is not defending one's own view against others; integrity is working integrally with others for the well-being of creation. This calls for respecting, debating, and negotiating difference, but not battering others who are different.

In that spirit, we turn now to explore diverse traditions of ministering with the earth, both ancient and modern. My hope is that readers will find, in one or more of these traditions, inspiration and guidance for their action. However important are the debates across traditions, the very concern for creation mandates that people struggle and work in covenant with others, bringing common concerns to bear on the ways we live in the world.

Ancient Traditions of Ministering with the Earth

Any work that accents covenantal relationships is obliged to look to partners of the past for wisdom. After all, we are called into covenantal relationship with ancestors as well as contemporaries. Ancient traditions were often more communal and respectful of the earth than traditions formed in later centuries of competition for religious and political power, rising industrialization, emphasis on rationality, and population growth. Thus, we turn now to ancient traditions for guidance in ministering with the earth. Of course, discerning ancient traditions is no small task, and discernment is inevitably influenced by observer bias. The danger of romanticizing ancient peoples is great, but an equally profound danger is to ignore the wisdom of the past, which undermines our self-understanding and limits knowledge that could save the world from self-destruction.[13]

NATIVE AMERICAN TRADITIONS

People in many parts of the world will think first of indigenous peoples when remembering communities that have lived carefully with creation. Every part of the world has its story of ancient peoples, and in some countries and cultures, the traditions of those peoples have been remembered and passed on more fully than in others. We could turn to the Maori people of New Zealand; the Polynesian, Melanesian, and Micronesian people of the Pacific Islands; the Masai people of East Africa, or Native peoples of North and South America. The stories of these peoples in the modern world are often ones of oppression, and the danger of seeking their wisdom is that we may perpetuate oppression by borrowing or stealing their wisdom without respecting and supporting their way of life in today's world. With great care, then, we will turn to some voices from one particular indigenous community—the Native American community—with the hope of hearing and honoring, rather than hearing and destroying.

To speak of Native American community is already oversimplified and distorted, because many nations and tribes exist within Native America, and many smaller communities exist within those larger ones. Further, many Native people experience diverse cultures within themselves. Steve Charleston tells his story:

> I come from Oklahoma…My grandfather and great-grandfather were Presbyterian ministers. Like most people in our tribe, the Choctaw Nation, they were Presbyterians who preached and sang in Choctaw. My own family was tied up with the oil fields. We moved out of Duncan and went up to Oklahoma City as the jobs changed. That means that I experienced a number of different churches. I was baptized a Southern Baptist, but I've known everything from Roman Catholic to Unitarian to the Baha'i faith…Things are very mixed in Oklahoma. It's a cultural patchwork quilt laid down over ranch land, red dirt, and eastern timberland.[14]

Steve Charleston is not only telling his personal story but is also communicating the reality of his inheritance. For him, as for many Native people, being Indian and being Christian involves "confusion, frustration, anger, and struggle."[15] This struggle leads him to seek a theology that is true to all of his heritage—both Native and Christian. He asserts that Native people have two ancient traditions from which they draw—traditions of America and traditions of Israel. When describing the traditions of his people, he says:

> They have their own original covenant relationship with the Creator and their own original understanding of God prior to the birth of a Christ. It is a Tradition that has evolved over centuries. It tells of the active, living, revealing presence of God in relation to Native People through generations of Native life and experience...Like Israel itself, Native America proclaims that God is a God of all times and of all places and of all peoples.[16]

Charleston explains that he has to work with at least three primary sources to do theology: "the Old Testament of Israel, the New Testament of the Christian scriptures, and the Old Testament of my own People."[17] Rather than replace the Old Testament of Israel, the Old Testament of Native America "stands beside it" in complementary relationship.[18] In fact, Native traditions have much to teach all peoples. Charleston concludes that "[o]ne of the guiding theologies of the second reformation will be from Africa, Asia, Latin America, and Native America."[19] Certainly, when we raise questions about the environment, we are turned quickly and soberly to traditions of Native America.

Another spokesperson of these traditions is George Tinker, who, like Steve Charleston, locates himself in relation to his heritage—Osage and Cherokee on his father's side and Lutheran on his mother's.[20] Like Charleston, he recognizes that conflict comes from standing in two worlds, not only for himself, but for his people, who have been exploited and missionized, and who live with enormous social problems—consequences of being uprooted from their traditions and their land. Tinker points out that Native traditions focus on sacredness of space more than sacredness of time.[21] This yields a way of life rooted in the land—the land of ancestors, the land that nourishes community, the land that gives spiritual power to the people. This naturally affects the way that Native Americans think of God, themselves, and the church.

In developing the theme of sacred land, Tinker refers to two central stories: the Corn Mother story and the Hopi creation story of Spider Woman. In the first, a story of long ago, Corn Mother was faced with the near-starvation of her family; she insisted that her husband kill her and drag her body in a circle around the clearing where her family lived. He finally did so, and the next morning corn had grown all around the clearing, wherever the woman's blood had soaked into the soil.[22] This story draws the attention of hearers to the power of a mother's love and to the sacredness of corn and Mother Earth.

In Tinker's second story, also of long ago, Spider Woman gathered the earth and her spittle and created the first people. Likewise she created the birds and animals, who "'all suckled at the breast of their Mother Earth, who gave them her milk of grass, seeds, fruit, and corn, and they all felt as one, people and animals....'"[23] In this creation story, the sacredness of the creative act, the creation of people and animals from the soil, and the significance of unity among people and animals are held together at the center. Tinker points out that the account of creation in Genesis 2 is similar; there, also, people are created out of the earth.[24] I suggest that the vision of oneness is also similar; the covenant theme of Genesis 2 is akin to the oneness theme in the Hopi story. In the Genesis text, the oneness of creation lies in the relationship of everything to God and to every other part of the world.

Tinker's introduction of Corn Mother and Spider Woman into the discussion of Native Americans and the land begins the process that Steve Charleston is urging for Native people—the process of telling and interpreting the Native traditions as a source of Christian faith. While people in Native American and Native Canadian Christian churches do this quite naturally, Charleston has challenged Native peoples to go further in interpreting those traditions in relation to the Old Testament of Israel and the New Testament of Christians. And Charleston has challenged the rest of us to look to Native Americans for serious interpretive work rather than exotic stories and rituals.

This kind of serious interpretation is what George Tinker offers when he challenges the time-dominated theology of the majority of the Christian world with the space-dominated theology of Native Americans. He notes that European immigrants in the United States often valued land for what it could produce, not for itself. He says, "The adhesive between white Americans and the place where they were born, the space in which their ancestors lived, the land of their childhood, was and is fairly weak."[25] Tinker identifies consequences of such thinking. In disputes over land, the immigrant peoples on the North American continent have often not understood the meaning of land to Native peoples, and Native people have often expressed concern for the immigrants' disregard of creation. Tinker quotes Seathl (or Chief Seattle) of the Salish peoples:

> The whites, too, shall pass—perhaps sooner than other tribes. Continue to contaminate your bed, and you will one night suffocate in your own waste. When the buffalo are all slaughtered, the wild horses all tamed, the secret corners of the forest heavy with the scent of many men, and the view of the ripe hill blotted by talking wires, where is the thicket? Gone. Where is the eagle? Gone.[26]

In this view, the earth is sacred; the destruction of the earth is desecration.

In Tinker's view of sacred land, the idea of ministering with the earth is taken for granted. As people care for the earth, they care for the Holy. This view leads Tinker to critique the global vision of the World Council of Churches of Christ—the vision of justice, peace, and sustainability. Much World Council discussion has gone into ordering the words of this vision, and Tinker has argued that sustainability should be listed first; in Native American traditions, creation is the beginning point rather than the ending point.[27] Tinker is not arguing that the natural environment is more important than human justice, but that creation is completely relational and is foundational to justice.

The Indian understanding of Creation as sacred, of mother Earth as the source of all life, goes far beyond the notion of such Western counter-institutions as the Sierra Club or Greenpeace. It embraces far more than concern for harp seals or a couple of ice-bound whales. It embraces all of life from trees and rocks to international relations.[28]

Economic, social, and environmental justice are inextricably linked. That linkage, as well as the linkage between time and space, is important to Latin Americans as well; for them, the passion for renewed and new creation is particularly strong.[29]

As one looks to Native American and other indigenous traditions, the challenges are inescapable. Christians will continue to debate sacred texts of faith and visions of the church, but Native traditions challenge Christians to focus on the Creator, revealed throughout history and in all creation. They challenge Christians to hallow the creation that is meant to be whole, and to envision a future of sustainability, justice, and peace.

CELTIC CHRISTIAN TRADITIONS

We turn now from the North American continent to the Celtic Christian traditions of the British Isles. Celtic traditions now live in memory, legend, and myth more than in living human communities, but in truth, they survive in the bones of many who still inhabit the British Isles (especially Ireland, Scotland, and Wales) and people long since dispersed to other parts of the world.

Celtic peoples and traditions thrived in Britain and other parts of Europe from ancient times, and in the first century B.C.E. their cultural contribution and identity were well recognized and documented. The Celts were a deeply religious people with ancient traditions, and they came to Christianity with a naturalness that led to a flourishing of Celtic Christianity from about 400 to 1000 C.E. The distinctive Christianity of the Celtic people stood in some tension with that which was transmitted and organized via the Holy Roman Empire, bearing more in common with the Christianity of the East, of Gaul, and of the desert fathers in Egypt, Palestine, and Syria.[30]

One quality of Celtic Christianity was its continuity with ancient Celtic traditions, shaped by traveling monks, missionaries and pilgrims, rather than by an imperialistic movement of armies. The transition into Christianity was a smooth one—a "grafting" of the new onto the old—and this contributed a continuity that distinguished Celtic Christianity from other branches of the faith that emerged within contexts of persecution and martyrdom.[31] The Celtic Christians were able to incorporate the creationist emphases of the earlier traditions and to see God as Creator and God as Christ already present in the lives of those earlier communities.[32] In this way, they were doing quite naturally what Steve Charleston describes and advocates in Native American Christianity—taking the ancient traditions to be a source of Christian faith parallel to the Testament of Israel. Examples abound, some conscious and intentional, and some drawn subconsciously from ancient traditions. The Celtic myth of the Grail was incorporated into Christian symbolism, and the art of Celts and Picts was adopted into Christian iconography. Similarly, Celtic legends of people such as the goddess Bridget were merged with stories of Christian saints such as Saint Brigid (also known as Saint Ffraid, Saint Isfryde and Saint Bride).[33]

At the same time, Celtic Christianity was influenced by interchange with other parts of the Christian world, particularly by Christianity of the East, of Gaul, and of the desert fathers in Egypt, Palestine, and Syria.[34] The influence grew over time, as missionaries traveled freely throughout Europe and western Asia, fueled by the Celtic love of wandering (*peregrinatio*). The journeys were given religious significance, often described as seeking the place of one's resurrection.[35] And though pilgrimages of the *peregrini* were valued for penance and mission, the Celtic asceticism was marked by a spirit of joy and a rhythm of activity and withdrawal; further, it was grounded in the belief that traveling is more important than arriving.[36] On the journey, an intimate relation with God and creation was nurtured, and caring for the earth and the mind were encouraged through the music, art, and poetry of the peregrini. Likewise, the Celtic structures of monastic life spread throughout Europe as the peregrini settled in new places. One glimpses already the spirit of sacred journeys, to be discussed in chapter 5.

The Celts had a temporal view of life (in contrast with the spatial view described by Tinker), but it was not a view of progress; it was a view of life as a journey, often circling back to origins. Thus, travel was a vocation, represented literally by the peregrini. Travel was a vocation of moving through life with a spirit of seeking, grounded in the spiritual quality of the journey. On a personal level, the worldview is captured in the phrase of contemporary theologian Nelle Morton, "the journey is home."[37]

On a cosmic level, the worldview is one that points to the future, seeing Christ as mediating God's purpose; the worldview also assumes thorough relatedness within God and creation, and between God and creation.[38] This cosmic view is represented in the intertwined patterns of Celtic art, the intimate relationships described between human beings and creation, and the dynamic relationship within the triune God—Father, Son, and Spirit. The themes come to expression in "The Three," a poem of Carmina Gadelica:

> The Three who are in the earth,
> The Three who are in the air,
> The Three who are in the heaven,
> The Three who are in the great pouring sea.[39]

What is revealed here is profound awareness of the triune God living in creation.

Celtic Christianity was thus pervaded with a theology of closeness with God and creation. Dominant theological themes included: the goodness of creation; the reality and intensity of evil in the world; the pervasive presence of God as Creator, incarnate Son, and ever-present Spirit; the sacredness of places and ordinary life tasks; the closeness and availability of angels and saints; and the possibility of knowing God through knowing the earth. From these themes, much insight can be drawn for ministering with the earth; three central insights are that human beings have much to learn *from* the earth, as well as the ability to commune *with* the earth, and much responsibility to care *for* the earth.

In terms of *learning from the earth,* many of the saints are described as people who learned from the land, sea and animals. Saint Patrick spent six of his young years in captivity as a shepherd in Ireland, living alone with sheep and mountains and forests; in this setting, he prayed and grew in his spiritual life.[40] Likewise, when Saint Cieran was a young boy, he was given the job of herding cattle "after the manner of David…for God knew that he would be a prudent herdsman to great herds, that is, the herds of the faithful."[41] Stories of saints' lives are filled with tales of their living with animals, close to the earth; these tales are used to explain the saints' spiritual depth and wisdom. Likewise, saints were portrayed as communing with nature throughout their lives; miraculous stories describe their communication with animals, even animals considered frightening or loathsome.[42]

The saints themselves testify in their poetry to their *communion with the earth.* For example, Saint Patrick begins and ends his famous hymn "The Deer Cry" with an invocation of the Trinity, and the center of the hymn is an invocation of the earth. Consider the opening and closing verse:

I arise today
Through a mighty strength, the invocation of the Trinity,
Through belief in the threeness,
Through confession of the oneness
Of the Creator of Creation.[43]

Framed by this verse, and surrounded by other verses regarding strength from God and Christ, and from angels and saints of the past, Patrick includes a verse on the earth:

I arise today
Through the strength of heaven:
Light of sun,
Radiance of moon,…
Depth of sea,
Stability of earth,
Firmness of rock.[44]

Here we see Patrick's testimony to what he receives from the earth. It is woven into the fabric of his trinitarian theology, not in contrast to what God gives, but as part of the fullness of God's gift.

Likewise, a theme running through Celtic literature is the importance of *caring for the earth.* The teaching of the Celts on this subject is summarized by

Saint Columbanus, "He who tramples the world tramples on himself."[45] Thus, ministry with the earth, from the perspective of Celtic spirituality, includes receiving *from* the earth and caring *for* the earth.

Modern Traditions of Ministering with the Earth

Just as ancient traditions described in the last section are still living, modern traditions described in this section are rooted in ancient soil. The particular formulations presented here have come to expression late in this century, however, so they are identified as modern. They represent only a small portion of recent thinking on human life in relation to the earth, but they do represent two perspectives. Viewed together, they stir thinking and communicate some of the diversity with which we need to wrestle.

Reflecting on diverse perspectives is an important aspect of ministering with the earth. The spirit of covenant suggests that people with different views may sometimes need to move their differences to the side in order to give reverence to the Creator and live in covenant with creation. On the other hand, differences are significant, and exploring them is also part of living in covenant. In the next pages, readers will surely find themselves akin to some views and foreign to others. Just being aware of one's responses can be an important starting point for deeper explorations of diversity within ecotheology.

THEISTIC AND CHRISTOCENTRIC TRADITIONS

The appeal to ancient traditions discussed above is itself controversial. The most vocal critiques are made by Christian theologians and philosophers who ground their understanding of creation in traditional theism or christology—especially in more orthodox or neo-orthodox perspectives. Their critique is often grounded in worldviews with sharp distinctions between God and the world. Their concern is that blurring distinctions is *not* helpful to the environment; it is actually misleading because the real source for respecting creation is God, and the relationship between humans and God needs to be understood as a relationship between creatures and Creator.

One recent critic of much ecological theology is Stephen R. L. Clark of Liverpool University in England. He objects that most environmental rhetoric today is pantheistic, identifying God with the world, and that such a view is difficult to translate into caring actions toward the world. It also obscures the imperfections in human beings and in the world.[46] In contrast, he argues that "Christian faith, along with the other great religions of the Book, does already teach respect for the dignity and sanctity of God's creation."[47]

Clark critiques recent patterns in ecological discussions—blaming inherited patterns of thought (such as Greek or patriarchal worldviews) for environmental destruction and romanticizing ancient traditions (such as the Native American and Celtic traditions). He argues that the real problem is the human desire to live better.[48] In short, human sin is the problem rather than faulty worldviews. Clark reviews several philosophical and theological models of ecology, critiquing each. He concludes that "a more resolutely orthodox approach has greater strength and subtlety than is usually acknowledged."[49]

Clark's writing is more focused on critiquing contemporary environmental theologies than in proposing an alternative, but he does give clues. He advocates that we flee from the language of progress, development, and stewardship, for these ideas exacerbate environmental problems. He urges that we appreciate God's distance from the world as well as God's presence, and appreciate human guilt without being overwhelmed by it:

> Better that we see incarnate beauties as real fragments of the god we
> can only gesture at. Better that we find some way of acknowledging
> our guilt without being poisoned by it.[50]

Finally, he advocates that we appreciate and respond to the world. The human vocation is not to save the world, but to sense God's grandeur and respond to it.[51]

A similar perspective is offered by Colin Gunton of King's College, London. Because Gunton focuses less on critique and more on a constructive alternative, his work could be seen as a companion to Clark's. For Gunton, the pivot point for reflecting on creation is the text of Genesis 1:26–27, in which God speaks of creating humankind in the image and likeness of God and letting humans have dominion over the rest of creation. Gunton lifts out two themes, the significance of interpersonal relationships for human beings, particularly male-female relationships, and human responsibility toward creation.

As to the first theme of *relatedness*, Gunton draws a correspondence between male-female relationships and the relationship of the three persons within God; he says, "To be in the image of God is to be called to a relatedness-in-otherness that echoes the eternal relatedness-in-otherness of Father, Son and Spirit."[52] As to the second theme of *responsibility*, he describes the human vocation as enabling creation to be that which it was made to be, thus, "to enable the creation to praise its maker."[53] The human vocation is to tend human relationships and relationships with the rest of creation.[54]

Several interlocking ideas are critical to Colin Gunton's interpretation. First, he argues for a view identified with "orders of creation"—a view in which relationships are patterned after the Genesis account of creation, particularly male-female relationships and relationships between humans and other beings. Secondly, he interprets creation as reordered through Christ. Christ is the One who redeemed fallen creation into obedience to God. He is the One who gave himself freely to his maker, thus opening "earth to heaven and heaven to earth." And he is the One who was with the Father from the beginning; therefore, he incarnates and mediates God in a unique way.[55]

In light of these basic theological tenets, Gunton accents human fallenness, as does Clark. Both the human race and the rest of the world fall short of the calling revealed in Christ; the most destructive toll is in human relationships with one another and with the rest of creation.[56] At the root of human failing is idolatry, or displacing God from the center of the universe and attributing divine value to human beings or other aspects of the material world.[57] Thus, at the root of human failing is a disrupted relationship with God.

From this idea, Gunton makes a natural move. He affirms that the human role is not to save the planet, but to give praise. Because the planet, like the rest of the universe, is "destined to come to an end," the Christian role is to raise awareness of the penultimacy of all things, alongside the capacity of the penultimate "to praise the God who made it."[58] Gunton is not altogether despairing of human action, however. Like Clark, he believes that we are not promised solutions to ecological problems, but we are promised "the freedom sometimes to share through the Spirit in particular transformations of the world" as signaled by the resurrection of Jesus Christ.[59] The church is, thus, a vehicle of God's salvation, not because of its purity, but because it is "placed by Word and sacrament under the rule of Christ and therefore in saving relation to God the creator and redeemer."[60] Through God's Spirit, the church seeks the restoration of God's image. Restoration involves conforming to Christ, thus reshaping human and ecological relationships.

From the theistic and christocentric perspectives of Stephen Clark and Colin Gunton, two major conclusions about ministering with the earth might be drawn. One is the importance of nurturing the worship life of the church. Worship is important if we are to praise the Creator and encourage all creation to give praise; worship is also the vehicle of Word and Sacrament, thus, a central mediator of God's transforming Spirit. A second conclusion is that ministering with the earth involves reshaping relationships with people and with creation, freeing human beings to participate with God's Spirit in building community life and in living well with the earth. In all actions of ministry, however, people will know that their actions are always flawed and transient in relation to God's.

ECOFEMINIST TRADITIONS

Ecofeminism is an emerging tradition—a movement that is scarcely twenty years old in the formal sense, but one that has brought women and men together with common concern for the earth. Ecofeminism has roots in feminist and environmental movements, and in uncovering nature-based religions, particularly goddess religions.[61] Ecofeminists actually represent diverse traditions, including Christian. The complex movement emerged explicitly out of concern for the cosmos and in response to disasters in local areas.[62] The result is that women have come together to act, to protect life, and to seek alternatives for policies and practices that destroy human life and the earth.

Searching for resolutions to cosmic malaise, ecofeminists often appeal to ancient roots. Riane Eisler sees ecofeminism as an integration of the three "leading-edge social movements of our time—the peace, feminist, and ecology movements," but at the same time, she traces these traditions back thousands of years.[63] She particularly appeals to goddess traditions, which yield evidence that prehistoric societies were more respectful of the earth and more just and peaceful than modern societies. She cites evidence that these societies were egalitarian systems, structured more by partnership than by domination. The Gaia hypothesis of biologists Lynn Margulis and James Lovelock converges with these early traditions, revealing the planet itself as a living system, functioning to support and nurture life.[64] The term *Gaia* is the Greek word for "earth" or "Earth Goddess."

When Eisler and others claim to draw from ancient sources, new questions arise: What were the earlier cultures, religious traditions and social structures *really* like, and how can we most fruitfully draw upon these traditions? Accessibility to prehistoric traditions is difficult at best, and the value of these traditions in relation to historic religions is a point of debate. Rosemary Radford Ruether, for example, critiques the alienating influence of Jewish and Christian male monotheistic traditions; however, she concludes that "merely replacing a male transcendent deity with an immanent female one is an insufficient answer to the 'god-problem.'"[65] Ruether, thus, calls her book *Gaia and God*, seeking to avoid a quick dismissal of either view. Encouraging critical interchange across traditions, she poses Christian traditions of covenant and sacrament as particularly rich for exploration as people seek to move toward an ecofeminist theocosmology.

The roots of ecofeminism are clearly drawn from many sources; these include: experiences of women with oppression (toward themselves, their families and communities); Native American traditions, ancient Greek mythology; goddess traditions; feminism in many forms; socialism; and postmodern analysis.[66] The multiple sources yield three major themes—diversity, critique of dualisms, and proposals for reconfigured relationships.

The first theme is *diversity*, which constitutes both a reality and an accepted value. The ecofeminist movement is a collective of diverse points of view and diverse forms of action in the world. The diversity is seen by some as a particular strength—one that should not be overcome by seeking for agreement, or what Lee Quinby calls "coherence, comprehensiveness, and formalized agendas."[67] Ecologists and feminists have actually formed dynamic alliances to challenge institutions of power, even without political agreement.[68] Effectiveness has emerged from working together across diversity.

The diversity of the movement can be seen in many forms. It is found in dialogue among liberal, radical, and socialist feminists; it is found within radical feminism between those who see the woman/nature connection as potentially emancipatory and those who see it as contributing to further subordination of women. Diversity is also found in the dialogue between white feminists and feminists of color.[69] Further, ecofeminists are in dialogue with others, such as deep ecologists—people who share many common passions but are not the same. The differences between these movements are particularly visible in their respective diagnoses of the root problem in environmental destruction; deep ecologists attribute the problem largely to anthropocentrism, and ecofeminists, to masculinism.[70] These differences are not really gender-oriented in the narrowest sense of men against women. The influence of gender is seen, however, in the way problems are defined, whether problems are seen as rooted more in personal consciousness or in destructive cultural values, such as the cultural value of domination.[71]

The differences we have been discussing are not merely superficial; different worldviews, social analyses, and environmental analyses lead to radically different views of what kind of action is needed. For example, the focus of radical ecofeminism has been more on the connection between woman and nature and the problems inherent in devaluing both; the focus of socialist ecofeminism has been on destructive social structures shaped by gender, social class, and race. For the latter, both nature and human nature are seen as historically and socially constructed.[72] Thus, radical ecofeminists are more likely to advocate for changes in worldviews, and socialists are more likely to work toward social revolution, or restructuring patterns of domination.

In addition to diversity, a second major theme appears in the ecofeminist movement—*critique of dualistic thinking*. This has long been a major theme in the work of Rosemary Radford Ruether and Susan Griffin; now Val Plumwood has identified dualistic thinking at the root of ecological destruction.[73] Plumwood argues that dualistic thinking leads people to interpret differences in terms of oppositional and dominant-subordinate relationships.[74] When people deal with difference in this way, dualism becomes a tool for setting two realities (such as nature and culture) in opposition to one another. Dualistic categories lead naturally to relationships of dominance-subordination, such as valuing culture over nature, or valuing some people over other people, particularly denigrating people who are closely associated with nature (namely, women, indigenous people, and people of certain races, classes, and regions of the world). When this happens, difference becomes a tool for dividing, judging, ignoring, and oppressing. Difference is no longer seen as contributing to the rich textures of the earth and the human community; it becomes a way of dividing and setting people over against one another and the earth.

The brief look at differences and dualisms within ecofeminism leads to a third theme; that is, *proposals to reconfigure relationships among human beings, and between human beings and the rest of the natural world*. The analysis of dominating relationships is the starting point, but not the end. What is needed is the cultivation of freedom so people will act responsibly in their relationships. Ynestra King urges human beings to make active choices, especially to exercise freedom and practice stewardship of evolution.[75] Val Plumwood advocates that people value difference and honor the continuity between humans and the natural world. She critiques the practice of describing women as the more nature-connected gender; instead, she encourages women to *choose* to identify *with* nature.[76] Plumwood also encourages people to cultivate virtues of friendship with nature, including openness, generosity, space-making, identification (the ability to place one's self in another's place), and responsiveness.[77]

These ecofeminist views place great responsibility on human beings and stand in contrast to the theistic and christocentric views of Clark and Gunton. The forms of responsibility will vary according to the particular ecofeminist perspective, but recurring themes are: to critique and reform worldviews by analyzing patterns of domination; to celebrate the relationship between women and the natural world; to reconnect human life with the rest of nature through story and ritual; to critique and re-form political structures, overturning patterns of domination and reconstructing patterns of equality and partnership; and to cultivate human consciousness and attunement to the natural world.

From these various ecofeminist perspectives, one can draw two immediate conclusions regarding ministry with the earth. One is that rational, theoretical agreement is not needed for people to join in ministering with the earth. Theological reflection and mutual critique are needed, but not theological unanimity. Earthbound ministries can, thus, stir theological conversation and encourage communities to open themselves to diverse points of view. A second conclusion is that ministry with the earth requires reshaping human relationships with one another and with the earth, not just in our immediate communities but also in large political structures. This conclusion coincides with a theme in the theistic and christocentric perspectives of Clark and Gunton, without their emphasis on heterosexual relationships. In both views, reshaping relationships is urgent for the well-being of life. Ecofeminists emphasize that relationships of dominance permeate the world; reshaping relationships requires social-environmental analysis and action in all social arenas to enhance mutuality, equality, and partnership.

Meeting God: Incarnation of God in History

The previous section ended with a plea to reshape relationships. The goal was not to eliminate diversity, but to enhance mutuality, equality, and partnership. This is more feasible if we recognize that God meets us in the diversity of ordinary life, with its pulls toward competing concerns. God is present, even in the most difficult confrontations. Such confrontations may evoke transformations in priorities, commitments, and perspectives, or stir a redoubling of energies toward existing priorities, commitments, and perspectives. The confrontations are sacred, not because truth always wins, and certainly not because people come to agreement (which they often do not), but because confrontation leads people to pause, rethink, ask questions, and discern new possibilities.

Consider the deaths of Princess Diana of the United Kingdom and Mother Teresa of India. No two women could be more different. They were from different countries, continents, and hemispheres; different social classes and life experiences; different vocations. Yet their two deaths rocked the world—confronted the world with the possibility of giving oneself for others, especially for those who are most poor, most oppressed, and most hurting. These two women did not have to agree with each other on all religious, ethical, and social matters in order to respect and admire one another. Their passions for people who hurt converged. They themselves converged. And when their deaths converged, the world was confronted with the boldness of their lives and the values they held dear. The world was confronted with the challenge of carrying on their work; indeed, the challenge was accepted for a time, witnessed by profuse donations of money and increased registrations for volunteer service. The very differences between Princess Diana and Mother Teresa intensified the public confrontation of their deaths.

The central argument of this section is that God is present in such moments of confrontation. God is incarnate in both ordinary and extraordinary beings, and very often, God confronts us through others. To understand God's incarnation more deeply, we turn now to the incarnation of God in Jesus Christ. Jesus reveals the compassion and concerns of God, as well as God's power and redemptive work.

God Walking among Us

Incarnation is God's presence with us. A primary image of incarnation is a road or path where we meet and travel with God. Mary and Joseph traveled a road to Bethlehem, where Jesus was born (Lk. 2:1–7). Three kings, following a star, traveled to the birthplace of this newborn king (Matt. 2:1–12). Jesus journeyed on many roads throughout his ministry, preaching, teaching, and healing. Jesus and the disciples traveled the road to Jerusalem, where he was to face death (Matt. 21; Mk.10:32—15:47; Lk. 19:28–48; Jn. 12:12–26). Jesus carried his cross on the path to Golgotha (Matt. 27:31–37; Mk. 15:20–24; Lk. 23:26–33). And the resurrected Jesus met two of his disciples on the Emmaus road (Lk. 24:13–35). These are roads where God walks with creation. In the midst of such ordinary life, God is enfleshed.

The presence of God is particularly full and "earthy" in Jesus, the Jewish carpenter from Nazareth, whose life embodies the vulnerability of God and the fullness of human life.[78] For Christian people, the incarnation is the power of this earthy Jesus to reveal God and to affect the flow of history. As the New Testament drama unfolds, Jesus enters the hurting creation, actively working for good and responding to the world through love. Larry Rasmussen argues that the way of Jesus, or "the way of God among us," is the way of entering the suffering of others with compassion.[79] It is the way of power and healing:

> The only power that can truly heal and keep the creation is power instinctively drawn to the flawed places of existence, there to call forth from the desperate and needy themselves extraordinary yet common powers that they did not even know they had. This is the power seen in Jesus.[80]

Similarly, Keith Ward sees the incarnation as relating God to human personhood, "involving the Divine in human suffering and taking human nature into the Divine."[81]

This view of God is compatible with the prophetic tradition of Judaism, as expressed by Abraham Heschel and others; in both, God is understood as passionately and intimately involved with creation.[82] Even the idea of incarnation—that God enters the world in a cosmic moment, associated with the final goal of history—is continuous with one form of Jewish mysticism.[83]

Thus far, the discussion of incarnation has focused on streams of tradition, but it is also important to focus on the efficacious power of a doctrine of incarnation. What does the incarnation of God in history communicate about what God can and will do in the future? Jay McDaniel recognizes that the significance of Christ can be understood in terms of redeeming fallen humanity or in terms of opening new possibilities for God's work in the future or both.[84] If emphasis is placed on the former, people can enjoy divine forgiveness and redemption; if on the latter, people can participate in a new consciousness and way of life, made possible through Christ.[85] Such a view suggests that the incarnation of Christ makes a difference not only in individual lives, but in the future of creation.

Just as the image of covenant inspires sacred meetings (chapter 3), so also sacred meetings are inspired by the incarnation of God in history, and such meetings are often sacred confrontations. Through God's incarnation in Jesus, many ordinary people come to expect that God will meet them in the midst of their ordinary lives, revealing the ways of God, affecting the flow of history, and pointing to God's new creation. Thus, we will consider incarnation here in relation to some of Jesus' significant meetings along the road, suggestive of the potential of sacred confrontation in earthbound ministry.

Mark is a good place to begin exploring this image of God on the road because in the book of Mark, Jesus was always traveling. To open the image, we will explore three Jesus stories that happened along the road. All are very familiar, but none of them ever let go of their tug. The first one is hard to hear; the second one is sweet and, therefore, is often *not* heard; the last one has been interpreted so much that we do not have to hear it.

The Woman Who Would Not Keep Quiet

Story number one comes from Mark 7:24–30. *Jesus was walking through Gentile territory on the way to Tyre. He went into a house, seemingly to get a break and hide away for a while. Maybe he was going on retreat. But people saw him, and immediately a woman came and fell at his feet. She explained to Jesus about her daughter, who was possessed by an unclean spirit; she pleaded with him to cast out the demon. But this woman was Syrophoenician. She was not just a woman (which would have been bad enough); she was a foreign, Gentile woman. Jesus responded to her quickly, "Let the children first be fed, for it is not right to take the children's bread and throw it to the dogs." The woman answered, "Yes, Lord, but even the dogs under the table eat the children's crumbs." He said, "For this saying you may go on your way; the demon has left your daughter." The woman went home and found her daughter in bed, the demon gone.*

This story is embarrassing to the Christian church. The woman just would not keep quiet. Her behavior rubbed against all social norms; she corrected Jesus, reminding him that Gentiles should be given God's blessings, as much as dogs under the table deserve a few crumbs. On the other hand, Jesus' response seems narrow—keeping his message just for the Jews and calling the Gentiles "dogs." Actually, Jesus healed two other Gentiles in Mark's Gospel, but one comes after this story of the Syrophoenician woman; some think that Jesus may have been more open to the Gentiles after this sacred confrontation.[86]

Most biblical commentators describe this story as a problem text, difficult to interpret.[87] The confrontation does not fit with stories of Jesus' overflowing compassion and wisdom. Some have said that Jesus wanted chiefly to reveal his true character to the disciples, and this is why he tried to turn the woman away.[88] Some speculate that Jesus' crude words in calling Gentiles dogs were added by later Christians, maybe by Jewish Christians who were prejudiced against Gentile Christians, or maybe by Gentiles who wanted Jews to appear exclusivistic. Still others argue that another healer met the woman and cast out her daughter's demon; only later did people attribute the healing to Jesus.

However challenging this story is, it cannot be avoided; Mark includes it and so does Matthew (15:21–28). The story actually communicates much about Jesus, especially as understood in Mark's community. It communicates that Jesus was willing to listen to a woman, even a foreign, Gentile woman who would not keep quiet—a woman who was not of his tradition and who was more than a little pushy. The story communicates that Jesus could see the faith of the woman, and he admired her courage. He said to her, "For saying that, you may go—the demon has left your daughter" (Mk. 7:29b).[89] The story also communicates that Jesus was willing to be corrected, even by someone of low social status, and he was willing to share God's gifts with her by healing her daughter.

The story is also revealing about the woman. It reveals that she loved her daughter and wanted to do her best to get help for her child; that she had faith in Jesus' ability to heal; that she had enough courage to break all social rules and risk complete rejection for herself and her daughter; and that she did not give up easily.

Taken as a whole, the story reminds the community that God listens and gives people courage to speak, and what people say may even change God's mind. It reminds the community that women are strong characters, not just as humble servants, but also as people who speak truth. It reminds the contemporary community that the historical Christian church has often ignored or belittled stories of strong women. The woman of this story is not even given a name. Further, her story has not been told so often in sermons and theological treatises as stories where women are pictured as sinners or needy (like the story of the woman caught in adultery in Jn. 8:2–11, or the story of the woman healed of her hemorrhage in Mk. 5:25–34).

Mark's story reveals a sacred confrontation with Jesus on the road—a meeting that disrupts social conventions and points toward a more inclusive community. At this point in the Gospel of Mark (chapter 7), Jesus was still a hero, performing miracle after miracle and speaking with simple eloquence. In this story, readers meet Jesus as vulnerable, open to correction by someone outside the mainstream, and willing to transcend himself and enlarge his own sense of mission. This picture of Jesus communicates that disruptive diversity affects even God. Jesus is affected by the deep pains and compassion of a strange woman in a complex and confusing world.

Jesus and the Children

But Mark tells other stories of confrontations with Jesus along the road. Reflect on the children who were brought to Jesus:

> *People were bringing little children to him in order that he might touch them; and the disciples spoke sternly to them. But when Jesus saw this, he was indignant and said to them, "Let the little children come to me; do not stop them; for it is to such as these that the kingdom of God belongs. Truly I tell you, whoever does not receive the kingdom of God as a little child will never enter it." And he took them up in his arms, laid his hands on them, and blessed them* (Mk. 10:13–16).

This story appears in Mark long after the disciples first confronted Jesus on the road. The twelve disciples and women who followed Jesus had already traveled many miles and asked many questions; yet, they still wondered who was the greatest and what Jesus' teachings really meant, especially the teachings about what was demanded of them as followers of Jesus. No sooner did they comprehend one teaching than Jesus would say or do something that perplexed them again. In Mark's telling of stories, Jesus stopped occasionally for a few precious moments of conversation with the disciples; even then, people kept coming and the world pressed in on them.

So it was the day that the children came to see Jesus. Parents had probably brought these children because parents through all times and cultures have followed the custom of taking their children to be blessed by persons of greatness. The disciples preferred to send the children away, however; they apparently did not have a confrontation with children in mind. Perhaps they thought discipleship was for adults. After all, Jesus had been speaking a *lot* in Mark about the cost of discipleship. Shortly before the story of the children in Mark is another story about taking up one's cross and following Jesus (8:31–38). Also, Jesus had had an interchange with the disciples in which Peter identified Jesus as the Messiah, and Jesus foretold his suffering and death. Peter rebuked him for such talk, but Jesus' response was to rebuke Peter and proclaim to the crowd: "If any want to become my followers, let them deny themselves and take up their cross and follow me" (8:34b). Between that confrontation with Peter and Mark's story of the children are other challenging stories. Jesus healed a boy with an unclean spirit after rebuking the disciples for their inability to do so (9:14–29), and Jesus taught that "Whoever wants to be first must be last of all and servant of all," responding to the disciples' argument about who was the greatest (33–35).

In light of such strong talk, the disciples may have been confused by this story of Jesus and the children, especially since it follows soon after another story of children in Mark. Jesus, responding to the disciples' aforementioned dispute about who was the greatest, had placed a child among them, saying, "Whoever welcomes one such child in my name welcomes me, and whoever welcomes me welcomes not me but the one who sent me" (9:37). Perhaps the disciples did not understand such teaching, or perhaps they simply did not like it. Perhaps the disciples were disturbed because mothers had brought the children to Jesus (a conjecture based on common practice). Maybe they thought Jesus' message was intended first for men, and only later for women.

Whatever their reasons, Mark tells us that Jesus let the children come. He said, "Whoever does not receive the kingdom of God as a little child will never enter it." He took the children in his arms and blessed them. He laid his hands on them, conveying that God's call was to them also. This was an appalling breach of convention. Children and youth were expected to look to adults as models, and Jesus was asking adults to look to children. The story thus reverses normal expectations and introduces two kinds of confrontation—confrontation by interruption and confrontation by children. What now do these confrontations suggest for earthbound ministries?

The story first *confronts by interruption*. The arrival of children was interruptive, and the incident raises issues that are interruptive—issues of belonging (who is included) and discipleship (what is the appropriate human response to God). Specifically, the story poses questions regarding whether children belong and, then, what it means to "receive the kingdom of God as a little child." [90] Such an interruptive scene surely calls up familiar images for leaders in ministry. Leaders often make plans with great care, only to have an unexpected incident or someone's unexpected mood turn the plans in quite an unexpected direction. Certainly, leaders in earthbound ministries experience this. They seek to nourish communion with God and engage people in significant action, but someone unwelcome arrives or an unexpected event disrupts what people are doing. The pressures of the world press in, and issues of belonging and discipleship are raised yet again.

Mark's story also *confronts people with children*, and this is the second time. Both of Mark's stories with children invite modern readers to reflect on their own sacred confrontations with children. Certainly, children and youth confront adults with a world full of *wonder*—a sacred creation. [91] One small story can be a reminder.

When our daughter was 6 years old, we walked by a house with an uprooted tree. Rebecca was full of questions; she was especially concerned about what was going to happen next. I told her that the people might plant another tree; then I explained that God plans for sun and rain to help trees grow. Time passed and the week after Christmas my daughter and I took another walk past the same house. This conversation followed:

Rebecca: That ground is still turned over.

Mother: Yes, it is.

Rebecca: No one has planted a new tree yet.

Mother: No, but maybe they will do it soon.

Rebecca: Jesus is going to do it.

Mother: He is? How?

Rebecca: Yes, he is going to get a shovel and dig a hole. Then he is going to put a tiny seed in the ground. He's going to put dirt on the seed and water it, and the seed is going to grow into a tree.

Mother: That's interesting. Do you really think Jesus can do that?

Rebecca: Well, he can do it when he grows up. He is still a baby now.

Mother: How do you know that?

Rebecca: He was just born at Christmas!

For Rebecca, God was physically present and real. She had taken my very general, carefully constructed theological statement about God's planning for sun and rain, and she had converted it into a vivid and concrete involvement of God in the world. Furthermore, she believed that God was going to step in and plant the seed because the replanting was moving slowly and intervention was needed. In Rebecca's unique six-year-old way, she knew that God was incarnate, and she confronted me with wonder.

Children and youth also confront us with *critique*; they often see the world with open and critical eyes—not toughened as most adults are to facts that seem irreversible. Our son, Cliff, asked us after the news one night, "Why do you hear so much on the news about a person dying in a well, when thousands of people die every day from auto accidents and even from starvation, and no mention is made?" Good question!

But maybe children confront adults most boldly with their need to receive. While the adults around Jesus were trying to earn Jesus' attention and love, the children were simply brought; they received. Perhaps these children confronted the disciples with their own need to receive from Jesus (justice, protection, blessing); Jesus' teaching confronted the disciples as well, communicating that disciples need to be like little children. This is highly suggestive for ministry. The call is to be as little children, and to be led by children.

Such interpretation sounds sweet, but most people do not really want to be like children. Once I participated in a camping conference where people made their name tags of wood and other materials. I chose to make my tag quickly, but someone shamed me, pointing out that no one could read my tag. I tried to fix it and made it worse. I realized that I had created the ugliest name tag in the meeting. I felt like a three-year-old klutz surrounded by adult artists. I did not want to be a child. I wanted to be in control and to produce a beautiful name tag in minimal time, to use my time efficiently. I did not want to play; I simply wanted to return to my room and review my presentation for the evening session. I finally did play, however, at least enough to laugh at my grotesque name tag; then, of course, I met someone in such a way that it made my day! Earthbound meetings can be just such times when the child within busy people is invited out to play, when people confront themselves and others in a significant way, and when people give up striving and just receive gifts from other people and the world around them.

But the stories of Jesus in Mark are not even that simple. They represent countercultural thinking; they challenge the church with a message that is often ignored. Christian churches, for example, often have difficulty supporting ministries with children, or ministries on behalf of children in the larger society. Churches often take little role in creating sanctuary for children, in addressing the abuses of children within their own congregation or parish, and even in addressing the abuses of children by representatives of the church. Some efforts have been made to call attention to the significance of children in the community and to urge the creation of safe havens for children in the church, but these challenges are heeded only minimally.[92] Further, churches have taken only a modest role in urging the ratification of the United Nations Convention on the Rights of the Child.

When related with sacred confrontations and earthbound ministry, the teachings found in Mark are radical indeed. They suggest the sacredness of being confronted with interruptions and with children. Interruptions become opportunities for blessing. And children are representatives of Christ (9:37), revealing how people are to respond to the reign of God (10:15). Ministry with the earth has to do with pausing when the interruptions come; it has to do with giving and receiving with children.

A Rich Man Approaches

A third story is found in the gospel of Mark immediately after the episode with the children. Picture the disciples sitting beside the road pondering these things, only to look up and see that Jesus was moving again. They probably had to run to catch up. Mark's Gospel is like a stack of stories which, like a stack of cards, could be put together in almost any order. Although Mark probably felt compelled to organize the accounts of Jesus' early ministry at the beginning, and accounts of the death and resurrection at the end, other stories could be organized for purposes fitting to Mark and his community.[93] Mark was probably intentional in putting the two stories of children close together, and placing the elaborated story of Jesus' blessing the children immediately prior to the now-familiar story of the rich man. Both deal with the kingdom of God, but the messages are strikingly different, as a look at the rich man story will reveal.

No sooner had Jesus left the children, according to Mark, than someone else came to meet him—a man who asked, "Good Teacher, what must I do to inherit eternal life?" (Mk. 10:17–27) Maybe Jesus was annoyed at the man's flowery speech, but he answered, "Why do you call me good? No one is good but God alone." But Jesus continued the conversation, perhaps sensing the man's sincerity, and also his limits. "You know the commandments," he said, "You shall not murder; You shall not commit adultery...." Now, the Jewish listeners would have known that the first commandment is that you shall have no other gods beside God. The man responded, "Teacher, I have kept all these since my youth." Jesus' compassion went out. Perhaps Jesus knew that the man realized something was missing. Jesus' response was a unconventional: "You lack one thing; go, sell what you own, and give the money to the poor, and you will have treasure in heaven; then come, follow me." This story turns traditional teaching upside down; wealth, in the rich man's tradition, carried an obligation to tithe, but not to give everything away. The man went away sorrowfully. And the disciples were left with Jesus and many questions by the side of the road.

At the very least, these three Markan texts reveal that meeting Jesus on the road is a risky business. In one moment, Jesus is humbled by a Syrophoenician woman, and not long after, he is showing compassion to children. In one moment, Jesus challenges the people to be like children and simply to receive from God; in the very next moment, Jesus challenges a rich man to give away his possessions and follow God. God's gift is presented as free, but also as very demanding. This seems contradictory, confrontational.

Even in confrontation, however, Jesus had compassion; he responded to the man's questions. Further, Jesus reminded people standing nearby how hard it is to enter God's new creation—harder than for a camel to go through the eye of a needle (10:25). Jesus reminded them, also, that what is not possible for people, *is* possible with God (10:27). The people were faced with impossible challenges and, then, assured that all things are possible with God. Such are the challenges and promises of sacred confrontation.

Sacred Confrontation: A Way of Ministering with the Earth

In this chapter, we have explored many forms of diversity, even within ecological theology. We have also reflected on the incarnation of God in Jesus, confronting people along the road. Taken together, the pictures are confusing and risky. They communicate that people need to listen to voices they typically ignore, and that even Jesus may change his mind and include people who are not really in his community. They communicate that people need to be like children, and that any one of us may be asked to give more than we are willing to give. But if the Christian community today is not willing to face these risks, maybe it should not be engaged in ministry at all. This chapter reveals that theological convictions and biblical stories do not give simple answers and moral rules. They offer us the diverse convictions of diverse people and the challenge of many questions and ideas.

Sacred confrontation turns us not only to theological traditions and Jesus stories, however. It turns us also to ordinary life with all of its messy diversity, to the incarnation of God in the most ordinary parts of God's creation. This awareness is communicated in the Jesus traditions themselves. Consider Matthew 25: 31–46, in which Jesus speaks of the end times, when the "Son of Man" will say to the righteous:

Come, you that are blessed by my Father, inherit the kingdom prepared for you from the foundation of the world; for I was hungry and

you gave me food, I was thirsty and you gave me something to drink,
I was a stranger…I was naked…I was sick…I was in prison (vv. 34b–
36).

When the righteous ask Jesus to explain, he will respond: "Truly I tell you, just
as you did it to one of the least of these who are members of my family, you
did it to me" (v. 40). In the ordinary life of messy diversity, Jesus is present;
God is present.

The temptation is to mystify incarnation, which helps people avoid sacred confrontations. The message of incarnation, however, is that the particularity of God's confrontations requires a response. Following Mother Teresa's
death, Edward Martin preached these words:

> There is a rush going on to make Mother Teresa a saint…But, regard-
> less of how fast Teresa is made a saint, remember she was just a
> woman—just a human being, a child of God, just as we are children
> of God. We should not let the 'saint' label so set her apart that we
> forget she was just like us and we, too, can be pencils in the hand of
> God, writing messages of the love of Christ for all.[94]

Martin speaks *against* mystification and *for* incarnation. He recognizes the
power in this remarkable life to incarnate something of God; that is the power
of sacred confrontation.

The challenges of chapters 3 and 4 come from exploring images of covenantal relationships and confrontations along the road. The images resound
with hopes for earthbound ministry, especially that diversity will be embraced
as a gift and confronted as a challenge. The hope is that people will engage the
disruptive stories that meet them in scripture as well as the disruptive stories
in their lives, and that people will face the challenge offered by these stories to
meet God and live radically in the world.

FIVE

Sacred Journeys:
Movements of Hope for God's People

A Native American elder spoke to a group of people at the conclusion of an evocative and emotional conference: "Do not expect us to be partners unless you plan to walk with us on the long journey."

⊠

In 1965, I was living in England as part of an international exchange program. My roommates in a small bed-and-breakfast hotel were two other college students, one black and one white. One evening I received a call from my dearest friend in the United States; he wanted me to know that he was leaving the next day for Selma, Alabama, where he was marching with Dr. Martin Luther King, Jr., in the march from Selma to Montgomery. I experienced pride, excitement, and a bit of anxiety about his journey, and when the conversation ended, I shared the news with my African American roommate. Her reply to me was simple, "We don't want or need you white folks on our marches; you come in like you are big heroes and get in the way of what we are doing." That night was the beginning of a long journey for me; my perspectives and friendships were revolutionized.

Many nights later, my roommate returned from a party very ill. She told people with her, "Just let me get to Mary Elizabeth, and she will take care of me." She and I were traveling a long road together; we had much to learn and enjoy with one another.

⊠

Mono Lake, on the East side of the Sierra Nevada Mountains in Central California, has been depleted of its water, wildlife, plant life, and soil life as part of a water distribution program, moving water from wetter parts of California to more arid parts. A major reclamation effort has been underway for some years now, and after many court cases, broad public support, and persistent efforts by a small group to support regeneration of the natural habitat, the waters are returning to Mono Lake. Trees are being replanted, and groups from Southern California (where Mono Lake water has been piped for many decades now) are active in the efforts. This is a project of many years past and many years to come—a long journey in which the people who origi-nally inspired the efforts have died, or will die, before Mono Lake is restored.

A group of women and men sit reminiscing about their lives. One after another, they describe camping and retreat experiences that were major junctures in their lives, times when a major revelation or monumental decision was made. They recall humor-ous stories, moments of inspiration, experiences of living closely with the natural world, stories of deepening friendships, and moments of overwhelming conviction.*

What do these stories of journey have in common? Each draws upon the metaphor of journey in describing life. Some speak of a people's journey, such as that of Native Americans; others speak of a short-term journey to a camp or retreat. Others speak of a journey through tumultuous times when the cre-ation is hurting and efforts are needed for regeneration. Yet, all of these jour-neys touch deep parts of life, and all have power to bind people with one another and the earth. All are transformative, or potentially so.

The purpose of this chapter is to *explore diverse forms of sacred journey and their potential for earthbound ministry*, drawing implications for future practice. In the quilting metaphor, this is the work of *basting on a backing*; journey is a practice and image that holds the many parts together. It is also a powerful leaven in the church community, stirring people to transformed life in the world. With that sense of power, then, we turn to sacred journeys through sacred places and sacred times, and to the movement quality of earthbound ministry.

Sacred journeys come in many shapes and sizes. They are sometimes iden-tified metaphorically as journeys through life, or literally as pilgrimages to a new land or to a special place away from normal environments, routines, and communities. In all of these journeys, people are transformed as they travel. In this chapter, we will *explore four kinds of journeys*. First, we consider the journeys of people through the cosmos. We will explore the action of *wonder-ing*, which arises from naked experience with the cosmos and gives birth to gratitude and sorrow for the wonders of creation. We move then to journeys through history; the primary action is *wandering*, and the attendant qualities are courage and hope. This is followed by journeys to sacred places, with the actions of *retreating* and qualities of renewal and transformation. And we close with journeys into moments of decision, with the action of *deciding* and quali-ties of risk and letting go.

Wondering: Journeys of People through the Cosmos

A new paradigm is needed for living reverently and justly with the cosmos. An important point of departure is the *journey of wondering—wondering at the magnificence of creation and at the sorrow of a hurting and longing world*. In this section, we will explore the journey of wondering as an important dimension of earthbound ministry, and we will do so largely through the literature of those who have wondered (including the psalmists), those who have contemplated the psalms, and those who have contemplated the writings of God in creation itself.

In calling for a new paradigm, we echo a motif similar to that of Paul Santmire, who urges Christians to focus on ecological metaphors, particularly on metaphors of fecundity and migration. Though the plea in this chapter is similar, the picture is not the same. Santmire reflects on two historical metaphors associated with mountains. First is the metaphor of ascent, in which people contemplate and yearn for the transcendent mysteries of heaven and high places; second is the metaphor of fecundity, in which people contemplate and yearn for the fullness of the world.[1] To these, Santmire adds a third metaphor of migration, in which people migrate to a good land. He argues that the metaphor of ascent follows a spiritual motif, and the metaphors of fecundity and migration follow an ecological motif.[2]

In exploring the writings of those who have wondered, we will discover some of their joy connected with fecundity and migration, but we will also discover metaphors of ascent. Perhaps Santmire's concern with the emphasis on metaphors of ascent, as in Karl Barth's theology, is fully appropriate, but not fully analyzed.[3] Perhaps the problem is not that metaphors of ascent have played such a part in Protestant theology (as in much of Jewish and Christian tradition), but that these metaphors have been allowed to dominate the metaphors of fecundity and migration. Perhaps we need, instead, an understanding of journey in which the movements of ascent, fecundity, and migration are seen in dynamic relation with one another. Such a journey might be symbolized by the Celtic high crosses, usually placed on a mountain or knoll, and understood as the place where heaven and earth commune. The interplay of the heights of heaven and the fecundity of earth becomes central; neither is isolated from the other. The journey of wonder leads into the interplay.

Journeys of Wonder in the Psalms

In chapter 2, the wonder of the psalms and the rhythms of biblical creation stories were fabrics gathered together to reveal the textures of sacred creation. We turn again to the psalms in this chapter, recognizing the way in which psalms reveal sacred journeys of the people of Israel. Psalms point to the sacred journeys of particular individuals and communities and, also, to the more inclusive journeys of all peoples through the cosmos. As discussed in chapter 2, the psalms are songs and prayers of sacred time, sacred place, sacred journeys, sacred people, sacred leaders, and sacred creation. As such, they point to the religious significance of ordinary human life in relation to God's creation.

The psalms themselves engage with the metaphor of journey; the interplay between temple and *sheol*, the presence and absence of God, confession and crisis, offers a kind of "sacred topography."[4] Thus, the human drama is played out in relation to the cosmos. The drama is intensified when one sees the dominance of praise and lament as the two major forms of address to God in the psalms.[5] Such a drama defies easy interpretation, and the interpretive frameworks that scholars bring to the psalms are myriad. Some recent scholars celebrate this dramatic power and warn against oversimplifying, a view expressed most eloquently by Walter Brueggemann, who encourages a hermeneutic of "abiding astonishment."[6] Such an approach to interpretation can inspire a journey of wondering.

The dynamics of praise and lament, like the dynamics of temple and *sheol*, suggest contrasts in human life journeys through the cosmos. These contrasts can be compared with the various kinds of psalms—psalms of orientation (hymns), disorientation (laments), and reorientation (praise).[7] Something basic about human life journeys is captured in the psalms, alongside their cosmic imagery and religious significance; thus the psalms are an earthy religious genre. No wonder they stir a sense of wonder in readers and interpreters.

The psalms are also active in the lives of people who read them. Three particular functions are named in the work of biblical scholars, and a fourth will be identified later. At the most obvious level, psalms *express the experiences of people as they journey through the cosmos*—the praise, lament, and sense of movement that people experience.[8] For this reason, they are important to worship in their expressive functions. They also *provide vehicles for reflecting on history and creation in relation to God*, a point that has been developed extensively in chapter 2. In this role, the psalms point to God's fidelity with creation and invite people into a relationship of fidelity with God.[9] They reveal God, and they challenge people to respond to God. A third function of psalms is constructive, that is, the psalms *contribute to the construction or reconstruction of the world*. Brueggemann explains, for example, that the psalms can be used to make and unmake a world. The psalms of recital construct a world that is "intergenerational, covenantly shaped, morally serious, dialogically open, and politically demanding"; simultaneously, they unmake a world that is "one-generational," "devoid of authoritative covenanting," morally indifferent, "monologically closed," and politically indifferent.[10] The world they create could be called a "counter-world."[11]

If psalms have such expressive, revealing, and constructive roles to play in the journeys of religious people, a community's approach to the psalms is important because it will affect the work of psalms in the journey of the community. Brueggemann critiques approaches to the psalms that remove awe or superimpose order, because these approaches undermine the constructive work of the psalms. Interpretations that accent historical reconstruction undermine the awe of the psalms by searching primarily for objectivity and human causes and effects in the historical texts.[12] At the same time, interpretations that recite history from a particular, ordered, and monopolistic perspective on the psalms deny marginality, tensions, and contrasts.[13] Both approaches fall into modernist traps of neglecting awe and complexity in favor of explanation and control. Brueggemann poses an alternative to the endless debate between social scientific analysis and theological protectionism; he proposes abiding astonishment.[14] One may appreciate both social scientific analysis and theological reflection, but one may still engage texts with a sense of mystery and awe. The psalms bear unfathomable riches but are never exhausted. They contribute to the journey of wonder but never explain or control it.

This leads to one further function of the psalms—to *touch mystery and open persons to a deeper relation with God and creation*. Nowhere is this experience of mystery expressed more vividly than in contemplative writings, where the deepest experiences of God are linked with psalms. Contemplatives seek the spiritual depth of the poetry by penetrating the actual words and literal sense; thus, the true meaning is often seen as hidden and allegorical.[15] Thomas Merton recognizes that the psalms, with all of their depth and hiddenness, reveal God and the poetic experience of the people who wrote them.[16] They "dispose the souls of men for union with God"; to do so, they must raise human minds and hearts to God and inspire people to give themselves fully to God.[17]

Because the psalms concern themselves with journeys of God's people through the cosmos, they inspire extravagant language, both in the psalms themselves and in contemplative commentaries. For Merton, then, "The God of the Psalter is 'above all gods,' that is to say, above anything that could possibly be represented and adored in an image."[18] He adds that the psalmists themselves "were carried away in an ecstasy of joy when they saw God in the cosmic symbolism of His created universe."[19] The cosmic symbolism points to God:

> Light and darkness, sun and moon, stars and planets, trees, beasts, whales, fishes and birds of the air, all these things in the world around us and the whole natural economy in which they have their place have impressed themselves upon the spirit of man in such a way that they naturally tend to mean to him much more than they mean in themselves.[20]

According to Merton, David was "drunk with the love of God" and sensed that human beings have a liturgical function as high priest of creation.[21] The psalms evoke such images in many commentators, and though the poetry records movements and cries of particular people, it also points to depths of life that transcend one people or one place.[22] The psalms bind all people and all places into a web of spiritual meaning.

Journeys of Wonder into God's Creation

We turn now from Psalms to the writings of God in creation. Here we find again the movements of ascent, fecundity, and migration; we find the actions of praise and lament; and we find experiences of orientation, disorientation, and reorientation. As we look to the earth, our home, we can be touched and transformed by what is revealed there.

What does it mean to think of Earth as home? Larry Rasmussen joins Walter Brueggemann and many others in bemoaning effects of the Enlightenment on human relations with creation. He argues that the dominant image of Western cultures since the Enlightenment is mastery, which encourages people to use the natural world, but not appreciate it. The quest for mastery finally denies "both our humanity and nature's essential character."[23] He urges people to abandon the mindset of mastery and go home—to take a good long look at the home in which they live, with all of its beauty and destruction.[24] This is similar to what we discussed in early chapters about knowing one's bioregion, but for Rasmussen, this knowledge is interpreted through a theology of the cross, which is thoroughly contextual and thoroughly aware that God redeems destruction. He advises:

> To experience the gracious God, go home and look around. And when you find putrid death there, together with remnants of life, take heart! God, in light of the cross, enters death to negate it; thus, life can emerge for those who, in humility, repent and believe.[25]

This may not sound like a journey of wonder, but in this journey people travel alertly toward what they know as home. They wonder at beauty but are tragically aware of hurt, placing hope in God's grace, which is manifested in the cross.

From a different theological angle, but with similar passions, John Muir has read the book of God's creation and left a record of his own journey of wondering. In some foundational ways, Muir's record bears striking resemblance to Rasmussen's. He began with a strong sense of place and respect for creation; even as a young man he interacted with mountains as living beings. Muir spent his life "looking around," as Rasmussen would say, and lived his life with an attitude of humility. Muir was not bound to home, however; he made home wherever he was. As a wanderer, he literally traversed thousands of miles on foot, and as a person, he understood his entire life metaphorically as a journey.

Consider Muir's physical pilgrimage through life. From his university days, Muir recognized he had much to learn, and when he left the University of Wisconsin after four years, he realized that he "was only leaving one University for another"; he entered the "University of the Wilderness."[26] His first journey was down the middle of the United States to the Gulf of Mexico, through Cuba and parts of the Caribbean, and finally into California—his thousand-mile walk.[27] This was followed by many journeys over fifty years through California, the Western United States, and Alaska. In his life as a pilgrim, Muir was inspired by the earth; he responded with inspired writing, through which he hoped to inspire others to act in accord with creation. Muir was no less a pilgrim than the people of Israel, who traveled as nomads and traveled through history with their God.

As with the people of Israel, Muir's writings emerged from his journey. His writings are parallel in many ways to the psalms, and they function in some similar ways. Like the psalmists, Muir *expresses the experience of his journey through the cosmos*, albeit a story of his experience rather than the journey of a people. Again and again, Muir invites his readers to share his delight in the creation. He writes during his first summer in the Sierras, "Another glorious day, the air is delicious to the lungs as nectar to the tongue; indeed the body seems one palate, and tingles equally throughout."[28] Muir's experiences of delight turn to pleas for preservation when he sees abuse of the earth. His experience is one of wondering at the magnificence of creation and lamenting wanton destruction.

Muir also *provides vehicles for reflecting on history and creation in relation to God*, drawing upon his own Christian heritage in interpreting the marvels of nature. As he describes his experience of the Hollow near Yosemite, he uses the language of baptism and resurrection: "Never shall I forget my baptism in this font. It happened in January, a resurrection day for many a plant and for me."[29] Likewise, Muir explains the movements of the natural world as part of God's plan:

> Along the sides of the glacier we saw the mighty flood grinding against the granite walls with tremendous pressure, rounding outswelling bosses, and deepening the retreating hollows into the forms they are destined to have when, in the fullness of appointed time, the huge ice tool shall be withdrawn by the sun. Every feature glowed with intention, reflecting the plans of God.[30]

Muir's poetic prose, like the poetry of the psalmists, interprets history and creation in light of his religious heritage and experience of wonder.

Similarly, Muir's writing *contributes to the construction and reconstruction of the world*. He describes a world that is interconnected and interactive, "'When we try to pick out anything by itself, we find it hitched to everything else in the universe.'"[31] He describes a world marked by movement and change:

> Gliding along the swift-flowing river, the views change with bewildering rapidity. Wonderful, too, are the changes dependent on the seasons and the weather. In spring, when the snow is melting fast, you enjoy the countless rejoicing waterfalls...In summer you find the groves and gardens in full dress...And so goes the song, change succeeding change in sublime harmony through all the wonderful seasons and weather.[32]

Muir's description of the world is filled with appreciation, but also with respect for the awesome power of natural forces. In describing floods, he explains natural cycles that contribute to flooding, sometimes accentuated by human actions. At the same time, he recognizes the value of such floods when viewed from the perspective of the natural world. Bemoaning that so few people "meet and enjoy storms so noble," he realizes that most people view storms from the perspective of their human bridges and houses that are carried away, rather than from the perspective of "the thousand blessings they bring to the fields and gardens of Nature."[33] Muir constructs and reconstructs the world as a beautiful reality before which human life is dwarfed, inspired and humbled.

The last function of Psalms described above is to *touch mystery and open persons to a deeper relation with God and creation.* Certainly for John Muir, a sense of mystery is strong. He even connects with biblical accounts of mystery, recalling, for example, Jesus' words to Nicodemus, that no one knows from where the winds come, nor where they go. Muir concludes that, even now, human knowledge is limited, and wind is a mystery.

> Though we Gentiles know the birthplace of many a wind and also 'whither it is going,' yet we know about as little of winds in general as those Palestinian Jews...The substance of the winds is too thin for human eyes, their written language is too difficult for human minds, and their spoken language mostly too faint for the ears.[34]

This sense of mystery is akin to what Walter Brueggemann describes as abiding astonishment—the natural response and preferred interpretative approach to the psalms.

The appreciation of mystery also leads to a fifth function of Muir's writing that is somewhat less visible in the psalms. Muir's writing *inspires people to be present with the natural world.* Consider the time when Muir discovered a deer-bed and sat for a long time watching the movements of an anxious doe. Muir was present not only with this doe, but also with the whole of that small spot of the universe:

> While I sat admiring her, a Douglas squirrel, evidently excited by her noisy alarms, climbed a boulder beneath me, and witnessed her performances as attentively as I did, while a frisky chipmunk, too restless or hungry for such shows, busied himself about his supper in a thicket of shadbushes.[35]

Note that Muir is journeying through the land, observing as he goes. The very experience of journey is critical; he is present to every moment. One can say that John Muir, like Paul Santmire, was more concerned with metaphors of fecundity and migration (the ecological motif) than with metaphors of ascent (the spiritual motif). On the other hand, Muir's fluidity in interpreting the work of God's hand, and baptism and resurrection, in the natural world suggests that these three motifs are interwoven after all.

Wandering: Journeys of a People through History

We turn now from wondering to wandering. One prominent image of Christian life is pilgrimage—a form of wandering associated with the history of a people, the metaphor of Christian life as a journey with God, and literal pilgrimages to holy places. In this section, we will focus primarily on the first two forms, turning to literal pilgrimages in the next section. In its multiple forms, the image of pilgrimage generally suggests movement toward a goal; experiences of joy, pain, and hardship; acts of faithfulness and faithlessness; and travel in relation with God. This image courses through history, and to understand it better we turn now to early pilgrimages in the Bible, pilgrimages through Jewish and Christian history, and pilgrimages toward repair of the world. All of these are in some sense earthbound, for they cross the rocks, deserts, and waters of the earth.

Pilgrimages in the Bible

The qualities of faith journey are nowhere more vividly portrayed than in the stories of Abraham, Sarah, and Hagar. We are told in Jewish and Christian scriptures (with other variations in Islam) that Abram and Sarai are called to leave their home in Ur and go toward an unknown promised land.[36] Abram is told that God will make of him a "great nation"; his name will be great and he will be a blessing (Gen. 12:1–3). Abram and Sarai (later, Abraham and Sarah) have probably been comfortable in Ur, but when they set out on their journey they leave all of that behind. When they finally arrive at the oak of Moreh, Abram is told that God will give this land to his descendants (v. 7). Still later Abram is told, "I will make your offspring like the dust of the earth; so that if one can count the dust of the earth, your offspring also can be counted" (13:16). Time passes before the Lord again appears to Abram, promising descendants that will number as the stars (15:5). The promises are recurring but not quickly fulfilled.

Furthermore, the future is not always pictured as bright and easy. God says to Abram: "Know this for certain, that your offspring shall be aliens in a land that is not theirs, and shall be slaves there, and they shall be oppressed for four hundred years; but I will bring judgment on the nation that they serve, and afterward they shall come out with great possessions" (15:13–14). In this pilgrimage of Abram and Sarai, you see many qualities of the future, which is the destination of their journey. The future is portrayed to them as unknown, great, blessed, promising, and oppressive.

Shortly thereafter, Hagar, the Egyptian slave of Sarai, appears in the story, and Sarai gives Hagar to Abram as a wife. In this part of the story, Hagar is used by Sarai, then by Abram, and then by Sarai again—so harshly this last time that Hagar runs away (16:1–6). Then, an amazing series of events takes place. The angel of the Lord comes to Hagar, asks her where she is from and where she is going (inviting her to speak for herself), instructs her to return and submit to Sarai, promises a multitude of offspring (as earlier promised to Abram), and foretells the birth and life of her son. Hagar responds by naming

God (*El-roi*, or "God who sees") and by wondering that she has seen God and lived (6:7–14).

In this narrative one can see clearly the oppression of Hagar, the power of God's presence in her life, and the strength of her initiative in making choices for survival (even returning to Sarai for a time) and for a better future life for herself, her son Ishmael, and their offspring. Delores Williams develops these themes and traces the continuing presence of God and persistent initiative of Hagar in Genesis 21, uncovering a pilgrimage that is lonely, but not alone, and harsh, but not without resources and power.[37] Williams describes parallels between the Egyptian Hagar and African American women as they experience abuse, strength, and hope.[38] Hagar's journey names brutality. It also names the invincible strength of a slave-woman and her ability to see God; these qualities endure.

Abraham and Sarah's journeys also lead down strenuous roads, in many directions and to unexpected stops. Though blessed and renamed by God, their journey is wrought with confusion and disappointment. Their story is certainly not a simple one of setting out to a destination God has chosen and traveling directly to a multitude of guaranteed rewards at the end. The journey is uncertain—full of smaller journeys. The faithfulness required is far more demanding than the decision to leave Ur, and Abraham and Sarah continue to follow God's lead through many years. They have to face unfulfilled promises, disappointments in a promised land which is already occupied, and a famine that forces them to keep moving.

At least three other qualities mark these journeys, however. Abraham and Sarah are not always admirable, but Yahweh stays with them and continually renews the old promises. Furthermore, the promises are fulfilled, though never in quite the way Abraham and Sarah imagined and never with finality. In fact, the fulfilling of one promise always leads to God's making a new one.[39] Another quality of journey appears more vividly in Hagar's life. Hagar is also given promises, but God acts primarily through Hagar's initiative to guarantee survival and quality of life for her and her offspring. In this nest of stories we can see the abiding presence of Yahweh, the promise-keeping of Yahweh, and the work of God through human initiative. The pilgrimages of the Bible, even in a few short verses, are not simple, but the motif of journey is indeed powerfully present.

Pilgrimages in Jewish and Christian History

In the Jewish and Christian traditions, people have always made sacred journeys, or pilgrimages, and these have served as interpretive frames for understanding the life of the community in history. The pilgrimage of Abram and Sarai from the land of Ur to the promised land is a metaphor for interpreting the journeys of early Hebrew people. Similarly, their pilgrimage became a metaphor for later Jewish and Christian journeys. We will see later, for example, that the spirituality of the Celtic Saint Columba was grounded in the Abraham-Sarah story.[40] Likewise, the account of Moses and the exodus became a paradigmatic story of Jewish and Christian people, past and present. And the African American church has drawn upon this particular story of pilgrimage as the central metaphor of deliverance from slavery.

References to pilgrimage in the First Testament, or Hebrew Bible, usually refer broadly to a life journey, emphasizing the sacred journey itself rather than a sacred place where the journey ends. In fact, the journey never ends. The Hebrew word for pilgrim means "stranger"—an image reminiscent of the wanderings of the early nomadic Hebrews. This image has also provided an interpretive frame for the Jewish experience of dispersion in more recent centuries.

Within Christianity, the pilgrimage has been most typically understood as a journey to a sacred place for religious reasons—to give thanksgiving to God, to do penance and ask forgiveness, to honor God with prayers and gifts, or to ask God for aid. Margaret Miles points out that both literal and metaphoric pilgrimages were important to Christians from the fourth century onward.[41] In that century, a Christian woman named Egeria traveled from Spain to Jerusalem, leaving a record in her letters to the women of her community; shortly thereafter, Augustine wrote his story of pilgrimage in *City of God*.[42] More will be said of these journeys later; what is important here is how the stories of Egeria and Augustine became popular interpretive lenses for interpreting Christian life.

The metaphorical use of pilgrimage for the Christian life came into play even more strongly after the Reformation and its consequent discouragement of pilgrim journeys for the sake of special blessings. Miles points out that Jonathan Edwards and John Bunyan led to an accent on Christian pilgrimage toward a spiritual world beyond the material one.[43] In modern times, however, both Protestants and Roman Catholics are reconsidering the vitality of pilgrimages. Gwen Neville Kennedy, studying Reformed communities, believes that kin religious gatherings represent a modern Protestant pilgrimage.[44] I would add that retreats, camps, and traveling seminars are also pilgrimages. More will be said of these in the next section; for now, we simply note that literal pilgrimages may raise possibilities for metaphoric interpretations of life journeys.

The two meanings of pilgrimage—literal and metaphoric—finally do come together. The particular journeys to particular places point toward the meaning of lifelong journeys where people travel as strangers, often into uncharted territory. These concrete journeys encourage us toward a larger perspective on life and prevent us from translating our life journeys into purely metaphoric, earth-denying realities. Likewise, the metaphors of life journey invite us to view our particular pilgrimages in larger perspective, both communally and personally.

Communally, the journey metaphor urges Christians to claim a communal understanding of the church as "people of the way," with all of the challenges that metaphor offers for religious formation and moral responsibility.[45] Personally, the journey metaphor urges people to see their lives as opportunities to face change with faithfulness, and to nurture other people in their growing as well.[46] Christian peoples sometimes describe this personal journey of transformation as a journey in relationship with the Spirit of God.[47] The very popularity of the journey metaphor suggests its power.

Christians, like Jews, have experienced themselves as a pilgrim people. Just as the Hebrew word for pilgrim is "stranger," so is the Latin word *peregrinus*. The Latin word for pilgrimage is *peregrinatio*, which means "wandering." Just as the stories of Abraham, Sarah, Hagar, and Moses have been paradigms, the stories of Jesus' wandering through Galilee and his last journey to Jerusalem have been pivotal for Christians. These stories of Jesus point to the meaning of his mission, and the stories of the early church and its missionary journeys point to the church's mission.

Analyzing these diverse biblical journeys, one can discern three common elements—leaving, moving, and going toward a vision. The same elements are present in medieval pilgrimages and religious journeys of modern times. Although the three themes sound simple, they do not communicate the pathos and dread of leaving, the vitality and uncertainty of moving, the hope and fear of moving toward something new. For this we need the journeys themselves and the stories of journeys, which are always richer than categories. No two journeys are alike, but one journey points to meaning in another. Jewish, Christian, and Muslim pilgrimages through history are interpreted by Abraham, Sarah, and Hagar, and theirs are interpreted by ours.

Pilgrimages toward Repair of the World

This chapter opened with a story of the long journey of Mono Lake toward destruction and preservation. As we continue reflecting on journeys of wandering through history, we turn to the tradition of repairing the world (in Hebrew, *tikkun olam*), shifting attention to the future of history. The idea of *tikkun olam* is not a casual look to the future. It is mournfully lamenting the world's pain and actively hoping for the regeneration and flourishing of all life. Thus, we turn again to Mono Lake:

> When we look upon Mono Lake,
> > We remember and repent
> > That we have destroyed the earth.
> The waters of Mono Lake—
> > Drained until all the streams were gone.
> The waters of Mono Lake—
> > Drained by thirsty people and lands afar
> The waters of Mono Lake—
> > Unable to sustain the fish and plants and birds
> > Who once made Mono their home.
> But when we look upon Mono Lake—
> > We can see our power to give new birth.
> The power of human creatures—

Rebuilding streams,
Returning waters to Mono Lake,
Restoring fish ponds,
Celebrating the regenerating earth once more!
The power of human creatures—
Re-imagining the shape of the land,
Restoring the free flow of waters,
Replanting indigenous plants in their home,
and letting justice roll down like waters—
justice for the earth teeming with life
and for people who call Earth their home.[48]

The human challenge is not only to wonder at the beauties of creation, and not only to wander with the courage and hope of Abraham, Sarah, and Hagar. The challenge is also to remember and repent the hurts of this earth, and to contribute to the regeneration and flourishing of life.

Here we return to Marjorie Suchocki and her earthbound understanding of sin as "the unnecessary violation of the well-being of any aspect of creation."[49] In so saying, Suchocki is identifying sin as violating creation, and thus, violating God, who is related with all creation. She identifies sin as violation—not against one being in a hierarchy of beings, but against the well-being of all beings in an interrelated universe. Further, she identifies the criterion of well-being as the presence of God's truth, love, and beauty in all of those relationships.[50] These qualities of God are also qualities that God wants for all creation. God knows creation as it is (truth), accepts creation as it can be (love), and integrates every being with every other in the divine harmony (beauty).[51] If God so treasures the world, how can we destroy it?

In such a view, God is maker and standard-bearer of the universe, and God is everywhere present and hurting with the world where violence prevails. Thus, to follow God is to participate in that which nourishes the well-being of creation—to participate in repairing the world. This is not empty rhetoric, but painfully real. As I was completing the editorial work on this book, I was involved in a conversation about cats. Attempting humor, one person joked about hitting cats with a car; others laughed. In that moment, I realized that to nourish the well-being of all creation is to eliminate such "jokes" from our vocabulary, and to joke instead about extravagant efforts to preserve life. God is maker of the universe, and all life is precious!

Faced with sinful realities, what do we do? One of the great flaws of modernism is to assume that repairing the world is rejecting all that is past and aiming toward new, improved ways of living. This could not be further from the truth. In fact, tools for repairing the world, and courage to persist, often come from the past. That which is new is easily heralded as a quick answer to problems, or denounced as heretical, when not seen in historical context. For example, the Re-Imagining Conference that sparked such controversy in 1993 was widely rejected as a heretical congress, and several years later is still being debated in some Protestant denominations in the United States. To some of those controversies, Gayle Felton replies with a reminder that the struggle with newness is not new, but is itself a part of our heritage:

> In 1620, Puritan pastor John Robinson (hardly a heretical feminist!) bade farewell to the Pilgrims who were sailing to the New World by saying: "The Lord hath yet more light and truth to break forth from his Holy word." Anna Howard Shaw prayed to God as Mother in her churches on Cape Cod in the 1880s. In 1910, the Women's Missionary Council of the Methodist Episcopal Church, South adopted the motto, "Grow we must, even if we outgrow all that we love."[52]

In recounting these moments in history, Felton recognizes a continuity between the "disturbing, troubling growth" of the past and that in the contemporary church; she warns that our great danger is when that growth ceases or is suppressed.[53] Growth is to be embraced, even when disturbing and troubling. It is part of our legacy.

The power of the sacred journey through history is that we are confronted with ourselves and realities of the world; we are called to respond with our best, meager efforts to repair the world wherever we are. We are faced, as well, with the repeated failures of the church to do so. Such awareness of failure is what leads Dorothee Soelle to think of the church as a changing community—not a house, but "a tent for the wandering people of God."[54] This tent image suggests that the past cannot be denied, but history continues to move. The stories of Abraham, Sarah, and Hagar, wandering through the wilderness of time, are stories that strengthen people with the sheer humanness and courage of ordinary people faced with extraordinary challenges. That is the strength that wandering people still need if they are to walk as pilgrims toward repair of the world.

Retreating: Pilgrim Journeys to Sacred Places

In order to probe more deeply, we turn now to literal, earthly pilgrimages. The *journey of retreating is composed of particular journeys that nourish a lifelong journey of faith.* From them, one can draw insights for earthbound ministries of retreats, camps, and travel to sacred places. We will look first to the pilgrim heritage within Judaism and Christianity, turning then to contemporary forms of pilgrimage and clues for the future.

Pilgrim Journeys of Yesterday

The focus of Hebrew short pilgrimages was usually on a central shrine. The shrine was in Jerusalem after David took the ark of covenant there. Later, pilgrimages were initiated to the tombs of Jewish leaders, to famous synagogues for prayer, or to famous rabbis for their teaching. The central shrine was always important, however, because it served to bond the tribes together; in fact, prophetic calls for centralizing were sounded if other shrines became too prominent. Jewish men were required to go to Jerusalem three times each year for the feasts of Passover, Pentecost, and Booths (Tabernacles). Such pilgrimages were intended to inspire spiritual and moral life and to bond the community.

As described earlier, pilgrimages became quite common in Christianity in the fourth century, inspired by the pilgrimage to the Holy Land of Constantine I and his mother Helena, and later by Egeria and Augustine. At the same time, early church fathers were writing of the possibility offered by such visits to understand scripture, to enjoy intense experience of God, or to meet and learn from the desert fathers and mothers. In time, Rome came to be a favorite destination of pilgrims, particularly the tombs of Saint Paul and Saint Peter, and the catacombs, where many Christian martyrs were buried. The purpose of such pilgrimages was to expand understanding, attain remission from sins, or inspire holy living. One additional benefit, which was real but often unplanned, was the increase of communication and understanding across cultural and geographical bounds.

The tradition of pilgrimages emerged in other parts of the early Christian world as well. One influential tradition in the sixth century (and earlier) arose in Celtic Christian communities of Ireland and Scotland. The Celtic pilgrimage tradition involved leaving everything you loved for a life of traveling, suffering, and fasting; it was identified as a form of martyrdom. It was also identified as traveling to a sacred place, a landscape with particularly potent spiritual powers; thus, the liminal experience of the journey was aligned with the liminality of particular places where one could feel closeness between the other world and one's world of everyday experience.[55] Celtic spirituality thereby embodied a paradox between a strong sense of place and kinship, and a love of ascetic wandering.[56]

The most famous of the *consuetudo peregrinandi* was Columba or Columcille, who was born in 521 in Donegal, Ireland. As one biographer reports, Columba identified his call to pilgrimage with God's call to Abraham: "The desire to go into exile began to grow in him, for he remembered the words of God to Abraham: 'Go forth out of thy country and from thy kindred, and out of thy father's house, and come into the land which I shall show thee.'"[57] Certainly Columba was aware of the inner and outer transformation associated with pilgrimage. He recognized the values of being a *hospes mundi*, "guest of the world," which awakens one to God and to the transitory nature of life.[58] He recognized, also, that God is everywhere present, and one can read the natural world as a book that reveals God.[59] His pilgrimage became a paradigm for many others.

This Celtic tradition of pilgrimages was also to bear much fruit in terms of spreading education and spiritual-cultural richness across sixth-century Europe. Christopher Bamford describes their influence as broad-ranging: "Many were the schools and monasteries these wanderers founded, the souls they saved, the kings they influenced, the beasts and birds they befriended, the poems they wrote."[60]

The pilgrimage motif was found in other earthbound movements as well. Saint Francis understood himself and his brothers to be pilgrims, likening themselves to Christ, who "condescended to become a pilgrim."[61] This is the same Francis who treasured holy places of solitude and who calmed animals, as when he tamed the wolf who had been marauding and killing.[62] In the story of the wolf, Francis is said to have made the sign of the cross over the wolf and addressed him: "'Brother wolf, you wreak much harm in these parts and have done some dreadful deeds, destroying creatures of God without mercy...But, brother wolf, I want you and them to make peace so that they may be no more harmed by you, nor the hounds further pursue you.'"[63] The wolf responded by bowing his head, and Francis asked for a pledge that the wolf, though clearly acting out of hunger, would not harm people or other animals again. The wolf put his paw in Francis' hand as a pledge and then went with Francis to the city to pledge again before the people. This is the story of a pilgrim, who lives with courage because he knows himself to be a transitory stranger in this world.

Pilgrimages were not without their problems, however. Some of the very people of the past who praised the potential benefits, such as Jerome and Augustine, were also vocal about the potential abuses. Particularly strong arguments were made against impure motives (such as the desire to see the world), excessive partying on the journey, neglect of families and responsibilities at home, and substitution of pilgrimages for holy living. Nowhere can the potential dangers of the pilgrimage emphasis be seen more clearly than in the Crusades, which were inspired initially by the spiritual yearning to journey to the Holy Land, but soon became an effort to Christianize people of other faiths and to protect the Holy Land for Christian interests, including economic interests.

Other problems emerged from pilgrimages when different Christian cultures and traditions came into conflict. This became quite a difficulty when the Celtic pilgrims were actively traveling across Europe. Because Celtic communities were often not structured around bishops, as in other parts of Christendom, holy people and spiritual guides were often the designated leaders of religious communities and churches in a particular locale. This pattern apparently spread with the pilgrims and met with the church structures of Roman Christianity. Nora Chadwick reports of problems in Gaul, for example, when *peregrini et extranei* sometimes usurped episcopal functions or were elected to vacant sees over local leaders.[64] The practice of pilgrimages can bring quite different church structures and Christian values into contact, stirring contentious, even violent, responses.

Although pilgrimages have continued, objections have continued as well. These objections reached great strength during the Reformation when the emerging Protestant churches spoke out loudly against the possibility of salvation coming from such visits and when they tore down images and shrines all across Europe. The objections were sometimes more politically motivated than religious, such as in the English Reformation; but in either case, the effect was to discourage pilgrimages.

This was not the end of pilgrimages, however. They never died in Roman Catholicism, and they have reemerged in Protestantism in different shapes. Each year, thousands of visitors pour into the great cathedrals of the world and sites of miraculous events. Persons journey long distances in order to increase their understanding, be healed, or seek forgiveness. Still, the church sponsors such journeys and even provides housing and hospitality along the way. Hostels exist in Mexico, Italy, The Netherlands, and so forth. These are all reminders of the journeys of old when travelers were required to get permission of the bishop, and because they were often in real physical danger, they were offered the church's protection in hostels along the way. Churches today sponsor tours to the Holy Land or Rome or the footsteps of our forebears. We see individuals and caravans traveling to Lourdes, France, and other sites of miracles with hopes for healing or spiritual uplifting. What happens there? Each pilgrim has a story to tell, but the fact of a healing or a favor granted seems to be less dominant in the stories than the inspiration and insight the pilgrims report.

The tradition of pilgrimages serves other functions in the modern world as well. Our Lady of Guadalupe in Mexico is not only a site of thousands of pilgrimages each year, but Our Lady has become a unifying symbol of hope and healing in Mexico and among people in other countries for whom Mexico is ancestral home.[65]

Also, in many parts of the world, places of retreat and campgrounds are developed around religious sites, and these serve as places of retreat for spiritual renewal. In Norwich, England, Saint Julian's Church has been rebuilt after wartime bombing, and the cell of the fourteenth century anchoress, Julian of Norwich, has been built into the wall in a way reminiscent of the earlier structure. Not only are regular services held in the small church, but also, quiet days and retreats can be arranged, with accommodation provided beside the church at All Hallows House. Another kind of historical shrine is found on the south coast of Georgia. At the campground of Epworth-by-the-Sea, sites of local and denominational history are marked, and a museum chronicles the sojourn of John and Charles Wesley in Georgia, along with stories of South Georgia church leaders. Local people also guide visitors to the salt marshes and other natural ecosystems nearby.

Alongside these pilgrim journeys, the pilgrimage metaphor itself has helped Christians interpret their experience as a people. African Americans have seen themselves and their visions of freedom in the journey of the exodus. Seventeenth-century Puritans, exiled from England, sought refuge in the The Netherlands, and later in the New World. They chose to call themselves pilgrims, for they were wanderers in a strange land (see Heb. 11:13–15). The journeys live on, and so do the metaphors.

Pilgrim Journeys of Today: Clues for Tomorrow

Why have we given such attention to historical pilgrimages, especially in light of the other-worldly tendencies of some metaphorical treatments? That is exactly the point; the earthbound qualities of human faith journeys can best be restored if people actually participate in retreats and pilgrimages. Likewise, the communal qualities of journey can come forth as people travel together, rather than construe the experience of pilgrimage in purely metaphorical terms related to individual faith journeys.

One of the most poignant critiques of historical pilgrimages comes from Margaret Miles, who objects to "historical suggestions that other people are to be seen merely as help or hindrance in one's individual pursuit of salvation."[66] In a nuclear world, Miles argues for a metaphor of pilgrimage grounded in spiritual meanings of the natural world and in nonpossessive love and enjoyment of others as beings before God. She offers an earthbound vision of "appreciation for the natural world, other living beings, and the natural world nearest home, human bodies."[67]

Alongside this historical critique are many reminders of the power of retreating and wilderness experiences. Delores Williams recognizes the long association for African Americans between wilderness and religious experience. The image is embodied in spirituals, such as: "If you want to find Jesus, go in de wilderness, go in de wilderness, go in de wilderness."[68] In addition, people have long traveled into the "wilds" for a sojourn of living close to the land. Henry David Thoreau lived alone on the shore of Walden Pond for two years and two months, and Mary Jo and Stew Churchwell were inspired to do the same on the shore of Sawmill Creek in the Idaho Rocky Mountains.[69]

People have also learned to bring the wilderness inside. A striking story is told of Irene, an elderly Greek woman living in a chronic care hospital. Irene had stopped communicating, even with her Greek-speaking family, who visited her regularly. One day an ocean program was provided for the residents of the hospital. Leaders brought in sand, shells, and piles of seaweed.

> When Irene saw the seaweed being lifted up out of the buckets, she wheeled her chair over, her expression shifting profoundly. Picking up handfuls of the kelp, Irene smelled its saltiness and began weeping. Slowly, haltingly, she began to speak. None of us understood her Greek, but we all understood her joy.[70]

Irene had been offered wilderness without even going outdoors; this was the wilderness of her childhood on a small Greek island. Irene began to talk, and her family later translated story after story, all unlocked with a bucket of seaweed. Such is the power of wilderness! The same people who told Irene's story are involved in Animals As Intermediaries (AAI); they visit hospitals and other institutions with animals, nature, and art to give access to the outdoors for people who would otherwise be homebound.[71]

The wisdom of wilderness is known quite well by psychotherapists as well. Howard Clinebell encourages people to tell their ecological stories, to spend time relating with the natural world, to make time for quietness, to grieve for the hurting planet, to engage with images and arts, to sojourn in the wilderness, and to act in earth-caring ways; all are ways of reconnecting with that which is natural and wild within and without.[72] The link with restoration of the earth and healing the mind is well documented and expanded by others, especially Theodore Roszak, Mary Gomes, Allen Kanner, Ellen Cole, Eve Erdman, and Esther Rothblum.[73] Of particular note is the reorienting power of wilderness experiences when incorporated into Peace Corps training, educational programs, and psychotherapy. Experiences of wilderness programs replicate medieval pilgrimages in terms of disconnecting people from the social structures and values of their everyday worlds and opening the way to radical transformation.[74]

Viewed in light of historical experience and contemporary theorizing, one can see why retreats, camps and pilgrimages have such power! They introduce people to a new world, often an idealistic or utopian world. They disrupt the normal social structures because people are not locked into their normal roles, power relationships, and patterns of relating. When a group of newly acquainted adults go on retreat, for example, they may not know one another's occupations; therefore, the normal occupational hierarchy is broken down long enough for people to explore new patterns of relating. One woman who went on such a retreat avoided telling anyone her occupation through the entire week. She was a nurse, and she wanted people to relate to her as more than a person filled with information about their illnesses.

In a similar way, when a group of youth go to camp their living patterns usually include several people their age in a cabin or home group, or on a church floor. They are living for a time in a predominantly teenage community, which gives them the opportunity to develop new skills of leading and relating, as well as to get to know themselves better in relation to their peers. This is especially important for those young people who spend most of their time at home with adults, or in jobs isolated from other youth.

Besides introducing a new world and disrupting normal social structures, camping and pilgrimages also disrupt the normal structures and hierarchies of church life. Informal relationships leave less control in the hands of the clergy and support less-structured patterns for worship, study, and fellowship.

These introductory comments are verified by the research of Gwen Kennedy Neville, who has engaged over several years in anthropological studies of Protestant kin gatherings in Scotland and the Southern United States (such as reunions and cemetery association meetings) and gatherings in close-knit conference centers like Montreat.[75] From her work and from other sources come clues for understanding retreats and pilgrimages in the modern church.

Clue # 1: *A pilgrimage is countercultural.* Neville calls it an "institutionalized antistructure," meaning that it exists in opposition to the social order.[76] She makes the point that in medieval societies, the pilgrimage was a journey *away* from home, a journey that took one temporarily out of the established social order. In fact, it was the only socially acceptable way for people to travel if they were not wealthy.[77] Medieval pilgrims lived in a much looser social structure when they were on a pilgrimage, without the strict hierarchy that existed back home. Their communal life was akin to what Victor Turner has called *communitas*—a community that is less structured, less differentiated, and more egalitarian.[78] This continues a pattern that characterized historical Christian pilgrimages as well. Margaret Miles describes them as a dehabituation from daily contexts and habits, which contributed to intense religious experience.[79]

In analyzing modern Protestant pilgrimages, Gwen Neville adds another striking insight. She argues that pilgrims today are more likely to *return* home to kin religious gatherings. People are so scattered that returning home is the more antistructural thing to do; it goes against the "bureaucratic rational system of postindustrial Protestantism."[80]

In light of this analysis, we should not wonder that churches sometimes give low priority to retreats, camps, and pilgrimages. These are antistructures. Also, we should not wonder that the Committee on Outdoor Ministries of the National Council of Churches of Christ (NCC) has made large claims for the possibilities of camping and outdoor ministries: "Church camping and outdoor ministries help bring about the reconciliation through Christ of oneself to God, one's neighbor and the environment."[81] Certainly, we should not be surprised that reentry issues are named in that same document as part of the uniqueness of outdoor ministries; people on a pilgrimage are always leaving, moving, and going toward a vision. Both the high hopes expressed for outdoor ministries and the awareness of reentry problems have something to do with the way outdoor ministries are often experienced as antistructure, or countercultural events.

If we take the work of anthropologists seriously, some of those antistructures or countercultural movements actually overturn normal structures, some provide an outlet for temporary escape from the structures, and still others provide a way for people to live with the tension.[82] In any of these scenarios, countercultural movements play a part in the social fabric, and the role can be threatening or complementary to dominant structures.

Clue # 2: *A pilgrimage can be an intentional community in which some social differences are leveled, and some daily habits are altered, at least for a time.* We have already touched on this interpretation, but Gwen Neville forthrightly describes religious summer communities as centers for "intentional *communitas*," using Victor Turner's term.[83] Retreats and camps offer opportunities for self-conscious communities in which normal structures and hierarchy are minimized and egalitarian social relations are maximized. This pattern of leaving social status behind, and the protections that go with it, was part of the Celtic pilgrim tradition as well, leaving pilgrims dependent on the status that comes simply from being faithful to God.[84] *Communitas* is also a central value in the wilderness experiences discussed earlier, with additional benefits from discarding modern, materialist trappings as people journey into a wildness.[85]

Such social realignment is sufficient argument in itself for retreats and pilgrimages, which can potentially stir social conscience and introduce new possibilities for community life.

Clue # 3: *Outdoor gatherings and worship are often anti-establishment and identity-forming events.* Churches in the past have often tried to limit or ban outdoor gatherings, particularly outdoor worship. Gwen Neville points out that such gatherings were frequently associated historically with religious communities that had great appreciation for nature and practiced outdoor meditation.[86] In the outdoor gatherings, closeness with nature could be celebrated and enjoyed. Also, the structures of worship and ministry were more difficult to control, again reflecting a countercultural dimension.

For these reasons, outdoor gatherings have historically been a political issue and probably still are. Neville documents how outdoor gatherings were used by Celtic communities to maintain their sense of identity and their independence from outside domination.[87] Perhaps retreating and camping are themselves political acts, offering a way to establish communal identity, identify with nature, and build communitas without strict hierarchies and social boundaries. These dynamics counteract dominant social structures.

Clue # 4: *A permanent, fixed place can be an important "sacred place" for persons in today's world of great mobility.* The sacred place may be a campsite, the annual meeting place of an organization, a homecoming site, a cemetery, or a conference center. The physical environment of the sacred place communicates something of its ethos. For example, at Epworth-by-the-Sea (described briefly above), the buildings are named for former United Methodist superintendents and bishops of South Georgia. Montreat, the Presbyterian retreat center that Gwen Neville studied, has a gate that Neville describes as a symbol of entering into a sacred world.[88] And some camps have meditation spots or points of silence. All of these physical features help communicate the ethos of the sacred place. Their functions may parallel the functions of Celtic spiritual places, inspiring a sense of living with the natural world.[89]

In addition to general physical features, the sacred place may also have historical connections for people. These connections can derive from the personal histories of campers and retreaters, or from the history of a church or region. Historical connections are quite obvious in camps and retreats when old-time campers introduce newcomers to their sacred campsite on the first day. The guided tours are often laden with stories of what happened in the various special places of the campground or retreat center.

Clue # 5: *Retreats and pilgrimages can link people with the past and represent the continuity of a community.* This linkage often takes place through the place itself or through the reminiscing of old-timers, perhaps explaining why camp properties are difficult to sell. Camps or retreat centers may also remain connected to the past by maintaining old traditions and lifestyles, choosing to remain close to the basics of life.

I asked one camp director, "What is camp like now; has it changed much?" She answered, "We have changed as little as possible; we want to stay simple, so we have decided to be almost regressive." She had earlier asked one of her most sophisticated friends to help her evaluate this decision. Her friend had responded affirmatively, saying that the world needs alternatives to modern living and young people need to experience simplicity. The ability of outdoor ministries to connect persons with the past may help explain why people sometimes feel that they enter a time warp when they step into the sacred place of a camp or retreat center.

Clue # 6: *Retreats and pilgrim journeys can offer a utopian community—an alternative community that looks to the future and what ought to be.*[90] I am not assuming an antagonism between linkage with the past and linkage with the future as some would do. In fact, I suggest that camps and retreats can hold together the past and future—wisdom of the past and vision for the future. I have even wondered if the prevalence of conversions and peak religious experiences at camp meetings has something to do with this visioning of what ought to be—the sense of God's pulling people toward something more. Many retreats and camps are planned in order to maximize the opportunity for visioning. For example, electronic devices and tape players may be eliminated; times of quiet may be included in the daily schedule; international and inter-religious interchange may be planned and supported; and interracial, inter-cultural communication may be nurtured. Such practices can open the way for communities to live toward the future—to be alternative communities.

Clue # 7: *Retreats, camps, and pilgrimages do carry much power to influence the people involved and the larger church, so we need to reflect critically on our practices—both facilities and program.* This last clue for interpreting pilgrimages in the modern church is important to name in concluding the others. With the kind of power and influence discussed above, camps, retreats, and travel groups can serve to perpetuate an in-group and out-group or to compete for power in destructive ways. The ongoing process of critical reflection and reformation are important if camps, retreats, and pilgrimages are to be responsible agents of transformation. We need for our countercultures to be healthy, our communitas to exist in caring covenant communities, and our alternative, utopian lifestyles to point in the direction of God's new creation.

As we reflect on the many faces of Jewish and Christian pilgrimages and on clues for the future, the action that we meet again and again is the action of retreating—a fundamental part of earthbound ministries. The values of retreating are myriad, but the qualities that never cease to surprise and inspire are the qualities of renewal and transformation.

Deciding: Journeys through Moments of Decision

The journey through this chapter has been a journey through wondering, wandering, and retreating; all are dimensions of sacred journeys. We are left with one last dimension of journey, which is a key to the others. This is the *journey through moments of decision—facing the tug of God and the realities of a moment in time, knowing that what we discern and decide will shape the future.*

Robert Frost describes the scene of two roads diverging in a yellow wood, concluding:

> Two roads diverged in a wood, and I—
> I took the one less traveled by
> And that has made all the difference.[91]

These images have startled and moved readers to see power in their decisions. Rachel Carson closed her earthshaking book *Silent Spring* with a chapter entitled "The Other Road," calling forth the imagery of Frost's poem. She writes:

> We stand now where two roads diverge. But unlike the roads in Robert Frost's familiar poem, they are not equally fair. The road we have long been traveling is deceptively easy, a smooth superhighway on which we progress with great speed, but at its end lies disaster. The other fork of the road—the one "less traveled by"—offers our last, our only chance to reach a destination that assures the preservation of our earth.[92]

Carson's book was remarkably effective in stirring North American people to express outrage at the use of DDT and other agricultural pesticides that were infecting baby food and most of what people ate and breathed. Her book was instrumental in curbing the use of these products to control insects, thereby protecting the health of all living things.

Rachel Carson's effectiveness lay in her love of the natural world and expertise as a marine biologist. It also resided in her ability to read poetry and write poetically; she dazzled people with life and confronted them with decisions to choose life over death. Paul Brooks writes of her:

> Rachel Carson was a realistic, well-trained scientist who possessed the insight and sensitivity of a poet. She had an emotional response to nature for which she did not apologize. The more she learned, the greater grew what she termed "the sense of wonder." So she succeeded in making a book about death a celebration of life.[93]

Carson used her art to face people with decision, either to accept death or support the flourishing of all life. She was neither naive nor romantic, but she was hopeful that people could be confronted by the beauties and health of the natural world, alongside the dangers of death; she was hopeful that the power of poetic language would stir people to decide for life. In fact, her book, more than any other single ecological treatise, evoked the passions of people, led to concrete actions against DDT and other pesticides, and introduced the word "ecology" into common parlance and political theory. Such is the power of one person who finds courage to let go of the way things have always been done and to communicate in unconventional ways about conventional, deadly practices that almost no one wants to face.

In many ways, Carson embodied the many forms of pilgrimage described in this chapter. She wondered at the beauty of creation as she traveled in her unique way through the cosmos. She wandered the earth through scientific studies, professional meetings, and the like. And she retreated to her seaside refuge in Maine to meditate and write. Out of her wondering, wandering, and retreating came her moment of decision. She decided, she acted—and that made all the difference.

Likewise, W. E. B. Du Bois was a man who dared read the world in which he lived, a world of 1903 that was economically, socially, and racially destructive. He read the people, the economic structures, the spirits of black folk, and the contours of the land. Faced with the oppressive realities that he saw, he dared to name realities that others talked about in silence. He also dared to offer hope—not a false hope, but the hope born of struggle and embodied in spirituals: "the hope that sang in the songs of my fathers well sung."[94] Between that hope of Du Bois's fathers, and the realization of their vision in children "singing to the sunshine," were many decisions. In a struggle for justice, people inevitably face a long journey, for which each person simply "girds himself, and sets his face toward the Morning, and goes his way."[95]

In that same spirit, scholars and activists who analyze environmental racism today begin with reading the people, the economic structures, the spirits of poor folk, and the contours of land. Faced with the oppressive realities that they see, they dare to name realities that others talk about in silence.[96] These are the people, along with Rachel Carson and others, who dare to decide and face others with urgent decisions on the journey toward Morning.

This, finally, is the challenge of a journey chapter for earthbound ministries: to wonder at each beautiful, painful, or tragic reality as we journey through the cosmos; to wander through history with courage and hope; to retreat to sacred places, seeking renewal and transformation; and to make prophetic decisions, however risky. A commitment to these journeys is necessary if we are to have courage and strength to enter the partnerships and vocations described in the final chapters. We close, then, with the words of the Native American elder with which we began, "Do not expect us to be partners unless you plan to walk with us on the long journey."

SIX

Sacred Partners: Listening to Suppressed Voices and Ministering with Forgotten Partners

In the 1970s, Paulo Freire consulted with leaders of Guinea-Bissau, a newly freed country in Africa, as they sought to reform their educational system. One initiative was to take urban children into the rural areas where they lived together in camps and worked with the farmers. The farmers taught them how to farm, and they taught the farmers how to read.[1]

⬙

A few years ago, a student minister was serving his first parish in a small town where he spent every weekend. He decided to get acquainted by visiting everyone in the church during the first year. On one such visit, he spent a pleasant time in the home of an older couple. He knew they were having a tough year because drought conditions had caused their crops to fail for the second year in a row. Normally they raised enough to sell and eat; this year they were barely surviving. During the pastor's visit the couple was festive, however, and no mention was made of their troubles.

As the young minister rose to leave, the woman asked him to wait a minute. He heard banging in the kitchen, and soon the woman appeared with a big box of canned fruits and vegetables for him. He expressed appreciation, but insisted that she keep the food. She spoke boldly in response, "If you take away my ability to give, you are taking the only thing that I have left." The young minister took the jars of food, saying thank you to the couple and saying to himself that he would never make that mistake again. This minister was learning early in his pastoral ministry that servant elitism is not well received; it is false charity. His parishioner introduced him to a ministry of partnership.

These two stories are testimonies to partnership. Freire's story reveals partnership between rural and urban people, children and adults, middle class persons and peasants. Similar stories dot the global landscape today, taking place on communal farms in India, Japan, Kansas, and Oregon, where partnership among people with different kinds of expertise and partnership with the land are highlighted. The second story reveals partnership between a pastor and parishioners, in which both give and both receive. The brief stories are snapshots of partnership, the ideal toward which this chapter points.

The very idea of ministering with the earth is that all aspects of creation are partners in ministry—the animals, plants, soil, and waters of the earth. The focus of this chapter is on those people and other beings whose voices are suppressed and whose partnership is forgotten. Hopefully, the writing will stir your awareness and memory of suppressed voices and forgotten partners in your life and in many parts of the world.

The purpose of this chapter is to *engage many partners in stitching designs for God's new creation*; the hope is to *strengthen and beautify the quilt of ministry with the earth*. To that end, we will: *attend* to the suppressed, *remember* forgotten partners, *stir* dreams of partnership, and *envision* a politics of partnership.[2] The underlying assumption is that ecology itself includes all of God's creations as partners. We, thus, join with Leonardo Boff, who describes ecology as "the relations, interaction, and dialogue of all living creatures."[3] The theological anchor is the Trinity, the community within God that gives origin and inspiration to the communitarian relationships of creation. According to Boff, "The entire universe emanates from this divine relational interplay and is made in the image and likeness of the Trinity."[4] Such a trinitarian vision will be embodied in the partnership of all God's creatures.

Attending to the Suppressed

Silence, when it is chosen, is rich in meaning and relationship; likewise, "silence" in the deaf community is filled with full-bodied communication. Silences imposed by social domination are different, however; they are lonely, isolating, and oppressive. Some of these will be explored here. Because metaphors of silence, hearing and voice are abundant in literature of oppression, that language will appear. Because of limitations in these metaphors, however, the term "suppression" will be used more frequently.[5]

A person or creature that is suppressed is often considered wild. Attending to the suppressed encourages people to listen to wilderness—to those aspects of the world that are considered wild, untamed, undomesticated, unregulated. Such a concern underlies much of the work toward preserving wilderness in the United States and elsewhere.[6] The issue is also symbolic. Ursula LeGuin proposes that women and children often represent wilderness symbolically; she invites people to listen and not be afraid.[7]

Suppression of People of Color

Reflecting on wilderness already has its dangers, most marked by the tendency of most mainstream environmental organizations to focus on wilderness and the preservation of wildlife and give little attention to race and social class as human issues intertwine with environmental ones.[8] The pervasiveness of environmental racism is now well documented, though it has not fully permeated the environmental movement.[9] Carl Anthony puts the issue starkly when he says of some ecologists: "Why is it so easy for these people to think like mountains and not be able to think like people of color?"[10] Anthony believes that these ecologists simply do not know the stories that would help them understand.

In a study by the United Church of Christ Commission for Racial Justice, forty percent of the country's landfill capacity was found to be located in communities of people of color: Emelle, Alabama (78.9 percent black); Scotlandville, Louisiana (93 percent black); and Kettleman City, California (78.4 percent Hispanic, or Latino).[11] The same study revealed that 60 percent of African Americans and Hispanic Americans live in communities with uncontrolled sites for dumping toxic wastes; approximately 50 percent of Asian Americans, Pacific Islanders, and Native Americans live in similar communities.[12] Many of these people live in communities with more than one site. In short, the study indicated that race was the dominant variable in the location of toxic dumpsites, and the pattern was consistent across the United States.[13] The very fact that the United Church of Christ conducted this study (the first of its kind) suggests an effort on their part to listen to suppressed voices, but the effort uncovered grim statistics indeed.

The problem of racial discrimination is complicated still further when matters of racial and social justice are posed over against matters of environmental preservation. The issues are clearly intertwined, and one is often abused for the sake of the other. In the case of the Gulf War, war was made on a people, and the consequent burning of an oil field will contribute to ecological destruction for decades to come.[14] As war rages in Rwanda, the rainforest is destroyed, along with many apes; war destroys an ecosystem and the economic and physical well-being of a people.[15] In other cases, the environment is used as a reason to oppress people. In South Florida, new immigrants, especially Caribbeans, are blamed for overloading the ecosystem; an attempt is made to address environmental destruction by curbing immigration.[16] In these cases we see the dynamics of silencing. Earth and people are suppressed at the expense of one other.

This leads to another aspect of racial suppression, namely, the way in which the mainstream environmental movement has ignored and suppressed mounting evidence regarding environmental racism. Although some positive change is taking place in this regard, the inability to listen to people at the grassroots who are most affected by environmental racism has intensified the problems.[17]

Suppression of Women

We turn now to the suppression of women. More than a decade ago, Mary Belenky, Blythe Clinchy, Nancy Goldberger, and Jill Tarule conducted interviews for their book *Women's Ways of Knowing*.[18] They discovered that some women relate with the world largely through silence, which is largely pressured from the outside. Though this experience is not unique to women, Belenky and her associates discovered that the phenomenon was very common among women they interviewed.

Responding to similar phenomena, Nelle Morton describes the significance of ministry that "hears others into speech."[19] She tells stories of women who gather to share. When someone speaks out for the first time about something deeply buried, emotions flow along with the words, and the person is heard into speech.[20] Drawing upon such experiences, Morton images God as the "great Listening Ear" at the center of the universe.[21] Morton's concerns are reinforced by the work of Carol Gilligan, Nona Lyons, and Trudy Hanmer, who have found that young girls around the age of twelve often make a shift from boldness to conformity.[22] Their research is not designed to identify a cause, but the cause may well be those same silencing forces that concerned Nelle Morton.

Similar forces also suppress women's gifts, such as literary or leadership gifts, which are submerged when women are restricted to limited roles.[23] The forces also silence women of color, subjecting them to double suppression and oppression.[24] Some women are making efforts to help others be heard. Ada María Isasi-Díaz and Yolanda Tarango have engaged in years of research to make public the passions, beliefs and concerns of Hispanic women.[25] Karen Baker-Fletcher has written the story of Anna Julia Cooper, which introduces an African American woman of power. And Cooper, in her time, also encouraged people to express themselves, drawing upon the metaphor of voice and describing human beings as "created in the voice of God."[26] All of these women, aware of suppression, seek possibilities for women to express themselves and move toward full partnership in human action and ministry.

Also among the suppressed are women affected by war. Consider the women of Sri Lanka, for whom war has been cruel; they and their children are the most displaced and impoverished.[27] Consider the women of Namibia, whose wartime life is well documented. These women were deprived of husbands and brothers, who entered the war as part of the S.W.A.P.O. or South African Army; they were deprived of children, who were often abused and killed in the destruction. They were left with full responsibility for their homes (both economic and child-rearing responsibilities) as male adults in their families entered war efforts. They themselves were often sexually and physically abused, but they were not able to come together for self-protection. They were not allowed to go out after curfew, gather to discuss their plight with one another, or protest to authorities. One woman said:

> During the time my husband was in detention, the South African soldiers broke into my house. I went to see the superior officer at the

military center in Oshakati, but after my visit, all that happened was that more soldiers came to intimidate me. They do not like us to report these things.[28]

No wonder the suppressed are often silent!

This suggests the need for a different approach to ministry, especially attending to women's suppression. For women to be free to express their deepest concerns, a different approach is needed to pastoral care and counseling.[29] Likewise, deep listening is needed if we are to recognize women's cries for justice, peace, and ecological integrity in the world. Women have long been leaders of action at the local level, and they have much wisdom to offer regarding poverty, war, the effects of development on women and children, population control, sexuality, living harmoniously with the land, collaboration with others, and local action possibilities.[30] Attending to suppression will enhance the lives of women, as well as contribute to the healing and regeneration of earth.

Suppression of Workers

Increasingly, the silences of workers around the world are also being heard into speech. Gustavo Gutiérrez introduces *The God of Life* by quoting two people in the Christian Workers' Movement. Victor and Irene Chero say, "We suffer affliction, we lack work, we are sick. Our hearts are crushed by suffering...But, despite all this, *we believe in the God of life*."[31] Gutiérrez builds his book on the Cheros' wisdom.

The church, on the other hand, has often been silent regarding social class and economics, not even having a language to discuss the struggles of workers, much less to heed their wisdom. The challenge begins with naming. Workers identify themselves variously—as peasants, working poor, working class, laborers, and so on—and some of these names have positive connotations in one setting and negative connotations in another. The name worker is used here because it is usually self-selected. Attending is another challenge, and it begins with honoring workers' wisdom. For many centuries, workers have been understood as receivers of wisdom offered by the educated elite. Forces of dominance have reinforced their silence, compounded further by issues of women, children, and racial minorities.[32] Workers, however, have much to contribute as they interpret the world and express hope and frustration, anger and vision.

Paulo Freire is especially mindful of this dilemma for education. He tells the story of his own conversion experience while lecturing across Brazil on children and discipline.[33] He was especially eager to convince parents not to spank their children. At the time, he was a university professor and expert on child development and child rearing. He had every reason to believe that his message was important and needed to be spread. One night he delivered his normal lecture; after he finished, a man stood up and asked how many children he had. Freire answered five; the man began to describe Freire's life. He said that Freire had a nice house, and though it was not luxurious, he probably had a room for his wife and himself and a separate room for his girls and one for his boys. In addition, the house probably had a living room and a kitchen with some modern appliances. The man went on to describe Freire's daily life. He said that Freire probably came home from work each day and sat down to relax. The children would go to their rooms to play. Freire listened carefully because this man was, in fact, describing his life very closely.

Now the man began to describe his own life. He said that his family lived together in one room. He got up at 4:00 every morning to go to work in the manufactory, skipping breakfast. The children had meager portions for breakfast themselves before going to school. The man said that when he came home from work each day his children were tired and cranky because they were hungry. He and his wife were tired and hungry too. He said that they all ate a small meal and then went to bed. Sometimes he had to spank his children to get them settled down so that he could sleep. He explained that if the children did not sleep, he could not sleep; if he did not sleep, he could not work; and if he did not work, they would not eat. Paulo Freire learned from this man that some wisdom is not written in books or speeches. Some wisdom comes from people who are suppressed.

Do workers need to be suppressed even more by the church's ministry? No! In fact, Paulo Freire represented the World Council of Churches of Christ in his collaboration with workers and leaders in Guinea-Bissau after it was freed from Portugal in the 1970s. The first story of this chapter was one of their efforts. It reveals an earthbound ministry in which urban persons met rural persons on their own ground; children were learning work skills, and partnership was fostered. The church was a partner.

Suppression of the Youngest and the Oldest

Consider children, youth, and seniors, whose suppression is attracting international concern. In recent years, we have witnessed the United Nations Decade of the Child and increased political participation by retired people in many parts of the world. Some researchers, like Robert Coles, have recorded children's voices in order to let children speak for themselves about their concerns. Young Freddy, for example, spoke to Robert Coles about his certainty that God favors the poor. He said that even the rich don't believe that God favors the rich.[34] Still other researchers survey or interview older persons before proceeding with public policies that will affect their lives. To these researchers can be added people who witness with their lives. Consider Marian Wright Edelman, who has dedicated her life to children, founding the Children's Defense Fund, speaking around the world, and writing on behalf of children.[35] Similarly, we turn to Mother Teresa, who dedicated her life to the dying, most often the very old or the very young.[36]

Many ecological issues affect children in particular, such as lead poisoning, toxic dumping, and destruction of small farms. Children are more vulnerable to the illnesses, genetic defects, and stunting of physical and mental growth that follow this destruction.[37] They are also more vulnerable to such practices as child prostitution when their families become desperate to survive. Likewise, the elderly are often victims of neglect as patterns of extended family are disrupted, and as the wisdom of elders is belittled and ignored.

In such a world, how might earthbound ministries include, nourish, and empower the youngest and oldest? How might people be taken seriously and engaged as partners with each other and the earth? Surely we need earthbound opportunities for all ages, but we also need to create spaces that are safe and comfortable for the youngest and oldest, and places where they might interact with the world and express their hopes and dreams.

Suppression of Local Knowledge Systems

We should not underestimate the degree to which some people and some parts of the earth are actively suppressed. The effect of this is not only the destruction of individuals but also the destruction of ecosystems. One of the best analyses of this problem is offered by Vandana Shiva, who describes the way by which local knowledge is negated, ignored, and supplanted by a dominant system (such as modern Western knowledge) that poses as the only alternative.[38] When this happens, people lose their ability to think of alternative ways to farm the land, choose crops, harvest trees, and so forth. Attention turns to miracle seeds and miracle crops rather than multiple seeds and multiple crops. If people listen to the suppressed voices of the natural forests, they will hear many voices—a virtual choir. What happens if the diversity is named as chaos and some plants are named as weeds?[39] The choir is reduced to a single voice or monotone.

Attending to the suppressed can make a difference in what we understand. *In 1985, a woman named Gwaganad of the Haida people in Queen Charlotte Islands, Canada, appealed to the British Columbia Supreme Court regarding a logging matter. She told the story of her people, who welcomed foreigners two hundred years earlier and shared the land with them. She described how those foreigners urged on them "a better way to live, a different religion, education in schools," and how their traditional potlatches were outlawed.[40] Then, Gwaganad described the ways of her people:*

> I was taught to respect the land. I was taught to respect the food that comes from the land...We are a nation of people at risk today...We almost lost ourselves as a people...The only thing we can hold onto to maintain that pride and dignity as a people is the land. It's from the land we get our food, it's from the land we get our strength. From the sea we get our energy.[41]

Gwaganad then described their food gathering, particularly the spiritual, bodily experience when the herring spawn; she and her friends go into the ocean to experience the spawning and harvest their food. She concludes, "And you don't quite feel complete until you are right out on the ocean with your hands in the water harvesting the kelp, the roe on kelp, and then your body feels right. That cycle is complete."[42]

Gwaganad's story reveals how people can be suppressed—by replacing their way of life, religion, educational system, and traditional cultural practices. Gwaganad's story communicates the importance of the land to indigenous people, helping them to maintain their culture.[43] The Haida way is to live closely with the earth, use only what is needed for life, appreciate the ways of other creatures, and feel spiritual relationships in your body. The wisdom of Gwaganad and her people supports their lives and the land. When their wisdom is lost, they suffer; so does the earth, and so do we.

Suppression of Victims

Increasingly, too, the suppression of victims of domestic violence and sexual abuse is being recognized, because people have discovered that suppression perpetuates the circle of violence. Silence about abuse keeps the abused syndrome within a person until that person can hold it no longer and abuses someone else. Persons who have no opportunity to express their suffering and anger almost certainly become abusers themselves.

Alice Miller has analyzed abusive punishments in Germany and presents a convincing picture that parents discipline their children harshly "for their own good," and the children keep silent, holding their anger in reserve for the next generation.[44] Adolf Hitler, for example, was an abused child.

What I say here about harsh discipline stands in tension with the earlier story of the peasant man in Brazil who challenged Paulo Freire. The tension represents the real issues that emerge when we pay attention to people who are suppressed. Earthbound ministries provide settings where such issues can rise. Retreats and camps are particularly good settings for open and safe self-revelation; relating closely and honestly with other persons; facing issues buried in the normal routines of life; living in alternative, nonviolent patterns of community; and participating in healing gifts of the natural world. In such settings, the ministry of other people and the earth can nourish healing.

Suppression of Animals and Other Beings

In earlier chapters, we attended to the sacredness of all creation and the inclusion of all creation in the circle of covenant. Yet, no voices are suppressed more than those that communicate in language without words—dogs, wolves, whales, dolphins, oak trees, native grasses, river waters. The suppression of these voices takes two forms; people either do not notice these beings at all or regard them only in relation to what they offer human beings. In either case, their subjectivity is denied.

Carol Adams and Marjorie Procter-Smith retell a nineteenth-century story of a visit to the United States by Pundita Ramabia, who was shocked to see a woman carrying a hen with its head down. Taking this to be the Christian way of "treating a poor, dumb creature," she cried out, "'O, how cruel to carry a hen with its head down." The woman replied, "'Why, the hen does not mind it,'" and Pundita Ramabia inquired, "'Did you ask the hen?'"[45]

Ramabia wanted to hear the hen's suppressed voice. Such listening for animals' voices can support animal liberation. Zoe Weil, for example, shows videos of animal abuse in her classes, revealing animals in slaughterhouses and industrial situations as they cry their suffering.[46] In seeing and hearing the animals' suffering, Weil's students can better comprehend the issues of animal liberation.

In addition to animals, we need also to respect the subjectivity of mountains and rocks, seas and rivers, air and soil, a subject explored in earlier chapters. These are all part of God's creation, capable of expressing themselves if we are prepared to attend.

Suppression by Selective Partnership

Failure to attend to animals and other beings is an act of selective partnership; people simply do not think of them as partners in ministering with the earth. Partnership among people can also go amiss. In the following case, several adults and youth were backpacking, and some in the group were excluded by an act of selective partnership.

The food was planned with care so that the inexperienced packers would not have more weight than they could carry. With jolly spirits the group traveled, and few complaints were uttered about the packed food. In fact, the youth seemed pleasantly surprised by good tastes. A particular hit were tubes of cheese squeezed on crackers; so popular, they were consumed early on the trip, leaving more boring items for later.

On the last day, the group hiked out along a beautiful riverbed. Between the ahh's and ohh's about the scenery, the youth began to talk about the luscious food they were going to eat on the drive home. By this time the food supply was nearly depleted, and they were learning the joy of combining dry hot chocolate mix with nuts and raisins. With four miles to go, the group stopped for their last trail lunch. Everyone was eating when one counselor called two other counselors aside. He had hidden two tubes of the cheese to share among the counselors on this last day; he proudly offered it, hiding so the youth would not see. The other counselors declined the offer.

Here we see a problem of selective partnership—partnership in which counselors were included and campers were not. The matter was as basic as food, and the decision was made by one to offer the food selectively to some partners and not to others. Partnership became an excuse for cliquishness and privileging one group over another. In some situations, these issues can become much larger. In the case of gay and lesbian persons, many denominations have actually formalized their exclusion from certain forms of partnership such as ordination.

Thus far, we have reflected on persons and creatures who are suppressed, who *wish* to communicate but are denied. Sometimes the very silence of these persons can speak volumes (such as the silence of Sarah in Genesis 22's account of the sacrifice of Isaac).[47] If we will just attend to what the suppressed are trying to communicate, we may find ourselves in partnership with some amazing people and beings of God's creation.

Ministering with Forgotten Partners

The very act of attending leads to partnership, so we move easily from attending to suppression to ministering with forgotten partners. This is important in all ministry, and nowhere is it more important than in earthbound ministries. The Aztec ideal of encouraging each student's gifts in serving the community is an ideal that inspires covenantal relationships and strengthens community.[48] This tradition has long been binding for monastic communities as well. How can people learn and grow in their faith if not in community? How can they learn and grow if no one takes them seriously?

Themes of community and partnership emerge repeatedly in the contemporary individualistic world. Consider a few examples. C. A. Bowers and David Flinders propose an ecological perspective on general education based in a relational view of people and the land.[49] The World Council of Churches of Christ focuses on ecumenical learning in community. Letty Russell and Lynn Rhodes call repeatedly for a ministry of partnership or co-creation.[50] The ministry of laity has received increased prominence in theological literature, and feminist writers seek to reconceive ministry in relation to community rather than hierarchical structure.[51]

For many years, discussions of ministry focused on ministry *to* and *for* the people. The time has come to capture a sense of ministry *with* the people and *with* the earth. A person who wants to do all of the serving and giving is denying others the privilege. In the second story of this chapter, the pastor learned how demeaning such servant elitism can be; this is a lesson to be learned again and again. On the next pages we will explore partnership through stories and draw implications for ministry. Most of these are ordinary stories where life-changing partnership takes place.

Partnership at the Grassroots

One of the major developments in movements for justice and ecological integrity is networking among local action groups. Groups across the world are concerned with issues as diverse as toxins, food production, protection of the water and land, economic stability, and outdoor experiences for urban youth. Dorceta Taylor calls this an "inclusive environmental movement" and notes that diverse groups emerge in response to local concerns.[52] Because multiple organizations keep diverse issues in the forefront, they need to continue, even as traditional environmental organizations diversify. Further, the multiracial environmental justice movement "provides the opportunity for people of color to lead instead of being led, to initiate and produce research instead of relying on someone else's, and to define the issues that are most pressing to them instead of having their issues defined by others."[53]

Without cooperation among environmental and justice organizations, little change will take place.[54] Leaders in these cooperative efforts have often been people of color and women, and the result has been to exercise greater influence on social structures.[55] In many parts of the world, the joint efforts have also strengthened the action and influence of small groups. One example is the Peasant Women's Federation (AMIHAN) in the Philippines. They act directly on particular issues and communicate women's experiences and visions to other workers' organizations and to the government.[56]

No mention has been made of the church in this discussion of grassroot organizations. Some churches are indeed involved in these efforts, but the church's role might be, in many cases, to support organizations and groups that form themselves, rather than to give proactive leadership. One example of such earthbound ministry was the United Church of Christ's (UCC) sponsorship of the First National People of Color Environmental Leadership Summit in 1991. This was a time of significant dialogue and planning for the future.[57] The UCC, in this case, was functioning as a partner, offering support and networking to people who were already leaders in their distinctive contexts.

Partnership in Congregational Life

In addition to such direct action, the church also has a mission to embody partnership in its daily life. In the Lahaina United Methodist Church on the Island of Maui, Hawaii, people practice partnership through hospitality. The church, 100 years old in 1996, began as three separate mission churches among sugar workers and their families, including a Japanese and a Filipino church. Worship services today are held in three languages (Japanese, English and Tongan) and the congregation represents many cultures indeed. Imagine a snapshot of a summer Sunday:

On Sunday mornings, someone stands on the front lawn to welcome folks to Lahaina Church. In the Sunday bulletin, you are greeted with notices:

ALOHA AND WELCOME to each of you who worship with us this morning. A special greeting to our visitors from the community and from around the world. Please…join us following our 10:30 a.m. worship for the "Aloha Hour"—a time of fellowship and refreshments on the front lawn.

WOULD YOU LIKE TO PRAY WITH SOMEONE? Immediately following our 10:30 a.m. service, worship leaders will be available in front of the sanctuary to pray with you in your special needs.

ENCOURAGEMENT CARDS are available on the back table for you to send a message/greeting of encouragement to someone in need. Write out your message…we'll mail it for you on Monday…Let us encourage one another!

In addition to these notices, visitors are also greeted from the pulpit. *On this Sunday, the pastor Piula Ala'ilima tells a story about some people who took a long journey away from home. Piula invites the children to take off their shoes, and he leads them on a brisk walk around the sanctuary. The scripture and sermon continue the theme, focusing on Jacob's story of running away from bad times. Piula closes, praying that people can face things from which they are running, and proclaiming that God travels with them. In Samoan, he adds, "Take it easy." When the service ends, people form a circle and sing "Hawaii Aloha." After the benediction, they share hugs and greetings, and conversation continues over punch on the front lawn.*

The Lahaina congregation is intentional in nurturing partnership within the congregation and with visitors, who come in large numbers to the historic church. It also nurtures partnership with the denomination and larger community. People are invited to picnic with other United Methodist Churches on the island, or to consider an issue before the Hawaii State Legislature or a joint effort in the state for responding to people who have been abused. The people also seek partnership with the past and future. Imagine a snapshot of their 100th anniversary plans:

For several weeks the Sunday bulletin of the Lahaina Church carried this reminder of the Church's mission:

> *For nearly one hundred years we have listened to God's voice and praised God's presence, we have learned and taught of our Christian faith, we have reached out in service and mission to those in our community and throughout the world, and especially to the hundreds upon hundreds of our sisters and brothers from around the world who visit us yearly....*[58]

The people prepared for their anniversary celebration by looking to the future. They pledged money for new churches and ministries in their annual conference "with the joy and confidence that one hundred years from now they too will be able to celebrate their centennial of proclaiming the good news of God's love."[59] *They also pledged money for maintaining the Lahaina Church "with the joy and confidence it will help sustain, and expand, our ministry here in Lahaina for the next 100 years!"*[60]

The Lahaina United Methodist Church is a community in which sacred partnership is recognized in many forms and nourished in many ways. The first thing they teach is that *partnership can be built through active celebration.* Worship is festive, the Tongan choir fills the sanctuary with beautiful music, and children are integral to worship. Second, the *people of this congregation interact regularly with scripture, the many cultures of their membership, peoples of the past and future, and one another.* They do so in worship and informal times, in stories and formal moments of remembering, and in folk songs that many people know from years past and from camps and retreats. Third, *the congregation extends hospitality to their multitude of visitors.* Instead of seeing these drop-in folks as a distraction, the congregation has made a conscious decision to welcome others through the spirit of their worship and through their greetings, bulletins, and informal gatherings. Fourth, *the congregation links with other churches, agencies, and institutions* as they participate in denominational gatherings and in collaborative work for justice in Hawaii. *They also link by praying for others,* naming friends, relatives, and troubled countries. The congregation invites people to be partners with one another and the larger world.

Partnership among Institutions

In addition to congregational life, institutions can also exist in partnership, whether the partnership is between denominations, religious communities, or local churches, or between these and public agencies. A particularly strong example is found in Auckland, New Zealand, where three theological colleges share a campus and common life. The founding college, Saint John's, is Anglican, as is the Maori theological college, Te Rau Kahikatea. Trinity College is Methodist. Although each college has community events for its own students and staff, much of what they do is shared.

Imagine this seminary campus where students, staff, and faculty worship daily and eat together at least one day a week (every day for many). For the required daily worship, they choose among many services: Morning Prayer; Wednesday Eucharist; Family Prayers one night every week; and a Taizé prayer service on Friday afternoons. No roll is taken, but participation is high. Students are also part of small community groups (mixed in denomination, age, culture, and gender) that meet biweekly with a staff member for sharing and prayer. Students and faculty rotate worship leadership, and the small community groups each take a turn in leading the Wednesday Eucharist.

Imagine Wednesday Eucharist, where many family members join the usual crowd of faculty and students. The welcome includes greetings to children, guests, and people who have been away and returned. Sometimes a parent sits in one corner with several children and some toys, and the liturgist cheerfully welcomes everyone in the "children's corner." Consistently, liturgists include the children in prayers of blessing.

Imagine, also, the common meals each noon. One of the College Principals blesses the food and makes announcements, especially regarding births, illnesses, deaths, and community events. Someone announces a campus-wide clothing exchange, a request for airport transportation, or an upcoming event in a nearby church. People rise enthusiastically to invite others to join campus groups, such as the Te Rau Cultural Group, Prayer Group for the Church Overseas, Walking Group, Women's Bible Study Group, Craft Group, Women's Association, and Renewal Group.

The consortium of institutions in New Zealand was not an overnight success story. Strong, positive relationships were born of pain, and they require continual work to nourish collegiality and negotiate the complexities of three institutions in relationship.[61] The students and leaders of the three institutions glow about their collaborations, however. Why? A few clues surface in the brief case study.

The three institutions embody partnership in several ways, some of which overlap with the congregation described earlier. First, *they worship and break bread together daily*. Their common life is bound with common praise and common meals. Second, *their common life has a regular structure and rhythm*. Not only do some things happen every day, such as worship and meals, but also the rites of the Anglican and Methodist Churches, the Anglican prayer book, and saints' days shape the rhythms of worship and celebration.[62] People learn the rhythms quickly and can thus participate fully. Third, *flexibility and diversity are encouraged and celebrated within the weekly rhythm.* Worship and community life has many forms, and whenever a group has an idea for a new project, such as a clothing exchange, they are encouraged to act. The three institutions offer common classes, but one morning a week the classes are separate by institution; this gives students an opportunity to reflect on what it means to be Anglican, Maori, and/or Methodist. Exploration of diversity is, thus, built into the structures; it is also welcomed in spontaneous variations on regularly occurring events. Fourth, *all students, faculty, administrators, cultural groups and denominations give leadership,* which provides rich experiences for everyone. Fifth, *the community life is organized to address and redress issues of justice in New Zealand.* All students, whatever their ethnicity, study Maori culture and language. They also relate to Anglican and Methodist churches, which have reshaped their polities to enhance the influence of Maori people, the original people of the land.[63] Sixth, *people in the community are regularly remembered and celebrated, including children of the community.* People are remembered at meals, and children are welcomed and encouraged to participate in Wednesday Eucharist. Further, *hospitality is offered to visitors.* They are introduced, invited to participate in everything, and invited informally to people's homes for meals and visits. Finally, *celebration is at the core of this community.* Parties and playful gatherings are common. Whether dedicating the offices of Te Rau in a formal Maori ceremony or gathering for a party in a denominational or community group, people gather constantly and celebratively.

Partnership among Leaders

One obvious form of partnership in ministry is often forgotten; it is partnership among leaders. When leaders work as partners, their relationships and creativity usually reward them and their communities. Consider one team-based church:

In a large Arizona church, the entire staff goes on retreat together each summer. They alternate between a reflective retreat and a recreational one. For the reflective retreat (2–3 days), they read in advance and invite a resource person to share with them on a theme, combined with worship, common meals, and a movie night. For the recreational retreat, they sometimes do very active things, such as river rafting. One year, members of their church sent them on a ten-day pilgrimage to Israel. In addition, the program staff meets weekly at 5:30 a.m. to hike on a nearby peak, all joining as they can.[64]

Because of such meetings, this staff has been able to work together through many transitions in their community and to give leadership in a concerted effort. In another church, the entire staff meets every few months with an outside resource person to reflect on their relationships and to play together for three-quarters of a day. In both of these churches, the regular retreats bear much in common with the earlier descriptions of sacred meetings and sacred journeys in this book.

This kind of partnership is often overlooked in earthbound ministries, even in ministries such as camping and retreats that are designed as intensive living experiences. One long-time camping leader describes the problem of "crisis recruitment."[65] Partnership is inevitably limited when leaders are recruited late, when they are chosen less for their special gifts and more for their availability at the last minute, and when they are not included in planning. Partnership is limited further when leaders are more interested in creating a following for themselves than in working as partners with others.

One camp director described one of her best camping seasons. She said that the weather was so bad all summer that most activities were totally disrupted. She had to trust the counselors to create alternative activities, and she encouraged their imagination and initiative. She said, "Fortunately, we had one of the best groups of counselors we have ever had, and they were able to make this a marvelous summer." She gave the counselors credit for making the summer work, but she, also, deserved commendation for entrusting the counselors with responsibility and respecting their gifts and actions.

Much can be learned from these community snapshots. First, *the mutuality of a leadership team can be enhanced by times set apart for renewal or planning.* The ability of a team to give leadership has much to do with their ability to know and respect one another and to develop collegial working relationships. Second, *the effectiveness of earthbound ministries is more dependent on the quality of community life than on external circumstances.* This is demonstrated by the camping story and by countless stories of local churches, youth groups, and retreat gatherings where a strong community life enables people to weather difficult external storms, and sometimes even internal crises. Third, *creativity, flexibility and imagination are essential ingredients of leadership.* These qualities are nurtured best in partnership, as team leadership often stimulates creativity and imagination and demands flexibility. Fourth, *a team working together can lead more effectively than a group of individual leaders* each pulling in a different direction. Elements of competition and resentment that pull energy from common work are reduced when people build mutual respect and common goals. Fifth, *wise leaders respect and encourage the gifts of others and acknowledge the contributions that others make to ministry.* Finally, *worship and play are critical ingredients in the building of community.* Worship and play have an opening quality, stirring people to see what they have not seen, to let go of their plans for a moment, to commune with God and one another. Jerome Berryman describes this quality as "Godly play," which can "awaken us to new ways of seeing ourselves as human beings" and can help us know God.[66] Worship and play can potentially open people to God's miracles at work in community life.

These truisms may be so obvious as to seem trite. They stand in tension, however, with the common tendency of church leaders to plan independently and then recruit a team who will follow their lead. The common practice denies partnership. The hidden assumption is that leadership is best done by a charismatic figure with a few helpers.

Partnership with Children and Youth

However well leaders are working, that alone is not sufficient for significant community life. Earthbound ministries include everyone. Cleaning a vacant lot of trash, collecting recyclable materials, organizing a campaign for better public education, hiking a mountain trail, discussing death or alcoholism in one's family, or sharing experiences of being rejected by friends are powerful when shared in a community of peers. This is communal power. People can learn from one another, experience mutuality, and realize that others face similar issues.

Children and youth can also help one another in countless ways. Each person has unique gifts that can be shared with others, and their perspectives on social and religious issues are vital. Consider this story of a river trip.

Once a young man went on a river trip with a group of other boys and their leaders. Each boy had a partner in his canoe, and each helped carry the troop's load. Everyone had to paddle, carry, cook, and clean in order to travel the 50 miles on schedule and spread the work. One boy was not accustomed to so much responsibility, nor to the vigorous pace in scorching summer temperatures. He dragged and complained. In the canoe, his partner did most of the work, and in camp he lay around and complained of not feeling well. The camp leaders urged him to carry his load. They suggested ways to build his energy; they offered empathy and encouragement. Nothing changed.

One day an older boy approached the fellow as he lounged on his sleeping bag. He said, "You know, you are not being fair to the rest of us; you are not carrying your load." Then, he asked if the younger boy would like to join him in his canoe. He said, "I can teach you how to paddle efficiently and have fun on this trip." The boy accepted the offer; he changed canoes and attitudes. Soon, he was carrying his load and more.

This story has much to teach. Most obviously, *children and youth need to be offered responsibilities and expectations;* they are important to the community. Also, *peers are important in offering accountability and friendship,* both of which are needed for persons to become full partners. Finally, *even the most reluctant partners can be invited, encouraged, and supported into partnership.* Children and youth are usually far more effective in inviting and encouraging their peers than are adults.

Partnership with People in Trouble

Spreading across the United States from Nashville, Tennessee, to Los Angeles, California, are gardening projects involving people whose lives are troubled in this threatening world. The projects include: community gardens where youth probationers work each week; high school gardens from which produce is sold for school projects; gardens initiated by neighborhood youth who make an agreement with their city to convert a vacant lot into a vegetable garden and sell the produce; farms where children with disabilities can play with farm animals who have disabilities themselves; and wilderness programs for youth and adults. One such program is the Garden Project at the San Francisco County Jail.

After 15 years of counseling with female prisoners, Cathrine Sneed was weary and discouraged by the recidivism rate (return to crime) of these women; the stress had effects on her body. She was diagnosed with a kidney disease and not given much time to live. Sneed describes what happened in her life when a friend brought her John Steinbeck's The Grapes of Wrath: "*After reading it, I felt that the message of the book was that if people have some connection to the land they develop a sense of future, hope, and even faith.*"[67]

The seed was planted in her mind, and when she returned to the prison, still unable to move freely on her own, Sneed requested permission to work with prisoners in clearing land that had become a dump and storage area. On this land, a former farm, she watched while prisoners cleared debris and created a farm. The farm eventually produced vegetables for soup kitchens and other programs feeding seniors and homeless people. After some time, Sneed's own health improved, and she credited her healing to the time outdoors and the joy of seeing the women's joy.

In time, this project spread, and Cathrine Sneed initiated another garden outside of the jail where people could work after their release. Produce from that farm is now sold to the Farmer's Market and restaurants in San Francisco. Yet another project has arisen from this one, and The Tree Corps employs many former drug dealers to plant trees for the city of San Francisco. The results include a lower recidivism rate among the prisoners, a long waiting list for people who want to work in the garden projects, a blossoming of self-esteem, and a deluge of testimonies. One man who has stayed out of prison for three years and gained the custody of his daughter is George. He says:

> When I was selling drugs...I felt ugly inside and so I acted ugly in the outside world, but being in the garden and watching things grow has helped me to see the beauty in life. This is what the garden does...It's about growing people.[68]

In Cathrine Sneed's miracle story, "growing people" happens through partnership, but why? One answer is obvious: *partnership is with the earth itself.* Sneed trusts the healing qualities of the earth, and her expectations are fulfilled in the lives of troubled people. Another answer is that *people are entrusted with the care of the earth and the creation of beauty and food.* People are given responsibilities with the earth, and their work serves larger purposes, such as feeding the hungry, filling a gap in the food cycle of a large city, and enhancing the beauty and air quality of San Francisco with trees. In addition, *these projects involve certain disciplines of responsibility.* People are expected to do their share of the work, and Sneed is strict. Former drug dealers are removed from the program if they return to selling drugs. Sneed's insights echo earlier themes regarding sacred meetings and covenant community.

Partnership with Denominational and Ecumenical Structures

Church leaders sometimes bemoan the fact that they do not experience much support from their denominations, and denominational leaders often do ignore earthbound ministries, whether in congregations, judicatories, or outdoor centers. In relation to camps and other outdoor ministries, denominational leaders are often frustrated by the autonomy of camps and retreat centers, or they respond to outdoor ministry as a decoration to more basic ministries. What a loss of partnership!

Once upon a time a leader in a United Church of Christ (UCC) camp became especially interested in the life of a young boy attending her camp. The leader happened to be aware of several activities for youth in the UCC denomination. Before the camp session was over that year, the leader had talked quite a lot with the camper and had inspired him to travel the following year with a UCC group to Just Peace, a multicultural event in Germany. She even helped the youth imagine and plan the logistics and to involve his own local church in sponsorship.

This story reveals that *networks are available if we seek them and spread the news.* Through networks, people can link local communities with denominational and ecumenical bodies, and share earthbound visions with larger bodies. Second, *personal invitations to persons can lead them into momentous decisions.* This story is small, but the functioning of networks is made possible by one small story piled on another. Finally, *no leader or community functions alone, but each is part of a network crucial to Christian life in the world.* Local churches and outdoor centers exist in a web of Christian community, and a web is strong only if each strand plays its role.

Dreams of Partnership

In light of the stories and reflections of this chapter, several themes emerge as marks of sacred partnership. As a prelude to dreaming possibilities for partnership, we begin with conclusions from the review of stories. The following themes suggest ways to nurture partnership: (1) engage in frequent celebration and worship; (2) attend to the quality of community life, as in sharing meals and negotiating conflicts; (3) practice acts of hospitality; (4) relate with people across time, age, and cultures; (5) establish regular structures, rhythms and expectations for community life; (6) encourage diversity, flexibility, and creativity; (7) share leadership and build mutuality; (8) engage in common actions to serve and reform the world; (9) play together; and (10) give and receive with the earth. Such proposals stir dreams! Sharing them begins a process that, it is hoped, readers will continue—the process of dreaming the future.

Dream first of *earthbound ministries in which a rhythm of celebration and worship, prayer and meditation, work, play, and sharing are part of every week.* This might take shape in small groups, or in a congregation or parish. Certainly, much can be learned from Benedictines and other monastic communities, some of which has already been translated into broader implications.[69] Much can also be learned from theological muses such as Leonardo Boff. Boff's enthusiasm for relationships leads him to identify sources of nourishment for people who seek to live well in natural and social ecologies. He especially names contemplation and meditation, discussion groups, prayer, celebration, and the marking of important occasions.[70] These ideas, embodied in the stories of this chapter and in traditions of Christian community, suggest a programmatic approach to community life that is not faddish or sporadic, but full-bodied and rhythmic. It has considerable room for novelty and spontaneity, but certain dimensions are a regular part of the community's life.

Another dream is *earthbound ministries that bring people together from different regions, races, social classes, ages, sexual orientations, or religious traditions.*

- Work camps often bring people into significant partnership, especially when work and expertise is shared with local people. Work projects bind people around common goals and draw upon many physical, technical, and social skills, thus requiring teamwork.

- Consider also ongoing groups, such as local action groups or youth groups, that bring people together across ethnic and cultural communities and across issues of concern. When diverse people play and work together, when they collaborate on projects, and when they share stories from their lives, they build deeper understanding and cooperation.

- Consider camps and retreats cosponsored by two denominations, or by a religious group and community group working together. The Nature's Classroom is such a partnership with the United Church of Christ and area schools in Ohio, with the camp providing ecological education for school children.

- Consider possibilities for interreligious events, especially in the modern world fraught with tension and violence across religious communities. The potential for building interreligious understanding is particularly great in a situation where people of different traditions live, play, and work together.[71] Near London, England, one consortium of colleges sponsors an annual meeting for teenagers on their campus, drawing students from Ireland and England—Roman Catholic and Protestant. The students live together for two weeks, engaging in worship, play, work, study, and meetings with religious and political leaders. Their lives are transformed in the process, and one wonders what these students will contribute to the future of justice and peace in their two countries.

A third set of dreams centers on *earthbound ministries that encourage silent time for listening to God and the earth.* This theme appears in many forms in this book, and it is echoed in Boff's appeal for meditation, contemplation, and prayer.[72] Silence is the work of monks and activists alike. Mother Teresa explains her rationale for silence:

> I always begin my prayer in silence, for it is in the silence of the heart that God speaks. God is the friend of silence—we need to listen to God because it's not what we say but what He says to us and through us that matters.[73]

Such silence can be offered through unstructured time for walking or sitting in silence. It can also be offered through special activities designed for listening, such as silent walks or times to sit quietly and meditate on the earth. People might be encouraged in these times to meditate on a sacred symbol in the natural world, and to offer and receive blessing.

Thus far, the suggestions for silence could be included in almost any form of earthbound ministry. Silent days might be offered one day a month in the church, or a half-hour every morning. Church members might agree during a troubled time to stop wherever they are and pray every night at 9:00 p.m. Camps and retreats can be totally designed as opportunities to listen to the earth, such as a camp focused on observing the life cycle of lobsters, or a camp in England that involves young people in counting beavers—a threatened species. In the English camp, the counting that youth do is not just for their own learning, but also to support preservation efforts for the beaver.

Another set of dreams centers on *earthbound ministries that give expression to people's bodies*, such as white-water rafting for persons with special physical needs. Imagine the thrill of rafting for someone who normally rides in a wheelchair and has no opportunities for active adventures.

Another group of dreams is more self-consciously political. Consider the possibility that *leaders in earthbound ministries might enter full partnership with the rest of the church*. What would happen if a consultation was organized with leaders across a region or denomination to discuss how ministries of the church could become increasingly inclusive, just, and earthbound? How might people address issues of spiritual renewal, intercultural communication, peacemaking, and ecological regeneration? What visions and recommendations could a consultation propose to denominational and ecumenical bodies?

The discussion thus far encourages people to be responsive to one another and creation, and to work together. Of course, partnership is easier with people we know and like; forgotten partners are easy to leave behind. Earthbound ministries depend on full participation, however, and if the bounties of God have been given to all of creation, then all creatures are called to make a difference. For this reason, the chapter ends with an exploration of how communities can organize themselves to maximize ministries of partnership for the preservation and renewal of God's creation.

Practicing Politics of Partnership

In order to support partnership, a community needs to be formed around a shared mission or shared concerns, not for the sake of homogeneity, but for the sake of ministry. What does that mean in terms of political structures and relationships among people of the community? To use the term "politics" may itself be controversial because it connotes scheming and power-building relationships to many people. On the other hand, politics has to do with the organization and practices of a community or organization. For sacred partnership to be a reality, we need to find ways to organize and practice community that are truly open to the fullness of humanity and creation.

Partnership often begins in common action rather than common ideas. Maria Mies and Vandana Shiva, for example, found that their desire and ability to co-author a book on ecofeminism arose from their activism. Mies—a German social scientist—and Shiva—an Indian physicist—were unlikely partners, but they discovered common concerns, which emerged from their participation in women's and ecology movements.[74] This dynamic is true for other women as well. Women often come together in local struggles related to nuclear power plants, logging, or chemically polluted food. When they discover common concerns, they "forge links in solidarity with other women, people and even nations."[75]

The calling to engage in partnership requires transformation in how we think and live in community, both in church communities and in all of life. We need to replace politics of combat with politics of partnership, and selective leadership with leadership shared among many partners. The challenge is to build churches that are purposive, communal, conversational, passionate and prophetic.

Purposive

First, churches need to be purposive. They need to wrestle with their purposes and challenge other social institutions to do the same, seeking together for the common good. We cannot deceive ourselves into thinking that purposes are altogether obvious. They often lie under the surface and need to be brought to consciousness, examined, critiqued, and reformed. We need particularly to ask *what* is happening in the community and larger world and *why*; then, we need to ask *how* a particular congregation or denomination can contribute to the repair of the world (*tikkun olam*).

These are significant questions, and they highlight the urgent need for religious communities to be purposive. Peter Senge speaks eloquently about the importance of a shared vision and reminds his readers, "If any one idea about leadership has inspired organizations for thousands of years, it's the capacity to hold a shared picture of the future we seek to create."[76] Why do people have such difficulty embodying this time-tested idea?

People are apparently not so gifted at embodying shared vision as we are at discussing this as an ideal. To move toward embodiment is risky, requiring shifts in politics and leadership styles. Perhaps the ideal of working toward shared visions is far more radical than most of us can envision, and perhaps it requires more risk than most leaders are willing to take. Real collaboration is more than meeting together to have a leader persuade everyone else to her or his ideas; thus, collaboration is not grounded in creative leaders who create exciting ideas and find ways to implement them. Real collaboration is not superficial either; it is not a general discussion for the sake of self-expression; rather, it affects decisions. Collaboration is mocked when a leader meets individually with key players in order to influence a decision before the actual "collaborative" discussion begins. Genuine collaboration involves genuine listening, genuine sharing of views, and persistent searching for the best possible way to respond to the diversity of concerns and approaches; this is not "politics as usual."

What is badly needed is an approach to politics and leadership that is collaborative, visionary, and constructive, so that institutional purposes can be grounded in the whole community. Such work involves generating ideas but also exploring, debating, and negotiating priorities. Building a community of collaboration is fundamental to the work of visioning, not only for dreaming dramatic changes but also for the quieter and more profound work of reforming the future of the community.

Communal

For a church to be purposive, it needs to be rooted in the matrix of communities in which it lives—communities within and outside the church. To grasp the fullness of this matrix of communities requires a new way of looking at social institutions, or what Peter Senge calls "systems thinking."[77] Churches need to think and act communally—thinking of themselves as related to a larger community (a mental shift), and working together to create community and repair the world (a shift in action).[78]

To say that churches live in a matrix of relationships is not to say that relationships are always healthy and joyful; they simply *are*. Thus, churches need to be conscious of relationships and ethically responsive to the many communities that affect, and are affected by, their actions. Churches are challenged to act justly toward others, and to engage as partners with other organizations in the repair of the world. Also, since relationships are not just with human communities, ethical responsibility is to the whole planet.

By speaking of a matrix of communities, one needs to recognize that some institutional relationships are grounded in intimate communities, but most are not. Within the matrix of any institution, the most urgent need is not intimacy, but the formation of an ethical response to the world. This does not require that people agree, or even like each other. What is required is for people to reflect critically on their situation and calling; what is required is for people to collaborate on common purposes and common action.

This also suggests that church leaders need to have qualities of leading *with* others, thus building up the communal leadership of the organization. In describing women's leadership, Barbara Hauser distinguishes between the old warrior/prince model of leadership and the newer caretaker/princess model, finding them both lacking. She proposes instead an interpreter guide model, built upon respect, interest, and trust.[79] A model of the interpreter guide is one in which leadership is relational and communal, not necessarily in an intimate sense, but in an integrated sense. Both the formal leaders and the organization as a whole are at their best when they are able to relate with honesty and vulnerability; otherwise genuine trust can never develop, nor can transformation.

Conversational

Accenting the communal nature of churches naturally leads to another challenge, the challenge to be conversational. The vision here is to live with others. Such conversation includes dialogue, but it is more than words (*logos*) and it is more than discourse. Rather, it is a living with (*con*) others, and that includes words and all other forms of human interaction and communion. It can also involve a communal turning around (*conversare*).

Of course, the word *dialogue* is often used in a way similar to what I suggest here with conversation.[80] My hope is not in the word, but in opening doors to fantastic possibilities for conversation—informal conversation, play, action projects, aesthetic expression. All are important for building community, and some conversations are particularly important for equipping churches to minister with the earth.

Conversation with the past is often seen as antithetical to the futuristic goals of organizations, but to converse with the people, movements, and events of the past is to experience a fullness of history. This is a source for self-understanding, social critique, novel ideas, and inspiration (both positive and negative). We see such conversation in the Lahaina congregation as they recall their 100-year history. We see this conversation in biblical scholars such as Vincent Wimbush, Cain Hope Felder, Phyllis Trible, and Elisabeth Schüssler Fiorenza, who revisit biblical texts in relation to ancient peoples and find fresh readings of Africa, African Americans, and women.[81] Conversations with the past are included in liturgies as well, including traditional liturgies of the church and newly created liturgies that converse with less-known figures and texts of the past.[82] The challenge in relating with the past is to cross enormous cultural gaps and relate with worlds quite different from our own. If we can do this, we will be challenged by the revelations of these other worlds, and we can, thus, critique and reform our own traditions.

Conversation across cultures is important for similar reasons. For a church to be concerned only with its members, or for an institution to attend only to its own constituency, is to narrow vision and thwart ethical judgment in the community. In order to have a large understanding of the world, people need to know the passions, concerns, and visions of people in different regions of the world. We need to learn from others and be at home in diverse cultural communities (racially, ethnically, socially, and otherwise diverse). Conversation contributes to self-consciousness and other-consciousness, and to the adequacy of ethical judgments.

Ideally, these conversations will sometimes be face-to-face, but they can take place through film, documentaries, drama, paintings, and literature as well.[83] Whatever the form, conversation will, it is hoped, inspire a spirit of humility and a journey over time. Some may even lead to acknowledging past hurts and reshaping social structures and attitudes.[84] People cannot casually meet one another, especially not meet repeatedly in situations where one group has power over the other, and expect to find genuine partnership. Partnership is born of many efforts over time and with abundant goodwill.

Conversation with the planet is living in the presence of the earth, interacting with the realities of life-bearing soil and water, life-saving acts of liberation, death-bearing oppression within human communities, and destruction of the environment. For churches and other social institutions to be in conversation with the planet requires them to engage in issues of war, oppression, waste and destruction, and in acts of caring for life. Practically speaking, this suggests that institutions need to care for their local soil, water, and human relationships, as well as to engage issues that affect the global community.

Passionate

In addition to being purposive, communal, and conversational, churches also need to be passionate—to be deeply affected by movements in the world and shaped by profound commitments. Passionate communities are animated by intense motivations and by the will to convert dreams into realities; in fact, their passions contribute to the realization of dreams.[85] The challenge is to be full of life, which is sometimes manifested in celebration and sometimes in conflict. To be full of life is to live in the messy middle, recognizing tensions as opportunities to embrace the complexity of human life. Tensions can be seedbeds for vitality. To be passionate is to seek ways for tension to inform and motivate the church rather than to destroy or debilitate it.

Prophetic

The last challenge for churches is to be prophetic. Of all the challenges, this is the most elusive. The challenge is to discern the prophetic pulls and set priorities for action. To be prophetic is to speak (*phanai*) before (*pro*); thus, prophecy carries a popular meaning of predicting the future and a typically religious meaning of speaking for God or for a cause. Both meanings are significant if we recognize the important role that churches and other institutions can play in anticipating, imagining, and contributing to the future, as well as standing or speaking for a cause, such as justice or sustainable development. The way a church makes decisions and sets priorities will shape the future of the community and related institutions. Discernment and courage are urgent.

To urge churches and social institutions to be prophetic is to recognize that they do bear power. Individual leaders bear power in the sense that they have "the ability to influence others, to shape events, and to achieve personal goals."[86] But leaders do not carry all of the power; institutions as bodies also influence others, shape events, and achieve goals. Institutions bear power in the sense of controlling resources, shaping cultures, and influencing human relationships (whether interpersonal, economic, political, or international). To call churches and social institutions to be prophetic is simply to call them to take ethical responsibility for the power that they have. Thus, the communal challenge described above is intensified in terms of ethical responsibility.

This chapter stirs hope that Christian communities will live communally and engage with all of God's creation as partners in ministry. For such hopes to become reality, massive reform is needed. We need to reform the ways we think about ourselves, plan our common lives, and shape the political structures of Christian communities. With such hopes of partnership and life-giving community dancing through this chapter, we move quite naturally to concluding reflections on sacred vocation.

SEVEN

Sacred Vocation:
Ministering with the Earth

The journey through this book has itself been a sacred journey, moving in the midst of God's creation. This is not to say that everything in the book or in creation is good. It *is* to say that everything—EVERYTHING—has been touched by God's presence. The challenge for people who care for the earth is to discern God's presence and guidance. And now as we move to the close of the book, the challenge is to discern God's calling—our vocation. Put simply, how might the end of this book point to a beginning—a renewal of ministry with one another and with the earth?

What is possible? The reflections of this chapter point to action; they *stitch the patches of insight from communities and traditions* discussed earlier in the book, as one would stitch a quilt. The metaphor of a quilt, elaborated in the retreat design of the Appendix, suggests that patches and pieces are stitched together and then quilted into a pattern, both for the sake of beauty and for the sake of usefulness. The purpose of this chapter is to *explore the Christian calling to minister with the earth,* and to *describe four particular actions for earthbound ministry: keeping Sabbath, tending cycles, engaging in transformative politics, and practicing stewardship with creation.* These proposals suggest directions for faithful response to God. It is to be hoped that the actions will be beautiful and useful in guiding the future of ministry with the earth.

We Are a Called People

What does it mean to say that we are a called people? This question emerges during a time when Christian churches and many other religious communities are seriously seeking—what does God ask of us and how are we to respond? The world is swirling with many questions and competing answers, and amid the swirl and competition the center of life is difficult to find. When the world is also swirling with the blight of abused air and land, abused animals, abused human relationships, economic inequity, and neglected needs, the center of life is even more elusive. For this reason, we begin here with a meditation on creation, with the hope that meditation will yield vision and action.

In the beginning
God created the heavens and the earth...
And at the end of the creating days,
God saw what was made
And said, "This is good!"

You are the people of that creation;
You are created by God,
You are created to be with God
And you are created so that you too may create.

You are a called people;
God has given you gifts.
You have received those gifts as a trust—
You are entrusted with them,
You are trusted to share them,
You are trusted to multiply them.

And the next time God looks around at the creation
That we have made *with* God,
God will surely cry at the sight of war,
And God will ache over racism, heterosexism,
        classism, sexism, ageism;
God will moan at the sight of earth being destroyed
And air filled with pollution;
But *surely*, God will smile at the love you have shared
And the difference you have made in someone's life,
And we can hope that you and others together
Will even make a difference in warrism, racism, heterosexism,
        classism, sexism, ageism, ecological destruction.
The next time God looks around, let us hope
That God will smile and say, "This *is* good!"[1]

This meditation does not answer all the questions that Christian people raise about a calling to minister with the earth, but it does point to the urgency of living as a called people. It also suggests that within creation itself, and in human interaction with creation, we find clues for the vocation of Christian peoples. One clue is the covenantal relationship that binds people to God and the earth. Another clue is the human hope for living well with the earth—awaking to our relationship with the earth, accepting the trust God has given, and participating in the healing of creation.

Further clues can be found in the explorations of this book—in the basic insight that all of God's creation is sacred; in the diverse traditions of ministering with the earth; and in the very possibility of sacred hopes, meetings, confrontations, partners, and journeys. The Jewish and Christian traditions are rich with an ethic of justice—the human calling to act justly in our most intimate relationships, in communal life, in relation to animals and trees. The traditions are also rich with an ethic of care—the calling to care for, and be cared for by, the earth. Some of these traditions, and the eschatological pull to God's new creation, are the foci of this chapter. But questions abound.

What qualities are needed for a new beginning in ministry with the earth? The qualities of ministry that seem most needed are hope, presence, action, and humility: *hope* that God is active in the world and we can participate in God's new creation; *presence* to God, one another, and the wonders and pains of the world; *action* that points toward God's new creation; and *humility*, both in relation to God and in relation to other people and beings of the earth. These qualities stand as possibilities and challenges as we seek to repair the world. The qualities are rich soil from which earthbound ministry can grow.

What actions of ministry are needed for a new beginning? The actions of ministry are many, but three emerge again and again: *compassion*, or feeling with God and creation; *reflection* on God and the world and the relationship between them; and *active participation* in reshaping community, social, and environmental life. To experience compassion is to feel the passions of God and creation, and to share in the joy and suffering that attend those passions. To reflect is to intuit, imagine, analyze, synthesize, and seek harmony; it is an attempt to understand and respond to God and creation. To participate actively is to live in the world with awareness that our lives affect the earth even as we receive from it, and with hope that we will contribute to the creative and redemptive work of God in creation. If earthbound ministries could enable people to experience compassion, to reflect and to participate, then the ministry of the church might indeed contribute to the community's ability to receive from and care for the earth; it might contribute to the ability of the creation to praise its Creator.

How, then, might we engender passion for ministering with the earth? To build upon what has been said about compassion, reflection, and participation, we turn now to four particular actions—keeping Sabbath, tending cycles, practicing transformative politics, and engaging in stewardship with the earth. Earthbound ministry is most alive when we invite people into Sabbaths and cycles, and into transformed politics and stewardship. The Jewish and Christian traditions of keeping Sabbath and tending cycles have faded in the memory and practice of many faith communities, and they have been distorted into rules and requirements in others. The pull to radical transformation in our ways of living together—our politics and stewardship—are easily ignored in cultures that reinforce competitive politics, individualism, materialism, and ownership. These practices are very important, however, to our sacred vocation of ministering with the earth.

Keeping Sabbath

For six years you shall sow your land and gather in its yield; but the seventh year you shall let it rest and lie fallow, so that the poor of your people may eat; and what they leave the wild animals may eat. You shall do the same with your vineyard, and with your olive orchard.

Six days you shall do your work, but on the seventh day you shall rest, so that your ox and your donkey may have relief, and your homeborn slave and the resident alien may be refreshed. Be attentive to all that I have said to you. Do not invoke the names of other gods; do not let them be heard on your lips. (Ex. 23:10–13)

A time of Sabbath is a gift—a gift to the land, animals, and people. Repeatedly in the Hebrew Bible, the Sabbath tradition is described as a gift of God. To keep Sabbath, then, is to care for a gift of God (Lev. 19:3; chap. 25; Deut. 15:1–18; Gen. 2:1–3; Ex. 20:11; 21:1–6). The Sabbath tradition transcends an anthropocentric focus on human activity and human benefits.[2] The Sabbath is a day of celebration—thanksgiving. It is a day of pause to be attuned to the Creator and wonders of creation. Thus, it is a day of mourning to grieve destruction of the world; it is a day of hoping for God's new creation; and it is a day of renewal, preparing us to participate in the creative and liberative work of God. As such, the Sabbath is the crown of creation. Drawing from the first creation story in Genesis 1—2:4a and from his Lutheran theological tradition, Larry Rasmussen remembers that creation is complete not with the creation of humans, but with Sabbath.[3]

Compassion

Sabbath is a way of life in which people nourish compassion, attuning with the movements of God, subtleties of creation, and hopes for God's future. Sabbath is much more than law; it is a way of living respectfully with creation. As an accent in Jewish and Christian tradition, it is a time of celebrating God's works, sanctifying the present, and discerning God's hopes for the creation. It is not a time for accomplishing tasks, but of letting go, waiting, and seeking the call of the future. Maria Harris recognizes this in reflecting on Jubilee (the Sabbath of Sabbaths as described in Lev. 25:8).

Eventually, Jubilee ushers in an era of forgiveness, freedom, justice, and jubilation. It begins, however, with a not-doing: the decision to pause and to let the land lie fallow. It begins in stillness. It begins…with a Sabbath that readies us for the next decade, the next century, and the next millennium.[4]

For this reason, the value of Sabbath is not measured by what is accomplished, but by what is inspired and envisioned. For this reason also, the fact of whether or not a Jubilee year was ever enacted is not the most important issue. What is far more important is what we can know of God and God's call to human beings through the Jubilee traditions.

The power of Jubilee to reveal and motivate is well supported by the renewal of Jubilee traditions by Christians in diverse traditions (Roman Catholic, World Council of Churches of Christ, Evangelical Lutheran Church in America) and diverse parts of the world. The Pope, for example, has declared the year 2000 as a grand Jubilee year, and the Roman Catholic Church is planning a year of prayer, repentance, and hope for the new millennium.[5] Another example comes from Korea, where Jubilee is a time of waiting, hoping, and working for the reunification of North and South Korea.[6] The year 1995 was declared as a year of Jubilee in Korea; this was the fiftieth year after the country gained independence from Japan (1945), followed by the division of the country into North and South.

The Jubilee and Sabbath traditions are powerful traditions of reversal— reversals from action to release of control, from ownership to forgiving debts, from stratified social relationships to equity. In these traditions, people seek to attune themselves to God and God's creation, and this is a far more radical vision than modern life can hold. Even someone so practiced in letting go of material goods as Saint Francis (in the twelfth and thirteenth centuries) found himself challenged by the need to let go of control. When Francis was fretting about some wayward brothers and their negative influence on the Order, he was reminded in prayer that God, and not he, ruled the Franciscan Order.[7]

Letting go and practicing Sabbath is challenging in most times and places. A personal story can underscore the radicality of this idea and the irony (or hypocrisy) of my writing a book that concerns itself with keeping Sabbath.

When I received a happy telephone call from Chalice Press accepting this book for publication, I had three weeks before a scheduled departure for two months in Europe (the culmination of my sabbatical). The time in Europe was prescheduled with conferences, plus an extensive plan of research and writing in European libraries and church centers. The time before my departure was also prescheduled with planning two major conferences, attending to urgent mail, ordering textbooks, responding to various expectations of my institution, and spending time with our children and grandchildren. I had no time to gather the materials I needed for revising this book; it was complete but far from its final form. I had no hope for revising the book with any kind of sanity; I would return from sabbatical to dive headlong into a new fall teaching term.

Never fear! My elation at the acceptance of the manuscript was sufficient to fuel my native optimism and determination. I did gather the materials, reshape my writing schedule, plan the conferences, attend to mail and institutional matters, order texts, and spend time with our children and grandchildren. I loaded an extra case with books and papers; I listened to family members call me foolish; I left home, exhausted but hopeful.

Then, the last straw fell onto my load. My computer crashed! Loaded with telephone numbers and computer books, I cried briefly; then, I proceeded to seek "technological support." The fact that we were beginning a writing retreat in an Austrian village complicated matters. The village was ideal for writing, but the pickup of my ailing computer was slowed by our long distance from major cities. Then the company itself kept the computer far longer than expected; they had a communication breakdown within the company, and two promised return dates passed with no computer in sight. With each disappointment, I would sag for a few hours and then bounce back. I had no choice but to bounce back, for I had gone to great trouble and expense to preserve time for this project. That precious time was finally absorbed in toto by the crashed and missing computer. Thus, my workload doubled, and I juggled the remaining sabbatical time between this book and other writing deadlines.

Of course, the supposed last straw was not the last straw at all. Amidst the computer delays, one of our children had a crisis back home to which we were responding long distance, and wondering all the while if we should go home. With assurances from our adult child that the crisis was passing, we continued our journey and continued our extensive long-distance communication. Toward the end of this time, I found a computer to borrow for two days, only to discover later that it was infected with a virus, which destroyed my work and my document disks as well. By this time, I was convinced that neither this book nor my life as a scholar was meant to be. And this was the time set aside to revise and edit a chapter on keeping Sabbath and tending cycles. I finally had to stop and practice Sabbath before I could continue writing.

This story reveals some of the challenges of compassion when the forces from inside and outside mitigate against it.

Reflection

Reflecting on my story, I realize it is insignificant in relation to the universe, but it *is* revealing of the technological morass and lifeways of the modern era. Not all people overprogram themselves as I often do; not all people base their choices on overly optimistic judgments about time; and not every project is plagued with so many unexpected impairments as this one has been. On the other hand, the extreme case can reveal something about common cases. What was missing in this particular case was empathy with the Spirit of Life. The rush of living was undermining the well-being of creation. Whatever neuroses my rush reveals in me—a yearning to belong, to excel, to be accepted—is not nearly so important as the deeper yearning it reveals—to be connected with life. Insofar as the summer events forced a work stoppage and a reshaping of the work process, they invited me to a Sabbath rest and renewal. They gave me opportunity to reconnect with life. Insofar as my behavior—and that of various companies, institutions and family members—contributed to frenzy, our actions were actually counteracting that deep yearning for life. Insofar as the debilitating events of the summer reveal larger patterns in the modern world, these patterns of modernism also undermine the human yearning for life; inevitably, the patterns undermine the well-being of creation. Sabbath is needed if well-being is to be restored.

To speak of Sabbath as a way of life is to recognize that frenzy is not the only way to live. But what are the alternatives? One alternative comes from human cultures that have lived more compatibly with the earth, particularly early human cultures and indigenous cultures in the modern world. The dangers of romanticism are great, but Jerry Mander offers evidence that prehistoric human existence was richer in economic stability, leisure, and food supplies than is commonly thought.[8] Further, the ways of earlier cultures in balancing between work and play, and between the use and preservation of natural resources, are impressive compared with modern practices of over-emphasizing work, distributing work inequitably, harried play, and overused natural resources. Many indigenous peoples continue to choose not to produce as much as they can and not to use all of their environmental resources, leading to frequent assumptions that these people are primitive, impoverished, and ironically, in need of outside help in resource management.[9] Perhaps, instead, these people have learned to practice Sabbath as a way of life—to empathize with the movements of God in creation.

Within the Jewish tradition of Sabbath is a persisting witness to the covenantal relationship between God, humanity, and the rest of creation. God is understood as the One who creates and holds the world; human beings are stewards; and all creation is valued by God. These values are expressed through narratives, rituals, and practices. To understand the Hebrew view of creation is to study many texts, stories, rituals, and interpretations of the history of Israel, and many of these relate to Sabbath and Jubilee.[10] The three elements of Sabbath observance are also telling reminders of the kind of stewardship that humans are called to exercise in the context of covenantal relationship with God and creation: "We create nothing, we destroy nothing, and we enjoy the bounty of the earth."[11] These are actions that remind people that God is the Supreme Creator, that the world does not belong to human beings, and that God is the Provider of all natural goodness.[12] Human beings are called, thus, to be responsible stewards, but neither owners nor dominators of the creation. This is at the heart of Sabbath.

Active Participation

All of the Sabbath traditions in Jewish and Christian communities involve practices. Although these vary somewhat from text to text and community to community, some of these practices have been summarized in recent literature. Sabbath practices do not involve vigorous work, but they can be quite demanding and challenging. Thus, the term "active participation" is appropriate, although practices include the so-called "passive" actions of resting and waiting. Prominent Sabbath practices are silence, worship, cessation of work, and letting go, which, in turn, nourish other practices. Tilden Edwards sees Sabbath as "an incubator for nourishing our being in the image of God," thus contributing to human service in the world and to what he calls "the co-inherence of work and leisure."[13] The time of resting is, thus, a companion to a time of movement.

In light of what has been said, the daily movement from evening to morning in the first story of creation is stunning. Each day in the first story of creation begins with evening ("there was evening"), and then with morning ("and there was morning"), thus framing the workday with rest, renewal, and hope on both sides. According to Luke, Jesus' ministry was also framed by Sabbath, with Luke 4:16 at the beginning and Luke 23:53–54 at the end.[14] Sabbath is a doorway for beginnings and endings.

Sabbath practices are named in different ways, but certain themes appear again and again. Maria Harris identifies the Jewish and Christian Sabbath practices as attunement to holiness in time (listening to what we are called to do in time), cessation (letting the land lie fallow and engaging in "not-doing"), and recreation in community.[15] These are quite similar to the practices described by Tilden Edwards, namely rest, worship, and the practice of community awareness, whether in community-gathering or in solitude.[16] Similarly, both authors recognize that these practices are important to a weekly rhythm, to daily pauses, and also to extended periods of Sabbath during special times of retreat or transition.[17]

In similar fashion, the Jubilee tradition involves practices—letting the land lie fallow, practicing forgiveness, proclaiming liberty, prophesying justice, and practicing jubilation (singing a new song).[18] Again, the quietness of letting go is combined with the active acts of forgiving and proclaiming liberty, justice, and jubilation. This is a moment in time, and attunement to the movement of time is important; it is also a moment in community, and both renewal and restoration of justice are done with and for the community. They are also done for the larger world, for the vocation of Jubilee is *tikkun olam*, or repair of the world. Jubilee is not a vocation that can be accomplished in some glib program of action; it involves all of the practices that we have identified, plus the reality of suffering, which arises when people are present to pain and brokenness.[19]

Underneath all of these Sabbath traditions is gratitude. According to Erazim Kohák, the Sabbath is celebrated in the act of honoring or giving thanks: "Not the absence of activity, but the act of honouring, of giving thanks, is what restores the human soul and puts it at peace."[20] In this sense, a large part of earthbound ministries can be understood as Sabbath time—time for the community to engage in the Sabbath practices described above, thus honoring and giving thanks to the Creator and creation. The Sabbath promise is not only restoration of human life, but restoration of the cosmos.

In light of this discussion, what practices of Sabbath are needed? Rather than begin with a set of rules or laws, a community may ask itself questions to guide its Sabbath practices, whether for weekly Sabbath observance, daily Sabbath pauses, or Sabbath seasons in the lives of an individual, community, or nation:

- How can we practice thanksgiving and joy during this Sabbath time?
- How can we rest and await renewal, letting go of needless doing?
- What recreation can we practice to recreate ourselves and our community?

- How can we listen to God and to God's call to the future?

The challenge of keeping Sabbath is the challenge of living in a new way so that the ways of God might become more clear.

Tending Cycles

Just as we said that keeping Sabbath is a way of life, so is tending cycles. And just as the root of Christian Sabbath traditions lies within Judaism, so does the practice of tending cycles. This theme is a bit less obvious, however, because both Judaism and Christianity are historical traditions with a strong focus on the linear movement of time. Even so, a more cyclical view of the universe creeps into the narratives, poetry, and wisdom teachings. Some discussion of the circles and cycles has been offered in earlier chapters, and the purpose here is to explore the ethical dimensions of these traditions. Consider this text of instructions from Exodus:

> Three times in the year you shall hold a festival for me. You shall observe the festival of unleavened bread; as I commanded you, you shall eat unleavened bread for seven days at the appointed time in the month of Abib, for in it you came out of Egypt. No one shall appear before me empty-handed. You shall observe the festival of harvest, of the first fruits of your labor, of what you sow in the field. You shall observe the festival of ingathering at the end of the year, when you gather in from the field the fruit of your labor. Three times in the year all your males shall appear before the Lord God...The choicest of the first fruits of your ground you shall bring into the house of the Lord your God. You shall not boil a kid in its mother's milk. (Ex. 23:14–17, 19)

Here we see an early Hebrew text in which festivals of the people of God are described in relation to cycles of the agricultural year. The ritual practices and remembrance of the community are done in a yearly cycle, shaped by the cycle itself, as well as by the history of God's work. The historical dimension is represented in the practice of eating unleavened bread for seven days in the month of Abib, commemorating the Hebrews' deliverance from Egypt. The cyclical and linear (historical) views of God's work and human response are thus conjoined, echoing themes of earlier chapters. In the Exodus text, the tending of cycles and the tending of history are an interwoven whole.

Compassion

The Exodus text suggests the theme of compassion for the earth, rooted in agricultural cycles and the history of God with the people. This theme appears in certain strands of the Christian tradition as well, suggesting an ethical guideline for tending cycles. Through earthbound ministries, we might come to see God's work in the movements of the seasons, and we might enable and encourage people to live in tune with those seasons, especially through rituals that follow cycles of the day, the month, the year, or a lifetime.

The whole of early Hebrew tradition was grounded in an agricultural cycle, and although the people made distinctions between their faith and that of more nature-based Canaanites, the earth's cycles influenced their religious life. Thus, the festivals of the year were festivals of receiving of the law, destruction of the temple, repentance (Rosh Hashanah) and new beginnings (Yom Kippur), harvest (Succot), light in darkness (Chanukah), letting go and going wild (Purim), and deliverance and rebirth (Passover). These holy days correspond to events in the history of the Jewish people, which are recalled in a cycle of remembrance every year. They also correspond to seasons of the earth—deliverance and rebirth in spring, planting, destruction in summer heat, autumn remembrance and regrets, late autumn harvest, winter darkness, and spring's bursting with life again. How might Christians, along with Jews, remember and return to these earthy roots and participate in repairing a severely damaged world?

Among other practices, we might recover the medieval monastic tradition of praying in relation to hours of the day and times of the year. Celtic monks were acutely aware of the rhythms of nature through a day and a year. One Celtic hermit, writing in about 806, saw the birds as joining in the canonical hours and singing the responses to one another. He wrote:

> The chanting of birds I hear—
> Good to draw man's tears:
> Each of them answers the other:
> Does not the whole Church do so?
>
> The birds of the world, power without ill,
> Come to welcome the sun,
> On January's nones, at the different hours,
> The cry of the host from the dark wood.
>
> On the eighth calends of noble April
> The swallows come on their pure tryst,
> (Till they depart)
> On the eight calends of October.[21]

Here we see the poet's sense that the birds are singing with the church and with the cycles of nature—the daily, monthly, and yearly cycles.

These recollections from Jewish and Christian traditions yield a vision of simpler life and closer harmony with cycles of the natural world. The ethical actions include practices of liturgy and prayer, as well as simplified living. The danger, of course, is that we can easily idealize times past, dismissing them as beyond reach or oversimplifying their accessibility as a pattern of life for modern or postmodern peoples. Nora Chadwick, one of the most prominent Celtic scholars of the twentieth century, describes the dilemma with sobering realism. She recognizes that the very looseness of Celtic organizational structure contributed to the disappearance of the Celtic Church, and their premodern lifestyles are impossible to envision or repeat under the force of modernity.

> The disappearance of the idiosyncratic Christianity of the Celtic Church was inevitable, owing to the absence of central organization; but it is impossible to reach the end without a feeling of regret. A Christianity so pure and serene as that of the age of the saints could hardly be equalled and never repeated...

> The Christianity of the Celts has a marked spirituality of its own. Having no towns, no currency, no large-scale industries, it had little temptation to material and worldly ideals. It retained to the end a serene inner life which could never be repeated in a rapidly changing world.[22]

With that note of realism, the question before us is how we might live in the modern world that *does* have towns, currency, large-scale industries, and much, much more. How might we find a serene inner life and tend the cycles of the earth?

Reflection

As I wrestled with that question, I became aware that compassion does not depend entirely on being removed from the flutter of modernity; it requires simply that we find moments of silence, aloneness, and meditation in the world. This leads into the act of reflection. Reflection can take the form of analysis and synthesis, common to Western theology and philosophy; however, the form of reflection most significant for tending cycles is what Kwang-Shik Kim describes as harmony and unfolding.[23] The poem "Autumn" represents such reflection; it was written as I walked alone in autumn, wrestling with adjustments in my life. It emerged in a reflective pause of the sort I hope to encourage in myself and others.

> The leaves of autumn quiver with brilliance—
> Sparkling yellows, transparent orange, raging red;
> The colors are so intense with joy
> That I want to hold them—
> To urge them not to leave,
> To photograph them,
> To remember every tree on every day
> And preserve the memory forever.
>
> Indeed, the colors of autumn are hardy this year;
> For many weeks, they hold their brilliance—
> Some leaves falling

And some becoming more brilliant still;
On sunny days, they are luminescent as they convey the sun,
On dull days, they make a canopy of soft brightness
    to mark my path.

But forever is never
And the leaves begin to fall,
Slowly, imperceptibly at first,
Then, dancing wildly in gusts of wind,
They fall in numbers grand
Until, tired with holding on,
They fall with no wind at all.

And yet, a few leaves remain,
Holding for weeks after the others have moved on,
And these hardy leaves hold the memory of what once was—
What could not be preserved,
What cannot be forgotten,
What cushions the ground now
So that we can walk more lightly.

Today I walk under the late autumn canopy
And know that the time has come
To let go of the full-colored beauty
Which I have wished so madly to preserve.
I know that the days of gold and orange and red
Are swiftly coming to an end.

But in the moment of letting go my desire
To hold the autumn trees so tightly,
I have met another moment of life
With those treasured trees
That I have come to love;
The trees have a different luster now—
A luster of transparent branches
Revealing the fullness of the sky,
And revealing the strength and delicacy of the limbs
Which hold the tree and reach upward and outward—
Toward me and toward the universe.

The trees stand almost stark now,
Pure and simple, undisguised;
And they live on, not in the splendor of color
But in a testimony to strength
And endurance and circling seasons.
They hold within their branches
The memory of their living past

And the hope of what is to come,
But first is the silence and beauty
Of bareness.[24]

This poem was itself inspired by the simultaneous reality of a fading autumn and the adjustment my husband and I were making to his retirement that had begun a few months before. The very fact that these words were inspired in me as I meditated on his first retirement months and on the trees that I loved suggests a correspondence between human life cycles and cycles of the earth. One could say that this association is a socially constructed reality, long engrained in the thinking of Western cultures, but regardless of how the correspondence is formed, it is quite common in many cultures to draw such associations between human cycles and the earth's seasons. Tending human cycles and tending cycles of the earth are often intertwined.

Sometimes the human life cycles and earth cycles are also intertwined with the cycles of Christian faith traditions, like the braiding of a rope. Hear the words of Ruth Ziedonis, who discovered closeness with Christ in the midst of a storm:

> I was swimming in the water when a storm rolled in. As the storm approached, the air temperature got cooler. The dark clouds were rolling in, and the wind picked up speed. Then light rain began to fall and became heavier. The water from the rain fed the land and cleaned the dust from the sidewalks. Since the Passion Week was approaching, I meditated on Good Friday and how the evening must have been when Christ was crucified on the cross! When the storm was over, a heavy mist covered the pool and the sky became clearer. The weather provided a context for me to meditate on Christ's death.[25]

In this moment, meditation on Christ's death was inspired by movements in the natural world, and cycles of tradition intersected with cycles of everyday living. Such meditative reflection is ethical action; it attunes people to God and creation in relationship.

Active Participation

Thus far, we have focused on compassion and reflection as ethical action, but active participation is also required for tending cycles. In the cyclical ethics of Judaism, some major principles are represented in the commandments. Consider, for example, the commandments regarding the settling of land (*yishuv ha-aretz*); they direct what kind of animals might be raised and what kind of trees might be burned on sacrificial altars.[26] Consider also the concern expressed for the pain of living creatures (*tza-ar ba'alei chayim*) and the requirement that humans care for the well-being of all living beings.[27] And consider, further, the commandments for humans to refrain from destroying (*bal tashchit*) other parts of creation.[28] Some of these were mentioned in chapter 2, such as the command to refrain from destroying trees in the siege of a city

(Deut. 20:19–20). This command, alongside the command not to slaughter a cow and her calf on the same day (Lev. 22:28) or to take a mother bird with her young (Deut. 22:6), suggests the importance of protecting creation and even conserving species.[29] In all of these commands, human participation is called for, whether in the form of making choices, giving active care, or exercising restraint. Although these particular commands may not be fitting in the present world, certainly the practice of discerning and practicing commandments is fitting if we are to make choices, give care, and exercise restraint.

Active participation in the cycles of the earth is suggested by the tradition of *imago dei* as well, the idea that people are created in the image of God. Larry Rasmussen develops this idea in a particularly cyclical way, suggesting that people are called to relate God with the world, and the world with God. As *imago dei*, our role is to mirror God's ways in our lives—in the ways we act toward one another and the rest of creation. We are to be images of God, and "imaging God is loving the earth as fiercely as God does."[30]

To love the earth fiercely is to participate in its circles of life with respect and compassion. How do we do this in earthbound ministry? Many suggestions have already been made, but the practices need to be more than a list. Tending cycles involves an ecology of action responses. This means that all aspects of the preaching, worship, education, pastoral care, fellowship, and service of the church are interwoven, and that each one has many dimensions. Thus, we do not practice many kinds of ministry, but one ministry with many faces, contexts, and practices. It also means that all acts of ministry should be grounded in ancient traditions, in pains and joys of the cosmos, and in communities where people live and serve.

Indigenous people usually understand these deep connections better than the rest of us, although some of the pastoral care literature has taken these connections seriously.[31] Gregory Cajete, a Tewa Indian, describes what he calls the spiritual ecology of tribal education, grounded in foundations that are mythic, visionary, and artistic, and in contexts that are environmental, affective, and communal.[32] In such an ecology, the practices of education are planted in the entire ethos and mythos of the people, with their stories, rituals, arts, land, feelings and attitudes, patterns of interaction and governance, and sense of who they are as a people. According to Cajete:

> Culture is the face, myth is the heart, and traditional education is the foundation for Indigenous life. All cultures have Indigenous roots bedded in the rich soil of myth from which the most elemental stories of human life spring.[33]

A spiritual ecology suggests that people participate in the fullness of human and earth community as connected beings. They follow the example of the Tewa people and "look to the Mountain."[34] Connecting is a particular challenge where cycles of relationship have been destroyed or abused. To look to the mountain is to ground ministry in all aspects of life—relating in all things with God and creation, with one's own distinctive people and land, and with peoples of the earth. This is the challenge of tending cycles.

Such a spiritual ecology is guided by traditions of the past, and it is also guided by recent ecumenical and global efforts to tend cycles of human and earth relationships so that all of creation might thrive. Consider the Earth Charter, adopted on March 18, 1997, in a Benchmark Draft; this will be studied in consultations for one more year and eventually presented to the United Nations General Assembly.[35] The Earth Charter begins with these words:

> Earth is our home and home to all living beings. Earth itself is alive. We are part of an evolving universe. Human beings are members of an interdependent community of life with a magnificent diversity of life forms and cultures. We are humbled before the beauty of Earth and share a reverence for life and the sources of our being. We give thanks for the heritage that we have received from past generations and embrace our responsibilities to present and future generations.[36]

The very language suggests interconnection with the present and a sense of history—connectedness across space and time. The principles of the Earth Charter continue this double-consciousness, and three principles exemplify its emphasis on tending cycles:

> (1) Respect Earth and all life. Earth, each life form, and all living beings possess intrinsic value and warrant respect independently of their utilitarian value to humanity.

> (2) Care for Earth, protecting and restoring the diversity, integrity, and beauty of the planet's ecosystems. Where there is risk of irreversible or serious damage to the environment, precautionary action must be taken to prevent harm.

> (3) Promote social development and financial systems that create and maintain sustainable livelihoods, eradicate poverty, and strengthen local communities.[37]

Such principles offer concrete guidance for earthbound ministry and the practice of tending cycles—human and earth cycles, cycles in this moment, and cycles across time.

This discussion connects yet again with the Jewish tradition of tending cycles—a tradition in which stories of the ancestors are important, as are the ways that people interact with trees and animals, seek justice for other human beings, and worship and sing. Tending cycles and keeping Sabbath are interwoven, for Sabbath itself represents a cycle of seven days or years. Respecting cycles and Sabbaths opens pathways for tending relationships. But what of movements in history? To this question we now turn.

Engaging in Transformative Politics

Blessed are those who do everything possible and furthermore dare
to try to bring about some small part of the impossible.[38]

Alongside the cycles of life are movements of history. The temptation to
choose a purely cyclical view of reality or a purely linear view is great, but the
hope of this book is to enhance complementarity. The dominant linear, historical view of Christianity has helped to justify Christians in taking what we
need from the earth without much attention to tending human and earth communities. On the other hand, the historical view has reminded Christians that
God is not finished with the world; God calls us toward a new creation. Thus,
transformation is central to Christian ethos and mythos—transformation represented in God's deliverance of Hebrew slaves from Egypt, and transformation represented in the contemporary Korean hope for a reunified country.
Here is where we hear a clarion call to transformative politics.

To say that the cyclical and historical views are complementary is not to
say that every community will accentuate these in the same way or to the
same degree; neither is it to say that the different accents will be tension-free.
The tension, and the different emphases of different communities, is part of
the reality of living in an ecosystem in which every part of the system makes
distinctive contributions. The distinctions are sometimes conflictual and challenging for the whole body, which offers protection against linear or circular
excess. Because the linear excess of Christianity has been particularly destructive in recent centuries, much attention has been given in this book to cycles.
We turn now to transformative movements; these are also part of Christian
response to God and the world, growing as they do from the historical consciousness of Jewish and Christian traditions.

The call to engage in transformative politics was touched, in chapter 6 in
relation to a politics of partnership. I urged a shift from combative politics to
partnership, with leadership by many partners and many communities. Qualities were identified for a politics of partnership; it will be purposive, communal, conversational, passionate, and prophetic. Continuing this theme, we turn
now to the political vocation of Christian communities, seeking to transform
human patterns of life and work—to reform existing patterns of social organization and action. This discussion builds upon the earlier one.

For a community to engage in transformative politics requires that the
people experience compassion for the world in which they live, reflect on the
complexity of that world and the pull of future, and actively participate in
transforming the world toward justice and care for all creatures. The interweaving of these actions is critical because each feeds the other. Gustavo
Gutiérrez urges that theology be grounded in contemplation and action, and
that all be grounded in compassion. As to the first claim, Gutiérrez says:

> God is first contemplated when we do God's will and allow God to
> reign; only after that do we think about God. To use familiar catego-

ries: contemplation and practice together make up a *first act*; theologizing is a *second act*.[39]

The circle is elaborated when Gutiérrez reflects on Job's conversations with his friends (as in Job 13–18); Job rejects their ways of doing theology, which do not take account of the concreteness and suffering in his situation or the compassion of God. Gutiérrez says, "Job's words are a criticism of every theology that lacks human compassion and contact with reality; the one-directional movement from theological principles to life really goes nowhere."[40] In so saying, Gutiérrez recognizes that compassion gives rise to reflection, which then gives rise to active participation and back again. Reflection without compassion and action is empty, even destructive. Transformative politics thus requires compassion *for* the world, reflection *on* the world, and active participation *in* the world.

Compassion

To experience compassion in the modern world is to feel the pains of the world, thus, to suffer with it. We are living through a period of history that reveals many signs of social disintegration. Longtime political structures are disintegrating, as are social programs that have been the mainstay of Christian denominations, national policies, and social structures in many parts of the world. In the United States, for example, programs of public education and social welfare are being attacked and dismantled, and people with small incomes face heightened vulnerability in face of these changes. The former Soviet Union has been dissolved, and the inheritor nations are struggling, again with considerable economic vulnerability. In the former Yugoslavia, religious communities that once coexisted in peaceful tolerance are embroiled in bloody warfare. In Haiti and Nicaragua, the ruling governments have shifted, and they have done so in the midst of bloodshed and continuing acts of terrorism. In the United Kingdom, national transport and healthcare systems are being drained of resources and pressured into dissolution or diminishment.

Some shifts are viewed more positively. In New Zealand, the government and churches are seeking to make reparation with the Maori people by giving preference to the Maori voice and vote, especially on issues such as water use; the efforts are filled with miscommunication, however, and people continually seek better patterns of social relationship. In such changing situations, the very discussion of politics seems anachronistic and hopeless, but the spirit of compassion can keep people at the table, seeking to understand one another and the fullness of the world.

Reflection

One of the very evident realities at the present time is the reality that projecting doom and evoking fear have limited value in changing the way human societies work. This form of reflection is inadequate as a pathway into the future, and the problem was well demonstrated by Robert Jay Lifton and Richard Falk in their analysis of what was known in the United States as the 1960s Cuban Missile Crisis.[41] They recognize that, throughout this crisis, some important actions and useful agreements emerged, but people remained within "the abiding framework of nuclearism."[42] Thus, transformation was limited and disillusionment easily followed. Thirty-five years of mutual blaming characterized United States and Cuban diplomacy, which reinforced, rather than resolved, antagonisms. Perpetuating existing frameworks has reinforced fear. The same is true for cries of justice, reconciliation, and integrity. Fear will never change people enough.

Lifton and Falk do not close with generalities, however; their reflection leads them to propose an alternative, a step-by-step movement toward a larger goal: fostering a political climate of action; encouraging gradual and partial steps directed toward long-range goals; being receptive to changes in leaders (however limited or opportunistic); challenging destructive thought patterns; offering alternative frameworks, e.g., a holistic world picture; avoiding narrow agendas and joining with others whose agendas are compatible; and encouraging actions of others (mobilizing "an energetic citizenry").[43]

Another evident reality is rapid social change, whether for good or ill. According to Peter Drucker, "No century in recorded history has experienced so many social transformations and such radical ones as the twentieth century."[44] He argues that the most influential social transformations have not been the most visible ones, but rather, those that brood below the surface. He adds that "extreme social transformations of this century have caused hardly any stir," referring to mass tortures, ethnic cleansings, genocides, and holocausts.[45] On the other hand, he believes that social transformations under the surface have had a lasting effect; they "have transformed not only the society but also the economy, the community, and the polity we live in."[46] According to Drucker, this age of social transformation will continue into the twenty-first century. Although I disagree with Drucker's argument regarding the minimal effect of extreme transformations, certainly the subterranean transformations are far more powerful than most people realize. Further, the devastation of the Holocaust (*Shoah*) and ethnic cleansings surely contribute to deep transformations that surpass human awareness. Genocide has been a major reality in this century, with victims among Armenians, European Jews, Serbs, and, less visibly, Native Americans in the United States.

Whether change is destructive or life-giving, it is always challenging. Social movements give rise to confusion and fear; they also undermine existing social systems and open the way for new systems. As people live with such massive change, they face massive pressures to redistribute power, to continue combative politics and combative warfare among nations and social groups (based in race, religion, socioeconomic power, gender, sexual orientation), and to seek more adequate forms of social organization. What kind of politics do we need in such an era? At the very least, people need to reexamine disintegrating social structures and to develop new structures that are more elastic and communitarian than those of the past.

Active Participation

In the context of these and other issues, the question of politics does indeed become important, because the actions of churches and other corporate bodies will either support creation, justice, and peace, or deny them. To that end, church politics needs to engage people with people, opinions with opinions. In the following pages, I will identify four kinds of politics that are important as people come together to seek God's future.

POLITICS OF SUSPICION

We need, first, a politics that is suspicious of powers that reinforce domination, oppression, and destruction. These powers are never completely clear, but we need a conscience that is wary of evil in the world and a politics that equips us to deal with the fullness of evil. A politics of suspicion is one in which we turn our suspicions onto ourselves as well as onto the society in general and the church in particular.

A politics of suspicion supports political action that is persistent in moving people and institutions toward a vision. One example of this comes from the 1992 General Conference of the United Methodist Church. In 1988, the Native American and Hispanic (or Latino) groups had not been able to get positive votes for the legislation they most needed to undergird their ministries. In preparing for 1992, the leaders of these two ethnic communities worked together and also with others. Together, they were able to convince the 1992 General Conference that the church needed a Comprehensive Hispanic Plan and a Native American initiative; the plans were approved. In the last hours of the Conference, however, the funding was questioned, threatening to undercut the earlier Conference approval. Some alert leaders had foreseen this possibility and rose to defend the budget items. The funding was preserved. Both the programmatic approval and the funding were possible because of a politics of suspicion. Because people joined in common action, and because they were alert to possible concerns and blocking actions, they were able to inspire the General Conference action and assure fiscal responsibility.

Reflections on human sin are particularly important to a politics of suspicion. Sin stands at the root of abuse, both of the environment and of human beings. Whether through greed, arrogance, jealousy, or fear, human sin marks its victims. It generates poverty, racial discrimination, gender prejudice, exclusion based on sexual orientation, stripping the land of its resources, and other ills that threaten creation. People will not agree on what sin is and what needs to be done in response, but they can at least agree to wrestle with their suspicions and to seek that which is good and just. A politics of suspicion is needed.

Sin can be understood as any action or attitude that destroys life. It may be social or individual, visible or invisible, dramatic or subtle. Rebecca Chopp has identified two aspects of human sin—depravation, which is "the destruction of the basic conditions of life," and deprivation, which is "the loss of the vision of flourishing."[47] Some sinful acts, such as murder or rape, have very visible and direct effects; others destroy the spirit, eating away hope. To practice a politics of suspicion is to be aware of both forms of destruction and, in all things, to act against destruction and on behalf of life.

In light of the reality of evil and these theological reflections upon it, what kind of resources do we need to support a politics of suspicion? We need, first, *resources that engage people in reflection on the pain and injustice in their own situations*. This includes themselves and their families, their communities and bioregion. We also need *resources that explore global realities and analyze the root causes of sin and evil*. As part of that, we need resources that offer analyses of the world situation—analyses that are theological, economic, ecological, sociological, and psychological. In addition, we need *resources that propose alternate visions for living in the world*, such as alternatives beyond capitalism and communism, biblical literalism and biblical illiteracy, political warfare and political passivity, and cultural isolation and cultural hegemony. To understand the world more fully, we also need *resources from different cultures, different parts of the world, and different points of view*. And we need the *resources of ordinary and forgotten people*—not just Moses, but also Miriam and the people of Israel; not just Paul, but also the early Christian communities; not just political and church leaders, but also the common people of nations and churches. This means that we need *resources beyond what one church can produce*—resources created by churches working together, by people in local churches, by diverse religious communities, by artists and authors of our time, by the news media, and by the groaning earth. All of these can open our eyes and our suspicions.

POLITICS OF GRACE

In addition to a politics of suspicion, we need a politics of grace—a politics that begins and ends with the Spirit of God, and church political action that begins and ends at the common table of our Lord, or in other acts of covenant. God's grace is already present before we act, but a politics of grace is attuned to the grace-filled movements of God. These movements of grace are ever present—revealed in the Spirit of God blowing through creation, revealed in Jesus Christ, who gave himself for the full life of creation, and revealed in us as we seek and act toward a vision of flourishing.[48]

The politics of grace is politics that discerns the mystery of God beyond the beliefs or values of any one or twenty communities. It is politics where people live and argue and respond passionately but keep returning to the communion table, and to the renewal of covenant. It is politics in which Christians seek hope in Jesus Christ—hope for redemption and for a vision of life *with* and *for* the oppressed, outcast, and neglected. And it is a politics in which people seek the face of God in the poorest of the poor and in the most ordinary of the ordinary to the end that we might all participate in God's work of shalom.

Practically speaking, a politics of grace is established when people: (1) foster the community's relationship with God and the earth; (2) build mutuality and encourage diversity within the community (through prayer and play, worship and study, action and reaction); (3) wrestle with incompatibilities across class, race, culture, and gender, allowing people to pull apart and come back together; (4) continually return to the communion table and other acts of covenant; and (5) build solidarity with other communities and institutions. In short, the community shares acts of God's grace with the earth and with people of all creeds and races, cultures, and socioeconomic groups.

What kind of resources do we need, then, for a politics of grace? We need *resources that foster a community's relationship with God and creation through meditation, prayer, and the arts.* And we need *language and cultural resources, pointing to God in diverse ways.* We also need *resources that pose questions and point to mystery,* and *resources that connect liturgy and ritual with formal study and action in the world.* Because God's grace is a movement in community, the *resourcing needs to foster covenantal living*—offering inspiration and guidance for intercultural, interreligious, interclass, and ecologically diverse community. Further, *resourcing is needed that will engage the community with its traditions past and present*—its stories, troubles, and hopes.

POLITICS OF FUTURE

A politics of grace already points to a politics of future. The life, death, and resurrection of Jesus always points to the future; therefore, Jesus is not just a historical figure from whom Christians gather their identity, but is also a future vision who points to a fuller identity ahead. The incarnation can keep people open to diverse cultures, points of view, and religious traditions because Jesus Christ has pointed to a reality beyond what people know in the present.

The experience of the oppressed also evokes a politics of future, often out of necessity. Such a politics can be tumultuous, with unanswered questions and elusive goals, but in a politics of future, present reality is always measured by hopes for a just and sustainable world to come. African American spirituals represent such moments of hoping in the midst of tormented human existence; spirituals in the antebellum United States embodied protest against slavery, as well as hope and movement toward a better future.

The politics of future is also born in communities that choose to focus their life together on a vision. We see the politics of future in the testimony of a small town pastor whose church has come alive in northern California since the congregation decided to focus on their ministry with homeless people. "We have a clear mission now," he says. We can also see the politics of future in the Center for Regenerative Studies at California State Polytechnic University, Pomona.[49] In this university setting, faculty, students, staff, and volunteers have created a model community for regenerative study and sustainable living. The actual physical setting was constructed from a futuristic design, but each step completed stirs more visions for the future. The Center will never be complete.

Practically speaking, a politics of future is politics where people: (1) look to God's future; (2) envision and work toward transformation in the world—ecological, personal, social, global; (3) involve the whole community in acting, critically reflecting, and acting again; (4) encourage people to wrestle with unanswered questions and negotiate their conflicting answers (rather than respond with avoidance or combat); and (5) see themselves in relation to the larger public world.

For such a politics of future, we need resources that invite struggling and imagining. Therefore, we need *resources that raise more questions than answers*, an anomaly in contemporary cultures oriented toward expecting simple answers and resolutions. Further, we need *resources that point to a future of hope, and inspire people to envision God's new creation*. For such a politics, we also need *church structures that provide space for questions and support for negotiation*. The form of these structures will vary among communities and cultures, but the need is urgent, especially considering the dominant mode of political action in the church and nation—political action by combat, in which one group strives to accomplish its ends by defeating other groups. What is needed is more than new answers, but a new way of doing politics in a world that cannot afford the luxury of having all issues framed as battles between "us" and "them." We further need *church structures that encourage and support inclusive communities*—interreligious and intercultural communities; communities living closely with the earth; congregations that welcome political refugees, gay and lesbian persons, and others pushed to the margins of society; communities living with and serving the poor, the disabled, and the outcast.

POLITICS OF FRIENDSHIP, ADVOCACY, AND SOLIDARITY

In a covenant community we are called also to a politics of friendship, advocacy, and solidarity. This involves befriending the stranger; offering hospitality to the outsider; working with and for the marginalized; advocating for those who are oppressed, rejected, or silenced; and building communication with all peoples and creatures.

The word friendship is important to this mode of politics because the emphasis is not on caring *for* others, but on being *with* others in their struggles for physical necessities, social justice, and the dignity befitting children of God. A stunning example of such friendship is offered by Taylor and June McConnell, who lived in Northern New Mexico for many years as students and teachers of multicultural relationships. Rather than writing volumes about the three cultures of the region, or teaching people what they needed to know, the McConnells spent many years in befriending. The result was deep, respectful knowing, and a lifestyle that placed friendship at the center of multicultural relationships.[50]

The word advocacy is important to this mode of politics because the emphasis is not simply on personal friendship, or even community friendship, but on mutual action in the social order for the sake of a sustainable world and a just and peaceful existence for all. Closely related is the word *solidarity*, which places emphasis on standing with another being, or another community, over time. One of the dangers of white liberalism has been the tendency to commit to causes and not to people and other beings. Liberals have often jumped from cause to cause, rather than walking with others until the soles of their shoes were worn out and their souls were hurting with pain. Genuine solidarity is found in someone like Gustavo Gutiérrez, who writes book after book as partner with the oppressed, respectfully speaking their cause and admiring their strength and wisdom.[51]

Gutiérrez recognizes that the life situation of people shapes their theology, and thus, he lives and works with people who are oppressed so that his own theology is shaped by their faith and life experience. Such a sentiment is also expressed by Ivone Gebara, who urges that theological reflection begin with shared experience. She recognizes that "discourse dealing with the important issues in life is the heart of every theology."[52] This, too, is the heart of solidarity—a way of being with people and creation so that the very way that you think and act is influenced by the realities of the other.

What kind of resources do we need, then? We need *communities of friendship and advocacy, both local groups and broad networks*. We need *experiences with people who stand in solidarity with others over time*. We need *opportunities for people to share themselves—their questions and passions and deepest commitments*. Further, we need *print and media resources that help people encounter the fullness of creation in the diversity of plants and animals and human peoples*. And we need *people and other resources that teach the practice of solidarity and advocacy*. Public knowledge of how to act in solidarity with others is very limited. For example, the practices of nonviolent protest and nonviolent living can be learned, and leaders of these movements know how to teach nonviolence. We have much to unlearn and much to learn. Finally, we need to hear some of the real *stories—lots of stories of friendship, advocacy, and solidarity*. Especially, we need to hear some of the real stories of friendship across dissenting groups (such as common actions by evangelicals and social liberals, Jewish statements against the genocide of Muslims in Bosnia, and so forth).

The challenge in all of these modes of politics is the challenge to seek unity with God, one another, and the world, at the same time valuing the particularity of all peoples and all creatures. Such politics is an effort to nourish both unity and particularity, particularity and unity. The road to holiness is not to avoid politicizing the church, but to act politically to nourish life—to walk together and stretch out our hands to the world, seeking to participate in a vision that is God's future.

Practicing Stewardship *with* Creation

The question of human stewardship for the earth has been much debated, as suggested in chapter 2. Some argue that this whole idea is so tainted with domination and superiority that it is a large part of the ecological problem.[53] Others believe that stewardship is one of the primary answers and hopes in the Jewish and Christian traditions, representing a humble respect and care-giving role for God's creation.[54] Jay McDaniel adds a particular twist by noting that humans do have dominion over the rest of the earth by the sheer weight of their numbers and powerful influence; thus, the central question is what kind of dominion is needed. He argues, then, for "dominion-as-stewardship."[55]

Add to these religious discussions the power that the concept of stewardship has in larger public discourse. Consider the statement of the Union of Concerned Scientists to the United Nations: "A great change in our stewardship of the Earth and life on it is required if vast human misery is to be avoided and our global home on this planet is not to be irretrievably mutilated."[56] Consider also the testimony of Bruce Babbitt, U.S. Secretary of the Interior, who realized the power of churches when he read letters from churchgoers of diverse denominations protesting a bill to weaken the Endangered Species Act. Regardless of their diverse faith perspectives, the people argued again and again that God has commanded people to be responsible stewards—an argument that was weighty, even in the national political community.[57] So, we turn to the practice of stewardship.

Compassion

Without rehearsing the Christian stewardship debate, I would add one accent that is often neglected, that is, stewardship *with* the rest of creation. Stewardship with creation grows from compassion—from feeling with the creatures of the earth. This sense of interconnection and responsibility, combined with the ability to feel with the earth, is found in Buddhism as well as in Christianity and other traditions.[58] This is compassion in its fullness. When stewardship theories focus only on human responsibility *to* God and creation, and *for* the care of creation, the idea remains human-centered. What is lost is the compassionate relationship and responsibility of *every* part of creation with the whole.

The way people understand these relationships shapes their perspectives on human responsibility in particular. If the relation of people with the land is defined in terms of possession, then the ethical ideal is to own and build up possessions over time; the ethical wrong is to steal. But if the relation of people with land is defined in terms of tending and caring in a mutual relationship, as embodied in the Australian Aboriginal tradition, then the ethical ideal is to care for the land. In this case, the ethical wrong is to destroy the land or to draw borders and fight for possession. Stewardship has to do with tending and caring in mutual relationship with the earth.

Reflection

Naturally, people will be preoccupied with the human role in creation, and practically speaking, we need to be. The Jewish and Christian traditions call people to this responsibility as a calling from God, who creates, redeems and sustains the world. In addition, the vast influence of humans on the rest of creation needs to be acknowledged, and for very practical reasons we need to give considerable attention to our responsibility for the world. On the other hand, our tradition also reminds us that God declared *all* creation to be very good (Gen. 1:31). And in the second creation story, God formed humanity from the dust of the ground and made trees to grow from the ground, and a river flowed through Eden to water the garden (Gen. 2:7a, 9a, 10a; cf: Ezek. 47–48). Not only is the whole of creation affirmed in the first story but also the distinctive roles of different parts of creation are confirmed in both the first and second stories of creation. Every part of creation has a part to play. This suggests that humans are stewards *with* the soil and sky, as the plants and animals are stewards with us.

As stated earlier, the picture of living with the earth has not been ideal in any culture, but some pictures, particularly from early cultures, have been more harmonious than others.[59] Although early peoples often lived in tenuous relationship with the earth themselves, their overwhelming sense of caring for, and living with, the earth was strong enough to point some directions for modern stewardship, even in the midst of population growth and technological temptations. In particular, the stewardship of early peoples was more often attuned to the rhythms of creation, less often guided by the spirit of ownership, and more often guided by a sense of partnership with the creation.

Active Participation

To speak of partnership and the stewardship of all creatures does not mean that creatures are all the same, undifferentiated. It means the opposite. Each has a role according to its kind. And what are those roles?

The first role is to worship and give thanks to God. Whether Saint Francis admonishes the birds and fish to praise God, or the psalmist enjoins all of creation to praise God (as in Ps. 96), the responsibility and joy of giving thanks and praise are accentuated. This particular theme is found in other religious traditions as well, and quite notably in Islam. In Islam, everything in the heavens and on earth is to give praise and glory to God, thus, joining human beings in worshipping Allah.[60] Roger Timm explains that, according to the Qur'an, the purpose of creation is to show signs of the power and goodness of Allah. The purpose is also to guide humans and test their faith and conduct, pointing them to Allah and God's will; to serve Allah and follow God's will; and to be used by humans and other creatures.[61] Timm recognizes the human-centered quality in many of these affirmations, but he recognizes, too, that the accent is on the devotional, or worshiping, function of creation. This has implications. Most notably, human beings should respect and act compassionately toward all of creation, because the creation *joins with them* in worshipping Allah, each having a distinctive devotional role to play. Also, the creation bears signs of God's power and grace, thus inviting people to care for and respect creation as a way of showing gratitude to the Creator.[62]

What vision is stirred when we consider that trees and seas have a vocation of praise and thanksgiving? Will people be more cautious with the natural world if they think thus? Just as Timm recognizes ambiguity in Islam regarding the actual ecological consequences in practice,[63] ambiguity is certainly present within Christianity and within most peoples who hold reverent views of the creation. On the other hand, the picture that emerges is the joining of all creation in worship of God—a sharing between humans and the rest of creation in acts of praise. It is to be hoped that one responds more respectfully to trees and seas when aware of their calling to praise God. One may even be humbled to realize that these creations mirror God simply by being themselves, without any embellishment from us. Thomas Merton says:

> A tree gives glory to God by being a tree...The more a tree is like itself, the more it is like Him [God]...No two created beings are exactly alike. And their individuality is no imperfection...This particular tree will give glory to God by spreading out its roots in the earth and raising its branches into the air and the light in a way that no other tree before or after it ever did or will do.[64]

Each tree is called in its unique way to give glory to God; in this way, trees and seas and the whole natural world are partners with humans in praising and serving God.

This suggests a second role of stewardship, namely, *for every being to fulfill its unique purpose*. If God creates all beings for a unique purpose, then, respect and encouragement are important if everyone and everything are to be free to fulfill that purpose. In the eighteenth and early nineteenth centuries in Britain and the United States, a major argument in the anti-slavery movement was that people who were being used as slaves were human beings with souls. For this reason, capture and ownership were not fitting; what was needed was respect for the souls of these human beings. Similar arguments were made regarding women during the same period, arguments that women have souls and thus should be liberated for full participation in the public world. Thomas Merton has expressed a parallel view regarding creation:

> The little yellow flowers that nobody notices on the edge of that road are saints looking up into the face of God...The lakes hidden among the hills are saints, and the sea too is a saint who praises God without interruption in her majestic dance.[65]

Because God has made these creatures, they are, by nature, sanctified and purposeful. Human beings have considerable freedom to make choices about our purposes and identities. According to Merton, "Our vocation is not simply to be, but to work together with God in the creation of our own life, our own identity, our own destiny."[66] Our unique purpose will be formed, then, as we pray and seek and give of ourselves, living with and for God.

This leads to a third role of stewardship: *to respect and enhance the work of every creature, and to work together in the ministry of God's creation*. We have thus traveled full circle and returned to the beginning of the book. The book began by gathering hopes for the church's ministry with the earth. The central hopes of such ministry are the heart of stewardship: to care for the earth, receive from the earth, and join with all creation to praise our Maker and heal our planet.

Conclusion

And so we conclude where we began—in meditation and in hope that we might indeed minister with the earth in such a way that the Creator will be honored and the creation will be repaired.

In the beginning
God created the heavens and the earth...
And at the end of the creating days,
God saw what was made
And said, "This is good!"

You are the people of that creation;
You are created by God,
You are created to be with God
And you are created so that you too may create.

You are a called people;
God has given you gifts.
You have received those gifts as a trust—
You are entrusted with them,
You are trusted to share them,
You are trusted to multiply them.

And the next time God looks around at the creation
That we have made *with* God,
God will surely cry at the sight of war,
And God will ache over racism, heterosexism,
        classism, sexism, ageism;
God will moan at the sight of earth being destroyed
And air filled with pollution;
But *surely*, God will smile at the love you have shared
And the difference you have made in someone's life,
And we can hope that you and others together
Will even make a difference in warrism, racism, heterosexism,
        classism, sexism, ageism, ecological destruction.
The next time God looks around, let us hope
That God will smile and say, "This *is* good!"[67]

APPENDIX
Retreat Design: Quilting a Life in Relation to God and God's Creation

The following retreat is designed to support people as they seek to relate deeply with God and God's creation. The design is based on the metaphor of quilting. It is built around six basic actions in making a quilt: gathering fabric; imagining a quilt design; cutting patches; stitching patches together; basting on a backing; and quilting (or stitching the quilt with designs). The retreat design includes prayers, poetry, interactive activities, and presentational material.[1] The design may be followed literally, adapted, or taken as a stimulus to others' imaginations. It may be combined with a discussion of *Ministering with the Earth*; it may also precede such discussion or stand independently.

Session I
GATHERING FABRICS

The theme for this session is gathering memories and hopes. That will become clearer as our time unfolds, but for now, we will begin with a circle of gathering prayers. *(Note to leaders: This session can be combined with a discussion of chapter 1.)*

Gathering Prayers

Greeting Prayer—According to John Wesley, everything you do in praise of God is prayer; therefore, greet one another in the spirit of praising God and with appreciation for the Spirit of God in another.

Silent Prayer—Thomas Merton instructed the brothers at Gethsemane to begin prayer with a sense of unity with God; then, they would know what to pray for. We will enter a time of silent breathing prayer: Breathe deeply, breathing Spirit in and out; let your prayers rise in silence; do not construct your prayers, but let them simply rise.

Prayers of Intercession—The following prayers of intercession are adapted from St. Ignatius of Loyola.[2]

> PREPARATION PRAYER—Dear God, grant us thy grace that all of our intentions, actions, and works may be directed purely to your service and praise. Amen.
> PRAYER FOR A PERSON WHO NEEDS IT ESPECIALLY TODAY—Imagine the person for whom you will pray. Think of that person's life—the person's gifts

and needs. Now, imagine what that person is experiencing right now. Speak your hopes to God for this person.

PRAYER FOR A PLACE IN THE WORLD WHERE HURT EXISTS—Think of what the physical place is like. Imagine the people, land, communities, individuals. What is needed here? Now, imagine yourself standing at the foot of Jesus' cross. Tell Jesus what you hope for this place…Speaking to Jesus as a friend, meditate on what you can do…Say your words of farewell…In the name of Jesus, the one who died because he loved the world and lived radically in it. Amen.

Gathering Prayer

We know that before we came together in this place,
    God was already here;
As we come together now,
    We bring our worries and gifts and uniqueness;
As we come together,
    We are connected with all those
        whom we love and like and know back home;
As we come together,
    We are bound with those who have gone before us—
our foremothers and forefathers
    And with peoples all across the world
    And with the bounties of the earth;
We know that as we come together,
    God is here and we will be blessed.
Thanks be to God! Amen.[3]

Re-membering Why We Are Here

Today is a day for gathering prayers and memories from our heritage, from our communities, from sacred places of our lives, from the earth. We have the privilege today of searching for spiritual depth in a world that pulls us to shallowness.

Today we have the gift of time
    to re-member ourselves with those we love
        far away and very near,
    to re-member ourselves with God who draws us near
        and stretches us far,
    to re-member ourselves with our deepest selves
        so that, near or far,
        wherever we journey,
            we make home
            and we live as family with those around us.[4]

We will spend time in this first session focusing on the art of quilting a spiritual life. We do not literally make our spiritual lives, for our lives are a gift from God. But in a sense, we *do* craft our spiritual lives with the fabrics that are given to us. Those fabrics may be oceans, mountains, people whom we love, people who love us, people who annoy or disturb us, communities in which we live, and most of all, the Spirit of God, who moves in and around and under our lives, crafting us, even as we seek to craft ourselves.

Among the Pueblo Indians of New Mexico live potters who make storytellers. They describe their art in this way: they begin sculpting by feeling the clay in their fingers and allowing the clay to communicate to them what they are to make. Now, these women have also been taught the patterns of their ancestors, and their storytellers often follow traditional patterns. At other times, their patterns vary. In either case, the creation is born as the artistic heritage travels through the artist's body as her fingers interact with the clay. Thus, artists craft the storytellers, and *yet*, the storytellers are crafted by a Spirit that is greater than the artists themselves. In the same way, we craft our spiritual lives, and *yet*, we are crafted by God's Spirit that is greater than we are.

Place a table in the center of the circle or in a place where everyone can see it. People will put their sacred symbols on this table during the next meditation.

Entering a time of silence, I invite you to bring something that you have with you that symbolizes stirrings deep in your soul—a hope, fear, dream, or commitment from deep inside yourself. Be spontaneous; do not spend too much time in analyzing this symbolic object, but bring it forward to the table and silently meditate on it. Bring the symbol forward and share your name with the whole group. You may briefly name your symbol, or not, as you are moved. Open yourself to what it reveals to you....We will leave these symbols here through this session, remembering that as we gather together, we gather ourselves—our very deepest selves—our whole selves—in this place.

Making a Quilt

In a sense, we are all artists who craft our lives with fabrics we are given and fabrics for which we search. Thus, the art of making a quilt is a fitting metaphor for a spiritual life retreat. Consider the basic actions that are important in making a quilt:

Gathering fabric—Some fabrics are old, some left over from earlier projects, some bought especially for the new project.

Imaging the design for your creation—Some designs are handed down for generations, like the hibiscus or pineapple designs of Hawaiian quilts; some are inspired by the natural world, and some are inspired by significant events, like wedding rings. Still others are created as you work, like the scrap-patched quilts that women of the rural United States made quickly for family needs.

Cutting patches—squares, strips, and triangles—Patches are cut from fabrics to create something new.

Stitching the patches together—Patches are sewn into a new form.

Basting on a backing—The backing adds warmth, support, or body.

Stitching the quilt with designs—Stitching adds durability; it can be sloppy and fast (when you need a utility quilt quickly), and it can be careful and fine for greater strength and beauty.

- Consider that quilts are often made by communities of people working together, using a quilting frame under which children play house and take naps while their elders work.

- Consider the AIDS quilt that inspires people all over the world to make AIDS quilts for their communities, and to make baby quilts for children born with AIDS.

- Consider the woman in Oklahoma who made nineteen quilts, one for each child who died in the Oklahoma City explosion on April 19, 1995. She did not know the children personally, but remarkably, the families of those children could see each child represented uniquely in one of those quilts, a testimony to the mystery of creation that was larger than the quilter herself.

Patching Together a Spiritual Life

Several basic actions are important in making a spiritual life:

Gathering fabric—We gather from those who have gone before us, from the fabric of our own lives, and from new fabrics that we discover along the way. When Gustavo Gutiérrez writes *We Drink from Our Own Wells*, he is aware that the people of Latin America are able to gather fabrics for their spirituality from their own wells; they do not need impositions from the outside.[5] Likewise, you gather fabrics from your heritage—your unique life journey and the journey of your people. Some will be worn and rough, and some will be bright and unblemished, but all will be yours to use—to craft into a beautiful and useful quilt.

Imagining the design for a new creation—New creation may be a new way of life for yourself or your community. Jesus' ministry was always looking to the future, to the possibility of new life.

Cutting patches—squares, strips, and triangles—People cut patches from the fabrics at hand to contribute to the new design.

Stitching the patches together—We bind ourselves into a community and bind the resources from our pasts into a new creation.

Basting on a backing—This is done for warmth and strength.

Stitching our lives with designs—This adds strength and beauty to the patchwork.

Gathering Fabric

During the next several moments, we will reflect on people and places from which we gather fabric for quilting our lives. Specifically, we will gather fabric from our ancestors, from sacred people and places in our lives, and from our unique experiences.

Gathering Fabric from Our Ancestors

All of us have ancestors, and whether we know them or not, whether we like them or not, whether they have been good to us or not, they are part of our lives. We will now enter a time of meditating on our ancestors.

Meditation—In a time of silence, reflect on one of your ancestors for whom you are especially grateful. This may be a mother or father, uncle or aunt, grandparent or dear friend. Remember the person, and allow the memories to flow…Now, reflect on a gift or blessing that this person has left for you.

Small Group Reflection—Gather in small groups (about three people), and share some of your memories and blessings. Remember to share only what you are comfortable in sharing. If you want to select only part of what you remembered, that is fine, and if you want to pass and be a good listener to the others in your group, that is also fine.

Meditation—Enter another time of silence, and reflect on one of your ancestors for whom you have ambivalent memories or conflicted feelings. This time, you will not be sharing the specifics of your memories, so do not worry about being vulnerable with the group. Remember this person, and allow the memories to flow…Now, reflect on the legacy *this* person has left for you, which may even be a negative legacy, or a blessing, or strength that has emerged from something negative.

Small Group Reflection—Gather in the same small groups, and share whatever you want to share about the inheritance you have received. What have you learned about your ancestors and their legacy to you? *(If this sharing time is eliminated, the group can move directly to the closing.)*

Ritual Closing—Sitting with your small group, silently pray for each person in the circle, and pray for yourself…Coming back together in the entire group, let us close this time by naming some of our ancestors, including not only those whom we have known, but also ancient people, biblical people, and historical people whose stories are part of our inheritance.

Gathering Fabric from Sacred People in Our Lives

The remainder of our time in this session is focused on gathering fabric from sacred people and places in our lives. This time of gathering will involve a rhythm of listening, meditating, and praying. *(The retreat leader may share the poems below for the group's silent listening, or you may substitute other poems, readings, music, or visual art. Whatever you choose, allow time after each offering for silent meditation.)*

I remember a woman who began tithing
    when she was young and poor,
Who continued to tithe when she became wealthy,
Who gave so much over her lifetime—
    to her family and church and causes,
That she died without wealth—a satisfied woman;
She lived well, and she was contented to die well.

I remember this woman's husband,
    who grieved his wife's passing after sixty-three years of marriage.
I remember how a young friend of the family
    came to him at the funeral
And thanked Papa for mentoring him many years ago
    when he was new in business and green,
        and when everyone thought he was bound to fail,
Except for Papa, who chose to be his mentor
    in business and in life.
I remember Papa and all that he gave of himself to his
    family and church and friends—
This dear man whose only regret now is that he has little
    money or energy left to give,
But who gives anyway, simply by being who he is.[6]

REMEMBER A PERSON WHO HAS REVEALED GOD'S SPIRIT TO YOU. Meditate on this person's life, and close the meditation when you are ready with a prayer of thanksgiving.

Gathering Fabric from Sacred Communities in Our Lives

We gather fabric not only from sacred individuals, but also from sacred communities. With that in mind, we continue to listen, meditate, and pray:

I remember a base community in South Central Los Angeles
Where five women gather every week
To read the Bible, pray, and reflect on their lives.
One night they were gathered,
And the youngest woman in the group read the text
    because the oldest woman could not read.
The story was about Jesus walking on water
    and Peter trying to follow,
        just moments before he sank;
As she listened, the oldest woman cried out,
"That story is about us; we are like Peter,
    only we are not afraid of walking on water.
We are afraid of walking out of our doors,

where gang members hang out
and threaten us."
The five women talked and prayed;
they all agreed with this wise old woman;
they knew their fear.
And so, these women decided on that fateful night
that they would *walk* into their fears,
open their doors to their neighbors,
stand outside to chat.
For one whole week, they stood on their doorsteps,
chatting with each other,
facing their fears,
until they gathered the next week for their study.
They read the Bible, prayed, and reflected on their lives;
They were proud of walking on water...
yet they knew their step was only tiny.
They vowed that during the next week,
they would *sit* outside on the lawn,
reading magazines, walking into the deep.
And so they did,
and each week was like the one before, but better;
Each week, these women took another step,
until they sponsored a barbecue for the gang members,
and a reaching-out plan for parents of these wayward youth,
and a coordinated effort with other base communities,
that continues even to this day.
All of this began with one quiet night when five women
gathered to read the Bible,
where the youngest woman read aloud
because the oldest woman could not read,
but the oldest woman could see visions
and the whole community was transformed![7]

REMEMBER A COMMUNITY OF PEOPLE WHO HAVE REVEALED GOD'S SPIRIT TO YOU. Let the memories of this community be present with you, and when you are ready, close your meditation with a prayer of thanksgiving.

Gathering Fabric from Sacred Places

As we continue the rhythm of listening, meditating, and praying, we will reflect on sacred places, considering places that inspire you.

Be Still

Be still and know—
The peaceful quiet beckons me
to be still,

But I cannot—will not—stop;
I think of things to do;
The things that must be done,
And yet, quietness calls to me—
Until I stop and sit and listen;
Then, I know—

Walking softly on a path,
    Again I know—
The forest opens into space,
A vast meadow stretches down the gorge,
Tumbling into the river far below.
I cannot walk on;
I can only stop and listen
And then, I know—[8]

RECALL A PLACE THAT HAS BECKONED YOU TO BE STILL AND KNOW... Remember the image of that place, and be aware of what that place has given to you...

Passing by the Sea

They stepped up and looked—
"How calm the sea!"
One said to the others;
Yet only a moment before
The water hurled against the rocks
And washed the stones with fury.
They walked on
And never knew.[9]

RECALL A PLACE THAT HAS BECKONED YOU, AND YOU HAVE RESISTED AND PASSED IT BY. *What do you remember about that place? How did your passing the place make a difference in the fabrics you are able to gather now?*

Hiddenness

The fog rolls in
    and embraces the coastline
We know the trees and sea are there
    beyond our sight and grasp.
We cannot imagine
    the contours of their bodies;
We feel their presence,
    even as they stand shrouded in mystery![10]

RECALL A PLACE WHERE YOU HAVE MET MYSTERY—a place that has communicated to you in ways that were beyond understanding...

A River's Journey

The water plunges down the gorge,
Carving a mighty path.

It rushes against rocks
Defying their strength.
The mad rushing water continues
Until the stream, purified and sparkling clear,
Flows gently into the river below.

Such a journey this is
That purifies the water
And polishes the rocks!
The journey seems quite simple
And the cost seems small enough,
But the stream leaves some of itself behind
And the rocks are slowly ground away.
Both the traveler
    and the ones along the way
        are forever changed![11]

Desert Mountains

This desert gave me strength
When nothing else was near.
The bold and craggy peaks
And the tiny tender plants
Witnessed to the movements of time—
And to endurance—
To endurance where water was slight
And heat and cold were plenty.

I came to these desert mountains
When I was young and fresh
And eager to explore them.
I became an adult here;
I birthed my children here.
Our family grew together here
And we met our crisis here.

This desert gave me strength
When nothing else was near.
The bold and craggy peaks
And the tiny, tender plants
Witnessed to the movements of time—
And to endurance.[12]

REMEMBER A PLACE THAT HAS ENTERED INTO YOUR LIFE IN A LIFE-CHANGING WAY.
What mark has that place left on your life?

Spirit
Spirit—

I know the touch of wind
     blowing over the mountains;
Spirit—
I know the chill of crisp
     breezes in autumn;
Spirit—
I know the refreshing calm of air
     moving on a hot day;
Spirit—
I know the wonder of love
     that is larger than those who love;
Spirit—
I know the power of grace
     moving in anger and in sadness;
Spirit, spirit—
I know your movements,
     but I will never KNOW you;
You are SPIRIT![13]

SPEND SOME TIME IN SILENCE, BREATHING IN SPIRIT AND BREATHING OUT SPIRIT...Thank God in your own unique way, and after a time, I will say amen... AMEN!

Gathering Fabrics of Your Distinctive Life

As we continue the rhythm of listening, meditating and praying, you are invited to reflect on yourself and the unique experiences of your life. *(Note to retreat leader: The following poem is about my life; you are welcome to share it, describe instead the fabric of your life, or both.)*

When I think on my life, I remember red—
The lifeblood that flowed through me from
     my family's love,
The dependability of their love, daily given,
The sense of extended family—grandparents, aunts
     and uncles and cousins,
Laughter and anger
In the midst of sureness that I belonged.

When I think on my life, I remember green—
The green of trees and grass,
The lush vegetation in my native Louisiana
     and my mother's native Georgia,
The precious spots of green in my father's
     West Texas,
The quiet green forest where I learned to pray
     in the camp I attended every summer,

The green earth that taught me to love it
and to care for its well-being.

When I think on my life, I remember gray—
The gray of disappointment when I realized I would
    always be an only child,
The gray of sadness when I realized that my aunts
    and uncles from Georgia and Texas were more
    excited and proud of my cousins than of me,
The gray of sadness when the teachers in my school
    told me I was special and then suggested
    that I marry a minister,
The gray of sadness when the leaders in my church
    always gave preference to boys over girls,
    when they excluded people of color,
The continuing gray of disappointment when I realize
    how often I play the role of worker who is rewarded
    with more work while others become the focal
    point of leadership and value,
The gray of realization that I am not at all charismatic,
    but I *do* have charisms or gifts
        and I am called to use them.

When I think on my life, I remember sunshine yellow—
The bright, ecstatic days on which my children were born,
The soft, mellow yellow of companionship
    with my husband—warming us and making us strong,
The glow of joy when I see people giving themselves
    to one another and to the well-being of the world,
The sparkling yellow when one of my students or former
    students touches other lives, takes a stand,
        makes a difference in the world.

When I think on my life, I remember black—
Not the black associated with despair,
But the black of depth—the moments of meeting God
    in the depths of my being—
The blackness of meeting God in the death of my father,
The blackness of meeting God in a moment of fiery anger
    at injustice,
The blackness of meeting God in the stillness of the early morning.

When I think on my life, I remember colors
I remember *many* colors
And fabrics of many textures.[14]

Quiet Time

I now invite you into a time of silence—a time to gather fabric from the sacred people and communities you have known, and to gather fabric from deep within yourself. *When you return (after 15 minutes, one hour, or whatever fits your retreat), we will have opportunity for some sharing.*

Closing

(When the group returns after a time of silence, invite them to reflect on what they have discovered.) What have you discovered about the fabrics you have gathered? What questions or concerns are raised for you by these explorations? What hopes are raised for your lives? for the communities dear to you? for the larger world?

Invite someone in advance to lead a closing prayer and close with that prayer.

SESSION II
IMAGINING THE DESIGN FOR
A NEW CREATION

The theme for this session is imagining a design for new creation. We will focus particularly on spiritual centering in a world tugging many different directions. (Note to leaders: This session can be combined with a discussion of Chapter 2.)

Gathering Prayers

In silence, wander outside and let the earth reveal God's dreams to you. Choose a symbol that communicates God's dreams (a symbol that can be moved without damaging the earth), and bring the symbol inside (to be returned later to its home). Place the symbol on the table in silence...We will close our meditation with people speaking single words and phrases of hope for God's new creation...Amen!

Re-membering the Purposiveness of Our Spiritual Lives

We gather fabric not just for pleasure or immediate needs; we gather because God calls us to be more than we are. As I read three texts slowly, I invite you to listen in the meditative style of *lectio divina*. Allow yourself to be caught by a word or phrase, and meditate on it without trying to analyze the text. After each reading, you will have time for silent meditation.

(1) From **Genesis 1:26–27:**

Then God said, "Let us make humankind in our image, according to our likeness; and let them have dominion [responsibility, care] over the fish of the sea, and over the birds of the air, and over the cattle, and over all the wild animals of the earth, and over every creeping thing that creeps upon the earth." So God created humankind in

[God's] image, in the image of God [God] created them; male and female [God] created them.

(2) From **1 Corinthians 12:4–7, 12–14, 24b–27:**

Now there are varieties of gifts, but the same Spirit; and there are varieties of services, but the same Lord; and there are varieties of activities, but it is the same God who activates all of them in everyone. To each is given the manifestation of the Spirit for the common good...For just as the body is one and has many members, and all the members of the body, though many, are one body, so it is with Christ. For in the one Spirit we were all baptized into one body—Jews or Greeks, slaves or free—and we were all made to drink of one Spirit. Indeed, the body does not consist of one member but of many...But God has so arranged the body, giving the greater honor to the inferior member, that there may be no dissension within the body, but the members may have the same care for one another. If one member suffers, all suffer together with it; if one member is honored, all rejoice together with it. Now you are the body of Christ and individually members of it.

(3) From **1 Peter 2:9:**

But you are a chosen race, a royal priesthood, a holy nation, God's own people, in order that you may proclaim the mighty acts of him who called you out of darkness into [God's] marvelous light.

God calls us to be and do that which we are called to be and do—in the image of God. We are to be: caregivers of creation; people baptized into Christ's mission; members of the body of Christ, each with our own unique gifts and callings; part of God's royal priesthood; God's own people; proclaimers of the mighty acts of Jesus Christ. This is why imagining God's new creation is so important. Our spiritual lives are important not only for ourselves and for God, but also for the well-being of God's new creation.

Explore Your Relationship With the Earth

The questions below are a guide for exploring your relationship with the earth. The first questions invite you to explore your own relationship with the earth through meditation; the later questions invite you to reflect on your church or community. You may later choose to take the questions beyond the retreat setting and involve a group in your church in systematic observations, analysis, and plans for action.

Reflecting on yourself:

1. Recall a moment in the last few days when you were particularly aware of God's movement in creation.
2. What was communicated to you in that moment about God and God's creation?

Reflecting on your community:

3. Think about your church or neighborhood (or home or other community). Notice everything that you can about the soil, air, water, animals,
   plants, and people. What do they want you to notice about them?
4. Where do you sense the pains of this sacred place?
5. What do you see as sources of joy here?
6. What in this place is calling out for repair (*tikkun olam*)—for justice,
   reconciliation, sustainability, regeneration?
7. What else do you observe beyond the scope of these questions?

Imagining God's New Creation: Gathering Mentors from the Past

Some people have been particularly important to the Christian community in helping people to image a new way of being. We will consider two
such people in this session—Howard Thurman and Julian of Norwich.

Howard Thurman—Meditating on a saint of a recent time and place

I invite you to listen and meditate on some stories of Howard Thurman, a
man who lived from 1900–1981 in the United States—a man whose life can be
considered a holy text. As we re-member Thurman, we live in community
with him and open ourselves to what God reveals through him about God's
new creation.

Howard Thurman was born in 1900 in Daytona Beach, Florida, where he
was careful to enter the white parts of town only during the hours when it
was allowed. Howard remembered his mother, Alice, as a "devout, dedicated
praying Christian."[15] He remembered his father as a good man, but one who
was not at all interested in the church. Howard's father was a railroad man,
who was gone for long periods when work was good, returning at intervals to
be with the family.

In his autobiography, *With Head and Heart*, Howard tells the story of his
father's death when Howard was seven years old. He came home with ty-
phoid fever; he rallied for a while but became gravely ill and died. Howard,
with his mother and grandmother, bathed his father and laid him out, because no one in town would embalm black folk. Also, the pastor of their Baptist church refused to bury Saul Solomon Thurman "from the church" because
he had not been a church-loving man. Howard's grandmother insisted that
the Board of Deacons allow the burial from the church, and they agreed, but
with the stipulation that the pastor would not conduct the funeral. Grandmother found a traveling evangelist, Reverend Cromarte, to preach the funeral. Unhappily, Reverend Cromarte used the occasion to explain what
happens to sinners who die out of Christ. As the sermon droned on, little
Howard leaned over to his mother and said, "Mama, he didn't know Papa,
did he?" Mama gently squeezed Howard's knee. After the funeral, Howard
decided, "One thing is sure. When I grow up and become a man, I will never
have anything to do with the church."[16]

After this time, Howard's mother and grandmother supported their family by washing and ironing, and later by cooking, for white families. Alice's work kept her away from home a lot, so Howard's grandmother, a former slave, did much of the child rearing. She was the one at home when Howard came in with his stories and questions about life, like the day he came home after being pricked in the hand by a white child at the house where he was raking leaves. He withdrew his hand quickly with a loud cry; the little girl said, "Oh, Howard, that didn't hurt you! You can't feel!"[17]

One day Howard came home very despondent. Having decided that he wanted to be baptized, he had gone to the deacons of the church for examination. He had answered their questions very well until they came to the last question, "Howard, why do you come before us?" To this question, Howard replied, "I want to be a Christian." The deacons shook their heads with disappointment. They explained to him that baptism comes after conversion, after you become a Christian. They asked him to go home and come back when he could tell them about his conversion. Howard went home dejectedly and told this story to his grandmother, who grabbed his hand and marched back to the church with Howard, swinging hands and huffing and puffing as she walked. She went in to the deacons, who fortunately were still meeting, and she said, "How dare you turn this boy down? He is a Christian and was one long before he came to you today. Maybe you did not understand his words, but shame on you if you do not know his heart." Howard was baptized the next Sunday.[18]

One last story will give some sense of the patches that Howard Thurman used to quilt his spiritual life. When Howard was finishing the seventh grade, his principal took an interest in him because he was very smart, and there were no high schools in Daytona for African American youth. The principal offered to tutor Howard through the eighth grade so he would be eligible to go to a missionary high school; Howard gladly accepted. His family was pleased, and the school officials agreed, as long as they could administer the tests. When Howard completed the year and passed the tests, his principal and family arranged for him to attend Florida Baptist Academy of Jacksonville. He was going to live with his cousin, doing chores in exchange for a free room and one meal a day.

Howard packed his trunk to go, and since the trunk had no lock or handles, he tied it with a rope. He went to the train station to catch the train to Jacksonville, approaching the train agent to buy a ticket. The agent told Howard that he would need to buy a separate, express ticket for his trunk; the rule required that a traveler's baggage tag be attached to a handle, not a rope. Howard was abashed, because he did not have enough money; all of his year's work and planning was about to be lost. He sat on the station steps and cried. After a few minutes, a large man in working shoes, denim overalls, and cap walked up to him and said, "Boy, what in hell are you crying about?"[19] Howard explained. The man said, "If you're trying to get out of this damn town to get an education, the least I can do is to help you." The man walked with Howard back to the window, bought an express ticket for his bag, turned and disappeared. Howard never saw the man again, but sixty-five years later he dedicated his autobiography "to the stranger in the railroad station in Daytona Beach who restored my broken dream sixty-five years ago."[20]

Howard Thurman was a man who lived in a swirling world—a world that did not want him to be educated, employed, or whole. Yet, he gathered the patches of his heritage and life experience and created a beautiful quilt that has inspired many others who are touched by his life and books. As a young man, Thurman lived close to the earth. He recognized that "the ocean and the river befriended me when I was a child," and the experience of raging storms provided "a certain overriding immunity against much of the pain with which I would have to deal in the years ahead."[21] Thurman's favorite oak tree had particularly inspired him. In storms, branches of the tree would fall, but the topmost branches simply swayed, "giving way just enough to save themselves from snapping loose."[22] This tree inspired Thurman's vision for his own future; he later said, "I needed the strength of that tree, and, like it, I wanted to hold my ground."[23] As an adult, Howard Thurman was indeed a man of strength like his beloved oak, and he was a man who had visions for the future of God's world.

Many years past childhood (at age forty-three), Howard Thurman and his wife, Sue, moved their family across the country from prestigious Howard University to a fledgling San Francisco congregation, calling itself the Church for the Fellowship of All Peoples. This church was committed to extending people's mutual understanding across nationality, culture, race, and creed, and to "seek after a vital experience of God as revealed in Jesus of Nazareth and other great religious spirits."[24] In this context, Thurman soon realized that the love he had experienced in his life "had to be communicated as a witness to the God in me and in our personal conduct as a witnessing congregation."[25] This led to other realizations, such as the need to ground goodwill in "a hard core of fact and understanding," which led him and his congregation away from sentimentality; they committed themselves to "thicken" their relationships.[26] This was done through Sunday lunches in different parts of the city, monthly intercultural dinners, an intercultural library collection, intercultural workshops for children, and other concrete acts of sharing through art, visitation, and special events.[27] In all of these actions, Thurman and his parishioners pointed to a new creation—a new way of being in an unjust world.

Julian of Norwich—Meditating on a saint of a long-ago time and place

Our second text comes from the life of another time and place. Julian of Norwich was an anchoress in the fourteenth century in central England. An anchoress is a woman who withdraws from the world, usually to a cell, to live in solitude, prayer, and mortification (deadening herself to things of the flesh through ascetic practices). A man who withdraws in such a way is called an anchorite.

Julian was an anchoress, living in a one-room cell in the wall of St. Julian's Church in Norwich, England (East Anglia). She took the name of the church, so we do not know her birth name. We do know that she was born in 1342, probably of an upper-class family, judging from her knowledge and ability to write. She was probably schooled in a Benedictine convent; at least, we know that St. Julian's church was connected with the Benedictine convent.

At about thirty years of age (May 8, 1373), Julian had a serious illness and experienced sixteen dramatic visions of God's love, which she called showings. She probably had not taken holy orders at this time, because she reports that her mother and parish priest were by her bed. The priest was prepared to administer last rites. She wrote the showings in brief form right away, and she wrote an expanded version 15–20 years later. *A Book of Showings* tells of her revelations and her theological reflections; they are also called *The Sixteen Revelations of Divine Love*.

Julian lived as an anchoress in one room, ten feet square. One window in her room faced the altar so she could participate in worship and receive communion through the church wall. Another window looked onto the road and perhaps a small garden. Through a third window, she interacted with servants, Sara and Alice, who shopped and carried on business for her. She could also interact with the world by watching people coming and going on the road and speaking to the many people who came to her window for counsel in this busy wool and market town.

Julian's times were turbulent. England had only recently unified after many years of fighting over the monarchy. England was still engaged in the Hundred Years' War with France, which began before Julian's birth in 1337 and ended after her death in 1453. The country also experienced the Peasants' Revolt in 1381, and three bubonic plagues occurred during her life. Further, the church was divided, with three people claiming the papacy. Julian's world was hazardous; yet she lived to be at least seventy-four, an age estimated from a record of her making a will in 1416.

From the patchwork of her world and her own life experience, Julian emerged with a vision of God's new creation—visions of God's love. That vision included a strong Trinitarian theology; she wrote repeatedly of Father, Son, and Spirit. Even more frequently, she described the Trinity as Maker, Keeper, and Lover, or as Father, Mother, and Spouse. Notice that she often related the mother image to Jesus. She said, for example, "The mother can give her child to suck of her milk, but our precious Mother Jesus can feed us with himself, and does, most courteously and most tenderly, with the blessed sacrament, which is the precious food of true life..."[28]

Another prominent theological theme for her is that God loves all of creation, even the smallest and most insignificant part. She writes of one of her visions in which she was holding something no bigger than a hazelnut: "In this little thing, I saw three properties. The first is that God made it, the second is that God loves it, the third is that God preserves it."[29] In short, Julian's theology was bodily, building upon her physical experience of the world. She was viewed with suspicion by church and theological leaders of her day, especially for being a woman who expressed herself freely. She herself protested when people tried to stop her from writing and offering counsel. She said, "Because I am a woman ought I therefore to believe that I should not tell you of the goodness of God, when I saw at the same time that it is [God's] will that it be known?"[30]

Now, we will enter meditation with Julian, so I invite you to pray with Julian. Take your symbol of God's dreams from the table and hold it while I read her words:

> And in this [God] showed me something small, no bigger than a hazelnut, lying in the palm of my hand, as it seemed to me, and it was as round as a ball. I looked at it with the eye of my understanding and thought: What can this be? I was amazed that it could last, for I thought that because of its littleness it would suddenly have fallen into nothing. And I was answered in my understanding: It lasts and always will, because God loves it; and thus everything has being through the love of God.

> In this little thing I saw three properties. The first is that God made it, the second is that God loves it, the third is that God preserves it. But what did I see in it? It is that God is the Creator and the protector and the lover.[31]

Julian's stories are stories of centering in a de-centered world—of knowing God, living radically, and writing boldly in a world that tried to suppress her. Her revelations from God guided her to imagine God's new creation. What she saw of God's love became the design of her quilt.

Reflection: What are some words that describe the design of God's new creation that Howard Thurman glimpsed? Julian of Norwich? What are some of the patches that each of them cut to help them live a life guided by that design?

Quiet Time: Imagining God's New Creation

In your quiet time in this next hour *(or whatever time is fitting in your particular retreat setting)*, imagine the creation that God is calling into being. I invite you to do two things. Meditate on pains of this world that trouble you, and meditate on the symbol of God's dreams that you selected earlier. Allow these to open you to what God is trying to reveal of God's new creation. Be aware that God often reveals a design for new creation through pain or through deep stirrings within the soul, whether those stirrings are questions, insights, aches, or celebrations. Before we come back together, return your symbol of hope to its home with a prayer of blessing.

Closing

Lay hands on each other, praying silently for the person whom you are blessing, and knowing that someone is praying for you at the same time. *(This can be done by asking people to stand in a circle, holding their right hands with the palms facing up and the left hands with the palms facing down. Then ask people to place their downward-facing palm on the upward-facing palm of their neighbor standing to the left. In this way, each person will be praying a blessing on the person to his or her left, while receiving a blessing from the person to his or her right. The retreat leader may close the silent prayer with a simple Amen. This approach to prayer is personal and, at the same time, respectful of persons who are nervous about too much touching.)*

SESSION III
CUTTING PATCHES—SQUARES, STRIPS, AND TRIANGLES

Our theme this session is cutting patches, preparing to make the design that we imagine. *(Note to leaders: This session can be combined with a discussion of chapter 3.)* Listen to the words of a Hawaiian quiltress, Pat Sims, as she explains, first, what quilting means to her:

> What has come over me? I'm all wrapped up in this art of Hawaiian quilt-making. It has taken over my mind, my time, and my energy. All in all, the whole experience is costing me my life![32]

The same person explained to a caller why Hawaiian quilts are so time-consuming and expensive:

> I explained that the flamboyant patterns are inspired from the beautiful nature here in Hawaii; the leaves, trees, flowers, and various other plant life. I told her of the long, tedious hours of basting the design to the background, the miles of intricate applique, and the months of quilting, all of it totaling 1–2 million stitches. I informed her of how the final dramatic design takes on a life of its own as it sits majestically on its background surrounded by the "ripple" quilting that depicts the waves of the ocean around the Hawaiian islands.[33]

Quilting is extravagant work—an appropriate image for spiritual life. Further, Hawaiian quilts are like Hawaiian volcanoes; they cannot be hurried. You can look across acres of black lava with cracks in it and realize that the lava took 1,000 years to develop those cracks, and then, when you see a few sprigs of grass, you realize that another 5,000 years passed before the grass grew. Creation takes a long time, and some work cannot be hurried. At the same time, one can participate fully in each moment of the process.

Note another aspect of Pat Sims's description, the way in which the designing and making of quilts is inspired by the natural world:

> Wherever I go on Maui, I watch the shadows of leaves and flowers that are cast on the ground hoping to get ideas for new quilt patterns...I feel the sway of palm fronds in the gentle trade breezes and, in turn, attempt to achieve that same rhythm with my quilts.[34]

With these reminders from a quiltress, we continue the inspiring, life-consuming, time-consuming, and rewarding art of making a spiritual life, turning *now to the act of cutting patches.*

The Act of Cutting Patches—Squares, Strips, and Triangles

How do people engage in the act of cutting squares, strips, and other shapes in the process of making a spiritual life? Let's begin with a very simple story, a parable.

A Parable

As people seek to relate to God and God's creation, they are faced repeatedly with parabolic stories and experiences—stories and experiences that turn ordinary ways of thinking about the world upside down. Consider the story in chapter 2 of this book about Rebecca and her snorkeling experience. *(This story, or another, could be told as a way of introducing the subversive action of parables.)*

Rebecca's story is parabolic because it turns the world upside down. It reminds us that no matter how careful we are, no matter how much we care for the world, we will always disturb and destroy it. Consider Rebecca's story as a prototype of what it means to cut patches for the quilts of our lives. We know that we cannot live our spiritual lives without affecting the world around us or even without causing some damage. Our challenge is to live with that vulnerability and to cut the fabrics we have gathered in the most responsible and caring way possible. Our challenge is to live with limitations and to contribute as much as possible to beauty, justice, and righteousness. Look at Rebecca's story. She rehearsed, expressed her lament for the coral and for her own carelessness, and then chose an action that seemed to her to be the best possible action for good in the situation. I suggest that she was cutting patches from her knowledge and experience. She was analyzing—cutting her heritage and life experience into pieces for the sake of reflection. She analyzed what she had been taught, what she had experienced, her remorse (or repentance), and then she made decisions about what she would do next to stitch the pieces together in a new way.

A Life of Cutting and Stitching—Julian of Norwich

Now, let's consider a particular spiritual life in which the cutting of patches is very clear. This is the life of Julian of Norwich, whom we considered earlier. Pause first to remember Julian and to call out images of her life that you recall…Now we can reflect on Julian's life as one of cutting and stitching.

Reflection: What are some words that describe the design of God's new creation that Julian of Norwich glimpsed? What are some squares and strips that she cut to help her live toward that design (e.g., living in a church cell)? How did she do her stitching?

A Communal Life of Cutting and Stitching

Consider the case study of Lahaina United Methodist Church, as told in chapter 6. Form yourselves into groups of 3–4 to read and reflect on the case. Consider the following questions: Which images of this church stand out for you? What words describe the vision of God's new creation that the Lahaina Church glimpses? What patches have the Lahaina people cut to help them live toward their vision?

Quiet time: Meditation on Cutting Shapes for Your Quilt

In eighteenth-century England, John Wesley initiated a ministry in small groups, or "classes." In these groups, people met to pray, sing, read scripture, and talk about their lives. The history of these classes is complex, with antecedents in other traditions, such as Puritan and Lutheran group meetings. For the sake of simplicity, we will draw from the tradition of Wesleyan class meetings to reflect on the kinds of cutting that help shape our spiritual lives. I invite you to reflect on the five questions below during your meditation time. The questions themselves are modified versions of Wesley's questions; his were expressed in eighteenth-century British language regarding the state of your soul. Also, the number of questions is larger than suggested for other sessions of this retreat because the cutting movement in making a quilt is a movement of cutting and analyzing.

1. What has been going on in your life in the past month?
2. What do you discern that God has been doing in your life during this time?
3. How have you been faithful to God?
4. How have you been unfaithful?
5. What do you discern that God is calling you to be and do now?

If you are moved to modify these questions, do so. If you are moved to draw or write or dance your responses, do so. Go into your quiet time with God's blessing. Amen.

Closing

What would you like to share that emerged for you during this quiet time? Feel free to share or not to share, depending on how you are moved…We will close with a robust THANK YOU, spoken three times with increasing volume and enthusiasm: Thank you, THANK YOU, *THANK YOU!* AMEN!

SESSION IV
STITCHING PATCHES TOGETHER

The theme for this session is stitching squares, strips, and patches together—stitching ourselves into a community and stitching the resources from our cultures and traditions into a new creation. One way of thinking about this is stitching ourselves together in such a way that we practice a just spirituality in a world of oppression, we practice spiritual community in a world shaped by individualism, and we practice harmony with all of God's creation. *(Note to leaders: This session can be combined with a discussion of chapter 4.)*

Steve Charleston, a Cherokee from Oklahoma, believes that his people have two Old Testaments—the Hebrew Bible and the ancient Native traditions. He also sees close ties between these two testaments. Whether or not you see your cultural and religious traditions as a second Old Testament, you can appreciate the kind of stitching that is necessary when people weave the traditions of their people together with the traditions of the early Hebrews and Christians. (See elaboration of this theme in chapter 4.)

Stitches that Bind

We bind with many kinds of stitches. We are bound, for example, by the liturgies of the church—the work of the people. Some liturgies have been passed down, and others arise spontaneously in different times and places. Worship means service to God, and the early uses of the word "worship" included service to God in daily life as well as in the gathered community. Thus, the stitches that bind are stitches that people sew when they gather for Sunday morning worship and other church activities, but also when they plant gardens, paint houses, lead meetings, mediate disputes, play with children, and so forth.

As a way of stitching ourselves together in this session, we will pray the Lord's Prayer with our words and bodies. Then in a time of quiet, I will share some prayers of the early Celtic Christians, who tried to weave their ancient Celtic traditions and closeness with the earth with their Christian traditions. In this circle of prayer, we will be stitching with our bodies and voices, and with voices of times and lands gone by.

The Lord's Prayer

Close your eyes and spread out so that you may move your bodies in prayer as you say the words. *(Note: This is spontaneous movement. No one will see what you do, so allow your movements to be a prayer and not a performance.)*

Celtic Prayers

Milking Croon[35]

Bless, O God, my little cow,
  Bless, O God, my desire;
Bless Thou my partnership
  And the milking of my hands, O God.

Bless, O God, each teat,
  Bless Thou each drop
  That goes into my pitcher, O God!

Loom Blessing[36]

(Note: A woman would hang her loom on Saturday night, placing a crucifix over it for protection. Columba was a Celtic saint.)

Bless, O Chief of generous chiefs,
My loom and everything a-near me,
Bless me in my every action,
Make Thou me safe while I live…

In name of Mary, mild of deeds,
In name of Columba, just and potent,
Consecrate the four posts of my loom
Till I begin on Monday...
Thus will my loom be unharmed,
Till I shall arise on Monday;
Beauteous Mary will give me of her love,
And there shall be no obstruction I shall not overcome.

I Lie Down This Night[37]

I lie down this night with God,
    And God will lie down with me;
I lie down this night with Christ,
    And Christ will lie down with me;
I lie down this night with Spirit,
    And the Spirit will lie down with me;
God and Christ and the Spirit
    Be lying down with me.

Celtic Christian people bound themselves with the ancient, nature-based religion of their people, but the Roman versions of Christianity, introduced alongside military settlement, became predominant. The Celtic prayers and spirituality were mostly lost before British and European peoples immigrated to what is now the United States and Canada. Perhaps the settlers' loss of relationship with their own indigenous ancestors made it more difficult for them to honor the indigenous peoples of North America.

The Act of Stitching Patches Together

A Communal Life of Cutting and Stitching—Lahaina Church

Now, we return to a story of a community's spiritual quilt-making. Consider again the Lahaina Church story. What patches have the people of that church cut for their communal quilt (recalling what we said in the last session)? Now, adding to what we said before, what kind of stitching have the people of Lahaina done?

A Small Act of Cutting and Stitching—A Sacramental Act

A few weeks ago, a young woman was traveling home on a mud-soaked, water-covered mountain road. She was headed down the mountain but had to turn around when the road washed out. Driving back up the mountain, she worried but proceeded with care. As she slowed at a curve, the car spun out of control, careened against the mountainside, and turned upside down. Slowly, the woman realized she was not injured, but she was hanging upside down in the protective grasp of her seat and shoulder belts.

Someone stopped and helped her from the car through a broken window. Another car arrived with a young family returning home from a mountain weekend; they stopped and offered aid. They waited with the frightened young woman for some time while the paramedics came and did their work, and then they offered to drive the young woman home, which, with the weather and washed-out roads, was to be a long drive. Further, the family lived nowhere near the young woman, and they had three young children to get home and settled into bed. They drove the girl home, however, and the next week, when the parents of the girl called to thank them again, the man of the family said, "We were happy to do it. We see that as what it means to be Christian. Besides, people have stopped for us before, and we *wanted* to do this for her." In this small act of cutting and stitching, a young family chose to stitch their past experiences with their basic faith commitments and to respond to an accident on the road. They were stitching patches together in an act of compassion—a sacramental act.

Quiet Time: Meditation on Stitching

In the quiet time now, meditate on the stitches that you sense God is calling you to make. Write, dance, draw, or empty yourself, as you feel called to do during the time of meditation.

Closing

What would you like to share that emerged for you during this quiet time? Feel free to share or not share, depending on how you are moved…We will close with the Lord's Prayer, praying with our words and bodies as before.

SESSION V

BASTING ON A BACKING AND STITCHING OUR LIVES WITH DESIGNS OF STRENGTH AND BEAUTY

We have two themes today as we near our close—basting on a backing and stitching our lives with quilting designs that give strength and beauty. These are the parts of quilt-making that take place when a quilt looks nearly finished. In life, of course, we never finish. We make new discoveries, return to issues that were once resolved, and meet new challenges. In responding to these experiences, we add refinements to our basic "quilts." These actions are the focus of the closing session. *(Note to leaders: This session can be combined with a discussion of chapters 5–7.)*

Basting on a Backing
Spiritual Disciplines as the Backing of the Quilt

Spiritual disciplines can be understood as the backing of our quilts—practices that add strength, stability, warmth, durability, and body. Today we will focus on one spiritual discipline—prayer—in order to reflect on the variety of backings that we can sew into our spiritual lives. Prayer is practiced in different ways in different situations and among different people. Just as a quilt may have a thick, warm backing for a cold climate, or a thin backing for a warm climate, so spirituality takes different forms in different situations. In fact, spirituality varies even within cultures and communities.

A Tongan student struggled to find a strong metaphor for God that would communicate with Tongan immigrant people; he concluded that God is like a can of coconut milk.[38] He explained that coconut is used by Tongans to prepare food; it adds nutritional value, brings out flavor in other foods, and so forth. Problems arise for Tongan people in California, who are removed from many of their natural experiences of spirituality and from their normal ways of living. One problem is that, when they run out of food, they cannot go onto the land and gather coconuts and other wonderful things. That is why Tongans living in the United States value a can of coconut milk; it nourishes and delights them. The can of coconut milk, then, is a strong metaphor of God for immigrant Tongans because it represents God as a presence, even far from home, and a source of nourishment and delight. Of course, canned coconut milk would have less meaning in Tonga itself where people have ready access to fresh coconut.

Similarly, prayers differ. Some people pray breath prayers on the run; others spend most of their day praying, like my friend, Aunt Dot. Aunt Dot had severe arthritis, reaching a point where she had to live in a hospital and have almost everything done for her. Aunt Dot had always been active in prayer, but when she reached the last months of her life, living in great pain, church members brought her a prayer list every day. She spent each day praying through the list. She told me one day when I was visiting that she had reached the time in her life when she could do nothing for herself or for anyone else, but she could still pray, and she prayed all day long.

Prayers also differ in terms of the flow of energy. Most commonly, some prayers are a flow of energy from us to God and from God back to a particular situation.

$$US \rightarrow GOD \rightarrow SITUATION$$

Other prayers are a flow of energy from us to God and back again, and the flow may move again from us into the world situation.

$$US \rightarrow GOD \rightarrow US \rightarrow SITUATION$$

Still other prayers are a flow of energy from the God within us to the God within others, like prayers I pray on an airplane, sending God's energy to the pilots.

$$US \leftrightarrow SITUATION$$
$$GOD$$

Of course, these various kinds of prayer are often combined as well.

Stitching Our Lives with Quilting Designs

Once the backing is basted onto a quilt, the actual quilting can begin. Quilting designs add strength and beauty, often catching some of the flow of life. As in Hawaiian quilts, they may reflect ocean waves, and they may be stitched with 1–2 million stitches. If people need a quilt quickly, however, they may simply tie the front to the backing in several places to hold it all together. What is important in this last step is that the quilt fit its purposes. The last step of quilting is intended to enhance the value of the quilt for the days, weeks, and years ahead.

We have talked a lot about God's future or God's new creation, but within that movement toward the future is a movement through cycles—day and night, Sunday through Saturday, spring through winter, birth to death. God is present not only in movements through history, but also in movements through these cycles of life. In such a world, God calls us to four responsibilities.

Keeping Sabbath

We begin by reflecting on the Hebrew tradition of keeping Sabbath. Let's read together from Exodus:

> For six years you shall sow your land and gather in its yield; but the seventh year you shall let it rest and lie fallow, so that the poor of your people may eat; and what they leave the wild animals may eat. You shall do the same with your vineyard, and with your olive orchard.
>
> Six days you shall do your work, but on the seventh day you shall rest, so that your ox and your donkey may have relief, and your homeborn slave and the resident alien may be refreshed. Be attentive to all that I have said to you. Do not invoke the names of other gods; do not let them be heard on your lips. (Ex. 23:10–13)

A time of Sabbath is a gift—a gift to the land, to the animals, and to the people. Repeatedly in the Hebrew Bible, the Sabbath tradition is described as a gift of God. To keep Sabbath, then, is to care for God's gift. The Sabbath is a day of celebration—a time of thanksgiving. As such, it is a day of pause to be attuned to the wonders of creation and the Creator. It is both a day of mourning to grieve the destruction of the world and a day of hoping for God's new creation. Further, it is a day of renewal, preparing people to participate in the cycle of another week. The seventh year is also a Sabbath—a year to let the land lie fallow and a year to forgive debts. The forty-ninth year (seven times seven)—the Year of Jubilee—is to be grander still. Jim Strathdee captures the spirit of Jubilee in his song:

> Once in ev'ry fifty year cycle,
> There must be a time of liberty,
> Slaves are released and their land is returned with the trumpets sounding
> JUBILEE! Let the slave and the captive go free

JUBILEE! Save the land and return it to me
JUBILEE! Let people stand in their dignity
In the year of God's Jubilee.[39]

When Maria Harris describes Jubilee, she argues that whether or not the Hebrews actually celebrated Jubilee is not the main issue; the vision itself kept
Jubilee values and challenges before them.

Tending Cycles

God calls us not only to contribute to the future but also to tend the cycles
of life. Our daughter, Rebecca, is great with plants because she tends them
day after day, and of course, she talks to them. She advised one of her Garden
Shop customers, a woman discouraged with her dying plants, that she could
try talking to her plants. Rebecca added, "It is really nice to talk to your plants
because they don't talk back."

Tending cycles is tending the daily routine, but it is also being open to
new seasons in your life or your family's life or your work. It is attuning to
seasons of the earth, to seasons of the church year, to movements of God in
your life. Dan Wakefield tells a story of Henri Nouwen in which a woman
expressed to Nouwen her anger at the church. Nouwen responded:

> All that is distraction…I don't mean to denigrate or even dispute your
> complaints, but those are beside the point. The only thing that really
> matters is your relationship with Jesus—I mean a personal relation-
> ship with the mystical Jesus.[40]

Seeing the woman's confusion, Wakefield asked Henri how a person re-
lates with the mystical Jesus. Nouwen responded:

> Just give me ten minutes a day…No—*five* minutes! Just take five min-
> utes a day, every day for two weeks, to sit quietly and ask to be with
> Jesus, ask for his presence. And then come and tell me what's
> important![41]

I am not suggesting that we would all agree with Nouwen's theological view
or his reflection on this woman's criticisms of the church, but he puts forth the
strong value of tending to the cycles of our spiritual lives—"Just take five
minutes a day."

Nouwen was also concerned with the cycles of human community, as
was very evident in the stories of his last years in the Daybreak community of
mentally handicapped adults, a part of L'Arche in Toronto, Canada. Nouwen
visited Trevor, one of the Daybreak members who had been admitted to a
mental hospital. When the hospital heard that this famous man was coming,
they invited him to a special luncheon. When Nouwen learned that Trevor
could not attend this luncheon because of a regulation against patients eating
with staff, he said that he would not join the lunch if Trevor could not be there;
the purpose of his visit was to see Trevor. The staff agreed, with some reluctance. As the story goes, "It was Trevor who broke the ice on this frosty occasion

by offering a toast with his Coke."[42] All of this took place in the Golden Room, where no patient had ever been admitted before. Nouwen was tending cycles of human community. In this same tradition, the eucharist at Henri's funeral mass was ecumenical, and despite the resistance of the church, no limitation was made to limit the receiving of bread and wine to "Catholics only." God calls people to tend to the cycles of life, and every part of it.

Engaging in Transformative Politics

We are called to act not only as individuals but also as communities. Read chapter 7 of *Ministering with the Earth,* and focus particularly on the four kinds of politics identified there—politics of suspicion, politics of grace, politics of future, and politics of friendship, advocacy, and solidarity. Spend time in silence remembering a moment when you experienced one or more of these…In small groups (about four), share some of those memories and reflect on what emerged from the various political practices in your communities…In the same groups, reflect on the kind of politics that is most needed in your communities in the future. You may choose one of the four in the book, or identify another. Sketch a picture of how that would look and help one another to develop the ideas and images…Pray in silence with one another as you close your circle.

What insights do you have for the practice of politics in your communities? What commitments do you take home?

Practicing Stewardship with Creation

We have been living as a covenant community throughout this retreat—called, led, and held responsible by God. Keeping covenant has to do with recognizing God, who calls us into being. Keeping covenant has to do with following wherever God leads. Keeping covenant has to do with caring for the bonds of human community and the bonds of God's creation. What kind of covenant is called forth in the Exodus 23 text? Covenant is with the land, the poor, wild animals, vineyards and olive orchards, oxes and donkeys, slaves and resident aliens *(see chapter 7)*. Covenant is with God—"Do not invoke the names of other gods."

Practicing stewardship has to do with keeping covenant. It is living with God and all of creation in such a way that every square of our quilt is valued. It is living in such a way that the pieces are stitched into a beautiful whole. It is living with the understanding that the pieces scattered are nothing but pieces, but when God calls us together, we can be whole, we can be just, we can spread love, we can be beautiful! May it be so!

Closing

The last step in making a quilt is signing your name. *(Close with a ritual of commitment that is created by the group and gives people an opportunity to sign their names to the blessings and commitments that they carry as they depart.)*

Notes

PROLOGUE

[1]Some striking examples of theological works do hold together the fullness of issues. See Leonardo Boff, *Ecology and Liberation: A New Paradigm* (Maryknoll, N.Y.: Orbis, 1995); Sean McDonough, *Passion for the Earth: The Christian Vocation to Promote Justice, Peace, and the Integrity of the Earth* (Maryknoll, N.Y.: Orbis, 1994); Shamara Shantu Riley, "Ecology Is a Sistah's Issue Too: The Politics of Emergent Afrocentric Ecowomanism," in *Ecofeminism and the Sacred*, ed. Carol J. Adams (New York: Continuum, 1994), 191-204; Dieter T. Hessel, ed., *After Nature's Revolt: Eco-Justice and Theology* (Minnesota: Fortress, 1992). In the last collection, see particularly H. Paul Santmire, "Healing the Protestant Mind: Beyond the Theology of Human Dominion," 57–78, esp., 60–5, 72–4; and George E. Tinker, "Creation as Kin: An American Indian View," 144–53.

[2]Sallie McFague, *Metaphorical Theology: Models of God in Religious Language* (Philadelphia: Fortress, 1982); *Models of God: Theology for an Ecological, Nuclear Age* (Philadelphia: Fortress, 1987); *The Body of God: An Ecological Theology* (Minneapolis: Fortress, 1993).

[3]Catherine E. Keller, *From a Broken Web: Sexism, Separation, and Self* (Boston: Beacon, 1986).

[4]Rosemary Radford Ruether, *New Woman, New Earth: Sexist Ideologies and Human Liberation* (New York: Seabury, 1975), 200–1; Ruether, *Gaia and God: An Ecofeminist Theology of Earth Healing* (San Francisco: Harper, 1992). The particularities of Ruether's action interests are visible in her own practices as well as in her writing.

[5]Hessel, 8–10, 17–18.

[6]Riley, "Ecology Is a Sistah's Issue Too"; Delores S. Williams, "Sin, Nature, and Black Women's Bodies," in *Ecofeminism and the Sacred*, 24–29.

CHAPTER ONE

[1]A fuller description of this church is offered in: Charles R. Foster and Theodore Brelsford, *We Are the Church Together: Cultural Diversity in Congregational Life* (Valley Forge, Pa.: Trinity, 1996).

[2]The terms "God-centered" and "earthbound" suggest that the ministry is inspired and guided by God, and attuned and responsive to God's creation. Larry Rasmussen identifies Martin Luther's theology as "earthbound," in the sense of recognizing God *in* the creation (pan*en*theism). See Larry Rasmussen, "Returning to our Senses: The Theology of the Cross as a Theology for Eco-Justice," in Dieter T. Hessel, ed., *After Nature's Revolt: Eco-Justice and Theology* (Minneapolis: Fortress, 1992), 42.

[3]This movement is complex, but Judith Plaskow's summary makes direct connections with eco-justice; Plaskow, "Feminist Judaism and Repair of the World," in Carol J. Adams, ed., *Ecofeminism and the Sacred* (New York: Continuum, 1994), 70–83, esp. 74–5.

[4]Gregory A. Cajete, *Look to the Mountain: An Ecology of Indigenous Education* (Durango, Colo.: Kivaki Press, 1994), 46.

[5]Ibid., 46–49.

[6]Selections from Mary Elizabeth Mullino Moore, "Puff of Wind," June 1995, based on Ecclesiastes 1.

[7]The author of Ecclesiastes, named by commentators as Qohelet, used the Hebrew word *hebel*, which is translated in the poem as "puff of wind," but can also be translated as "breath," "vanity," "worthlessness" and so forth. Seemingly, the rhythmic cycles of earth do suggest passing time to Qohelet, but whether his view of passing time is interpreted as acceptance, vanity, or worthlessness, depends upon which meaning of the Hebrew word is emphasized by translators.

[8]Thomas Berry, "The New Story: Comments on the Origin, Identification, and Transmission of Values," *Cross Currents* (Summer/Fall 1987) 187. Berry discusses this new story against the background of critiquing "the mythic power of the industrial vision" (184).

[9]Thomas Berry, "The Dream of the Earth: Our Way into the Future," ibid., 200. Brian Swimme, speaking as a scientist, sees Berry's contribution as providing "a functional cosmology that will

enable the human community to organize itself in a way aimed at planetary health"; Swimme, "Berry's Cosmology," ibid., 218.

[10]See, for example Nigel Calder, *The Key to the Universe: A Report on the New Physics* (New York: Viking, 1977), 181–185; Steven Weinberg, *The First Three Minutes* (New York: Basic Books, 1977); and John Boslough, Stephen L. Hawking, *A Brief History of Time: From the Big Bang to Black Holes* (New Yrok: Bantam Books, 1990).

[11]Rosemary Radford Ruether, *Gaia and God: An Ecofeminist Theology of Earth Healing* (San Francisco: Harper, 1992), 57.

[12]Ibid.

[13]Berry, "The New Story," 193.

[14]Ruether, 48; cf: 40–41. The exceptions would be the older hydrogen and helium atoms.

[15]Ibid.

[16]Ibid.

[17]James A. Nash, *Loving Nature: Ecological Integrity and Christian Responsibility* (Nashville: Abingdon, in cooperation with The Churches' Center for Theology and Public Policy, Washington, D.C., 1991), 23.

[18]Ibid.

[19]Leonard Weber, "Land Use Ethics: The Social Responsibility of Ownership," in Bernard F. Evans and Gregory D. Cusack, eds., *Theology of the Land* (Collegeville, Minn.: The Liturgical Press, 1987), 13–39. Wendell Berry describes the ecological crisis as a crisis of character and the agricultural crisis as a crisis of culture; Berry, *The Unsettling of America: Culture and Agriculture* (San Francisco: Sierra Club, 1996, 1986, 1977), esp. 3–26, 39–48.

[20]C. Dean Freudenberger, "Implications of a New Land Ethic," in *Theology of the Land*, 69–84; *Global Dust Bowl* (Minneapolis: Augsburg, 1990); *Food for Tomorrow?* (Minneapolis: Augsburg, 1984); Wendell Berry, *The Gift of Good Land: Further Essays Cultural & Agricultural* (San Francisco: North Point, 1981); *The Unsettling of America*.

[21]Cheryl Simon Silver, with Ruth S. DeFries, *One Earth, One Future: Our Changing Global Environment* (Washington, D.C.: National Academy Press, 1990). Silver and DeFries draw from the Forum on Global Change and Our Common Future in which scientists came together to explore a range of problems for purposes of analyzing and projecting futures. Problems analyzed included global warming; food, water, and changing climate; coastlines and rising seas; the ozone layer and ultraviolet radiation; vanishing forests and vanishing species; and lakes, forests, and acid deposition.

[22]Ibid., 16; Gro Harlem Brundtland, "Global Change and Our Common Future;" Afterword of Silver and DeFries, *One Earth One Future*, 149.

[23]Charles Birch and John B. Cobb, Jr., *The Liberation of Life: From the Cell to the Community* (Cambridge: Cambridge University, 1981); Jay B. McDaniel, *With Roots and Wings: Christianity in an Age of Ecology and Dialogue* (Maryknoll, N.Y.: Orbis, 1995); *Earth, Sky, Gods and Mortals: Developing an Ecological Spirituality* (Mystic, Conn.: Twenty-Third Publications, 1990); *Of God and Pelicans: A Theology of Reverence for Life* (Louisville: Westminster/John Knox Press 1989). Kenneth Leech focuses on human justice, and his understanding of spiritual deficiency requires judgment, prophecy, redemption, and struggle, as well as attunement; Leech, *The Eye of the Storm: Spiritual Resources for the Pursuit of Justice* (London: Darton, Longman and Todd, 1992), 140–199, esp. 152–3.

[24]Linda Filippi, "Place, Feminism, and Healing: An Ecology of Pastoral Counseling," *The Journal of Pastoral Care*, vol. 45, no. 3 (Fall 1991), 242, cf: 231–242. See also: Filippi, "Of Sweet Grapes, Wheat Berries, and Simple Meeting: Feminist Theology, Gestalt Therapy, Pastoral Counseling and The Earth," (Ph.D. Diss.. Claremont School of Theology, 1990). Howard Clinebell builds on similar ideas; Clinebell, *Ecotherapy: Healing Ourselves, Healing the Earth* (Minneapolis: Fortress, 1996).

[25]John B. Cobb, Jr., "Postmodern Christianity in Quest of Eco-Justice," in *After Nature's Revolt*, 27–30. This concern leads Cobb to recognize limitations in terms such as eco-justice and sustainability, which continue the anthropomorphic and dualistic tendencies even while trying to overcome them. The terms still imply the care of earth for the sake of human justice and well-being.

[26]Peter Mwiti Rukungah, "The Cosmocentric Model of Pastoral Psychotherapy: A

Contextualized Holistic Model from a Bantu African Worldview,"(Ph.D. Diss., Claremont School of Theology, 1994).

[27]C. Dean Freudenberger, "Managing the Land and Water," in Charles P. Lutz, ed., *Farming the Lord's Land: Christian Perspectives on American Agriculture* (Minneapolis: Augsburg, 1980), 123–45; *Food for Tomorrow?*; "Value and Ethical Dimensions of Alternative Agricultural Approaches: In Quest of a Regenerative and Just Agriculture," in Kenneth A. Dahlberg, ed., *New Directions for Agriculture and Agricultural Research: Neglected Dimensions and Emerging Alternatives* (Totowa, N.J.: Rowman & Allanheld, 1986), 348–64; *Global Dust Bowl*.

[28]This last point was made in a presentation of the Claremont seminar group who attended the Summit: Convocation on the Earth Summit, Claremont School of Theology, 15 September 1992. Team members were Frank Rogers, George Lakes, Boyung Lee, Michael Wallace, and Grace Newkirk.

[29]For a discussion of several religious traditions in relation to ecological perspectives, see Mary Evelyn Tucker and John A. Grim, eds., *Worldviews and Ecology: Religion, Philosophy, and the Environment* (Maryknoll, N.Y.: Orbis, 1994).

[30]Alfonso Ortiz, words spoken from San Juan Pueblo, 1972, quoted in Cajete, *Look to the Mountain*, 5.

[31]Ibid.

[32]Chapters 2–3 and 5–6 began as presentations for a National Council of Churches of Christ conference with leaders in camping and outdoor ministries. The conference (September 1989) was a look forward to the year 2000 with the theme "Sow Seeds: Trust the Promise."

CHAPTER TWO

[1]This particular language is mine. John Day argues that the God-human relationship of the psalms could be called mystical in the sense of "intimate fellowship and communion with God," but not in the sense of "absorption into the deity." See: Day, *Psalms* (Sheffield, England: Sheffield Academic Press, 1992), 128; cf: Hendrikus J. Franken, *The Mystical Communion with YHWH in the Book of Psalms* (Leiden: Brill, 1954). In seeking to understand the forms and functions of psalms in the Hebrew community, I deviate from strictly form-critical study and follow in the tradition of Patrick D. Miller, Jr.; Miller, *Interpreting the Psalms* (Philadelphia: Fortress, 1986), 3–11. Miller argues that the Psalms are not best understood in relation to particular contexts and authors, but as poetry which is open and metaphorical, thus speaking from and to multiple contexts (29–47, 51–2).

[2]Eric Katz, "Judaism and the Ecological Crisis," in Mary Evelyn Tucker and John A. Grim, eds., *Worldviews and Ecology: Religion, Philosophy, and the Environment* (Maryknoll, N.Y.: Orbis, 1994), 55–70; cf: Robert Gordis, "Ecology and the Jewish Tradition," in Marc Swetlitz, ed., *Judaism and Ecology, 1970–1986: A Sourcebook of Readings* (Wyncote, Pa.: Shomrei Adamah, 1990), 47–52. Both Katz and Gordis do textual analysis to communicate this point. For example, the fundamental theocentric ideas that God owns the earth and that human beings are to be responsible and caring stewards are reiterated in creation stories, Sabbath and Jubilee traditions, rabbinic teachings and so forth (Katz, 55–60). Further, specific laws govern the respectful, conserving, and longterm care that human beings are expected to offer for the well-being of the earth and the plants and animals that inhabit it (Ibid., 60–67).

[3]Other psalms also focus on Mt. Zion and the temple, such as 46; 48; 76; 84; 87; and 122.

[4]Day, 43, 61–64.

[5]Day, 88. Day describes this as an "irreducible minimum" list, as identified by H. Gunkel.

[6]The actual laments are listed differently by various scholars, but the presence of both communal and personal laments is widely acknowledged. The listing here is drawn from Day, 19–38, esp. 19 and 33. An alternate list is found in W. H. Bellinger, Jr., *Palmsody and Prophecy* (Sheffield, England: Journal for the Study of the Old Testament, Supplement Series 27, 1984), 32–77. Bellinger lists the individual laments as Psalm 6–7; 9–10; 28; 31; 36; 55; 57; and 64. He lists community laments as Psalms 12; 14; 60; 85; and 126.

[7]Day, 40; Walter Brueggemann, *Israel's Praise: Doxology—against Idolatry and Ideology* (Philadelphia: Fortress, 1988), 1. Day identifies this multidimensional theme in Psalms 19:1–4; 96:11–12; 98:7–8; and 148:3–11).

[8]Rolf P. Knierim, *The Task of Old Testament Theology* (Grand Rapids, Mich.: William B. Eerdmans, 1995), 322–50.

[9]Ibid., 342–45. Many passages in Proverbs also indicate that creation is founded in Torah or Wisdom; thus Torah can be learned by observing the world (e.g. Proverbs 8).

[10]Walter Brueggemann, *Israel's Praise*. This is the thesis of Brueggemann's book, and he elaborates it thusly: "'World-making' is done by God. That is foundational to Israel's faith. But it is done through human activity which God has authorized and in which God is known to be present" (11). See also: Miller, 70–76.

[11]Rolf P. Knierim, "On the Old Testament's or TaNaK's Spirituality of Human Existence," *HUMANITIES Christianity and Culture*, 27 (Dec. 1995), 20. Focusing particularly on verses 1–18, he marks that the psalmist is "totally guided by the awareness of the totality of the world . . . and by the equal awareness of the hidden presence of God in this totality." See also Knierim, *The Task*, 269–97.

[12]Ibid., 20–21.

[13]E. M. Blaiklock and A. C. Keys, trans., *The Little Flowers of St. Francis: The Acts of St. Francis and His Companions* (London: Hodder and Stoughton, 1985), 55. The book was originally written after the death of Francis by Brother Ugolino da Monte Santa Maria and unnamed others. Other stories tell of Francis' liberating some turtle doves (73) and his preaching to fish (122–124).

[14]For detailed analyses of these Genesis texts, see Walter Brueggemann, *Genesis: Interpretation* (Atlanta: John Knox Press, 1982); Conrad Hyers, *The Meaning of Creation: Genesis and Modern Science* (Atlanta: John Knox Press, 1984); Phyllis Trible, *God and the Rhetoric of Sexuality* (Philadelphia: Fortress, 1978); Claus Westermann, *Genesis 1–11: A Commentary*, trans. John J. Scullion, S.J. (Minneapolis: Augsburg, 1984).

[15]Knierim, *The Task*, 171–224. Knierim recognizes a fundamental theme in the Hebrew Bible that is often neglected by interpreters, namely, that cosmic space and historical time are intertwined; in fact, the act of creation described in Genesis 1 is the beginning of cosmic time as well as human history (193). Israel's worldview was not only historical and human, but it also described a close relationship between God and the earth, and a cyclic quality of time; such a view is not surprising for an agrarian people (176). The Hebrews understood cosmic time as cyclic, with historical dimensions, and they understood human history as historical, with cyclic dimensions (185–98). The important points here are the intertwining of cosmic story with human history, and the interweaving of cyclic with historic (linear) time.

[16]Deacon Boniface Perdjert, "Through Aboriginal Eyes," *Poverty Watch* (October 1993) 3.

[17]Sani Tavita Vaeluaga, conversation, Trinity Theological College, Auckland, New Zealand, 29 May 1994.

[18]Hans Küng and Karl-Josef Kuschel, *A Global Ethic: The Declaration of the Parliament of World Religions* (London: SCM, 1993), 13. The quote is from the abridged version of "The Principles of a Global Ethic"; the summary was read aloud in the closing plenary of the Parliament and used in public communication. The emphases are original.

[19]For a detailed discussion of the relationship between energy systems and social policies in diverse parts of the world, see Michael Grubb, Peter Brackley, Michèle Ledic, Ajay Mathur, Steve Rayner, Jeremy Russell, Akira Tanabe, *Energy Policies and the Greenhouse Effect, Volume Two: Country Studies and Technical Options* (Dartmouth, England: Royal Institute of International Affairs, 1991). For a popular discussion of the sun's warming, see Gregg Easterbrook, "Brighter Sun Warms Greenhouse Debate," *U.S. News and World Report*, vol. 123, no. 13 (6 Oct. 1997), 34. For discussions of economic debates, see John Carey, with Catherine Arnst, "Greenhouse Gases: The Cost of Cutting Back," *Business Week* (8 December 1997) 64–66; Exxon Corporation, "The Global Debate Over Global Warming: Uncertain Science, Real Costs," *Exxon Special Report* (December 1997). For a discussion of politics in relation to cultural construction and learning, see: Markus Jachtenfuchs, *International Policy-Making as a Learning Process? The European Union and the Greenhouse Effect* (Aldershot, England: Ashgate Publishing Co., 1996), esp. 16–41.

[20]James A. Nash, *Loving Nature: Ecological Integrity and Christian Responsibility* (Nashville: Abingdon, in cooperation with The Churches' Center for Theology and Public Policy, Washington, D. C., 1991), 33; cf: World Commission on Environment and Development, *Our Common Future* (Oxford: Oxford University, 1987), 176.

[21]Nash, 33.

[22]Ibid., 32.

[23]Ibid., 35. See also World Commission on Environment and Development, 178; Cheryl Simon Silver with Ruth S. DeFries for the National Academy of Sciences, *One Earth, One Future: Our Changing Global Environment* (Washington, D. C.: National Academy, 1990), 63–102.

[24]This idea is likewise developed by Nash, 37; Herman E. Daly and John B. Cobb, Jr., *For the Common Good: Redirecting the Economy toward Community, the Environment, and a Sustainable Future.* (Boston: Beacon, 1989), 361–381; C. Dean Freudenberger, *Global Dust Bowl* (Minneapolis: Augsburg, 1990); Larry L. Rasmussen, "The Planetary Environment: Challenge on Every Front," *Theology and Public Policy*, vol. 2, no. 1 (Summer 1990), 5–8.

[25]Larry Rasmussen, "Returning to our Senses: The Theology of the Cross as a Theology For Eco-Justice," in Dieter T. Hessel, ed., *After Nature's Revolt: Eco-Justice and Theology* (Minneapolis: Fortress, 1992), 50–54. Rasmussen identities mastery as "the master image in the West since the Enlightenment" (51), and he warns against the temptation of "assimilating the ethos of modernity" and identifying mastery as "the supreme human vocation" (53). Rasmussen, instead, is calling for a theology of the cross, which demands a practice of humility.

[26]Jake Statham, with Robert Houston, "Malaysia: Eco-Tourism—In Shades of Green," *Action Asia Magazine* (April/May 1994) 106.

[27]Ibid.

[28]Ibid.

[29]Ibid.

[30]Ibid., 110, 111.

[31]Ibid., 109.

[32]Ibid., 111.

[33]Eugene Linden, "Ancient Creatures in a Lost World" *Time,* (20 June 1994), 48. According to Linden, these discoveries are particularly noteworthy because they are not common in the twentieth century. He notes that "only three other new genuses have been documented in this century" (ibid.).

[34]Ibid., 49.

[35]H. Paul Santmire, "Healing the Protestant Mind: Beyond the Theology of Human Dominion," in *After Nature's Revolt*, 75; cf: 57, 61–65, 74–77. Santmire identifies the theme of human dominion as tied to the "the anthropological" focus of Luther and Calvin, the focus on God and humanity and their relationship. In this view, the relationship between God and the rest of nature is underplayed and the ideas of dominion and stewardship become distorted into domination. One particular expression of the problem is Karl Barth's reservation of I-Thou relationships to authentic human relationships, leaving only the option of I-It relationships between humans and the rest of nature (63–64). Santmire proposes, instead, a contemplative and cooperative relationship between human beings and nature, a relationship that he designates as I-Ens (75–76). See also Paul Santmire, *The Travail of Nature: The Ambiguous Ecological Promise of Christian Theology* (Philadelphia: Fortress, 1985).

[36]Dieter T. Hessel, "Eco-Justice Theology after Nature's Revolt," in *After Nature's Revolt*, 12. See also: Sean McDonagh, *The Greening of the Church* (Maryknoll, N.Y.: Orbis, 1990). Hessel's proposal is compatible with McDonagh's interpretation of stewardship as "standing before God in a posture of worship and joyfully accepting responsibility for the management of human affairs and well-being of creation" (McDonagh, 119). McDonagh adds that the biblical view presupposes an interrelated and interdependent world with God-given laws that people need to understand and follow (Ibid., 119–120). Thus, Hessel's idea of stewardship that is guided from below, from abroad, and from nature would be compatible with the spirit of the biblical texts.

[37]Anand Veeraraj, "God is Green," (unpublished essay, Bangalore, India, January 1988).

[38]Nash, 45.

[39]Ibid., 47.

[40]Ibid.

[41]Ibid., 50–51; cf: 52–53.

[42]This point has been emphasized and developed by many people, though full consciousness still dawns slowly. For helpful discussions, see Cobb and Daly, *For the Common Good* ; Carol

Johnston, "Economics, Eco-Justice, and the Doctrine of God," in *After Nature's Revolt*, 154–170; Heidi Hadsell, "Eco-Justice and Liberation Theology: The Priority of Human Well-Being," in *After Nature's Revolt*, 79–88; Sean McDonagh, *Passion for the Earth: The Christian Vocation to Promote Justice, Peace, and the Integrity of the Earth* (Maryknoll, N.Y.: Orbis, 1994).

   [43]Some stories of the Philippines are told by Sean McDonagh, *Greening*, 82–84; cf: 74–93.

   [44]Carol Johnston, 161, cf: 159–164. According to Johnston, such a system would be based on a recognition of internal relationships and the intrinsic value of all entities. She says, "Instead of more crisis management and more distribution, we need inclusive participation and power sharing based on the recognition of the inherent relatedness of every entity and on intrinsic value" (161). She refers to Genesis 1 as a biblical testimony to the inherent goodness of creation, which God recognized when "God saw that it was good" (161–162).

   [45]McDonagh, *Greening*, 96.

   [46]Ibid., 9–106. At the time of writing, McDonagh had worked for twenty years with tribal peoples in the Philippines. He identified the problems facing these people as a warning sign to the rest of the world: "a kind of microcosm of the problems facing other Third World people, the rest of humanity and the earth itself" (3). The very vulnerability of these people makes them more easily affected by the problems, but the problems will eventually be felt by all. McDonagh likens the warnings of tribal people to the warnings of canaries in nineteenth-century mining operations; the canaries were so sensitive to the toxic gases in mines that their illness was taken as a warning that miners needed to evacuate (3). The devastating experiences of tribal people today are warning signals, and one cannot listen seriously without recognizing how all of the issues are intertwined. See also McDonagh, *Passion for the Earth*.

   [47]Carol Johnston, 154–70. Johnston gives particular attention to internal relations; she critiques atomistic, individualistic worldviews that focus solely on external relations.

   [48]Knierim, *The Task*, 171–243; Dieter Hessel, 10–14; John Cobb, 21–7. Appropriating the biblical work to theology, Hessel identifies major ecojustice themes, and emphasizes that biblical thought does not generally pose an "either/or choice between caring for people and caring for the earth" (11). Similarly, Cobb asserts that biblical thought is not anthropocentric, individualistic, or dualistic" (27); in short, he finds the spirit of the Bible closer to postmodern thinking than to modernism.

   [49]Nash, 97.

   [50]Ibid., 98–100. This theme is echoed in Carol Johnston (161–62).

   [51]Rosemary Radford Ruether, *Gaia and God: An Ecofeminist Theology of Earth Healing* (San Francisco: Harper, 1992), 19–22. The connections to Egyptian creation stories may actually be closer, especially in relation to gods' speaking things into being.

   [52]Heinrich Bornkamm, *Luther's World of Thought* (St. Louis: Concordia, 1958), 189, quoting from the original in Martin Luther, *Dass diese Worte Christi . . .* (1527).

   [53]Rasmussen, "Returning to our Senses," 42–43.

   [54]Ibid., 40–46.

   [55]John Paul Heil, *Jesus Walking on the Sea: Meaning and Gospel Functions of Matthew 14:22–33, Mark 6:45–52 and John 6:15b–21* (Rome: Biblical Institute Press, 1981), 68–69.

   [56]David Bruce Taylor, *Mark's Gospel as Literature and History* (London: SCM, 1992), 170–73; D. E. Nineham, *Saint Mark* (Philadelphia: Westminster, 1977, 1963), 177–85, 205–59; John Bowman, *The Gospel of Mark: The New Christian Jewish Passover Haggadah* (Leiden: E. J. Brill, 1965), 155–59, 174–78.

   [57]Ibid. Taylor, Nineham, and Bowman all combine an emphasis on the glory of Jesus' miracles and the foreshadowing of the early church's eucharistic practice, associated also with Jesus' last supper.

   [58]Robert M. Fowler, *Loaves and Fishes: The Function of the Feeding Stories in the Gospel of Mark* (Chico, Calif.: Scholars Press, for Society of Biblical Literature, 1981), 91–148. See also Vernon Robbins, "Last Meal: Preparation, Betrayal and Absence (Mark 14:12–25)," in *The Passion in Mark*, ed. Werner H. Kelber (Philadelphia: Fortress, 1976), 21–40. For Fowler, the stupidity of the disciples suggests that the perceived success of their earlier missionary journey is discounted. He even sees some evidence in the first feeding story that the disciples were carrying contraband

money and food that Jesus had earlier instructed them not to bring (116–8). Fowler argues that the obtuseness of the disciples, and not a eucharistic theme (which requires a backward reading), is Mark's concern (134–46). Thus, if one reads the story of the last meal in light of the earlier feeding stories (a forward reading), the disciples' failure "assumes shocking proportions" (135). See also Burton L. Mack, *A Myth of Innocence: Mark and Christian Origins* (Philadelphia: Fortress, 1988), 230–2. Mack also questions eucharistic allusions and emphasizes Mark's miracle chains with the corresponding non-comprehension of the disciples (216–19).

[59]Heil, 118, cf: 118–44, 172–3. Heil sees the feeding stories as confirming these themes in Mark's sea-walking story, and he sees many correspondences with themes in Matthew and John. In Matthew the disciples are afraid they are seeing a ghost, but later when everyone is safely in the boat, the disciples proclaim "Truly you are the Son of God" (14:33b). Heil does not emphasize the disciples' ineptness as much as some interpreters do. He accents their privileged position in having Jesus explain everything to them, emphasizing the extraordinary significance of Jesus by pointing out the disciples' lack of comprehension, a situation that would shift later in the Gospel (123–27, 130–44).

[60]Hugh Anderson explains that the disciples' inability to understand will finally be eradicated by Jesus as the Messianic secret is unfolded, beginning with v. 8:31; Anderson, *The Gospel of Mark* (London: Marshall, Morgan and Scott, 1976), 194–202. See also Nineham, 181–82, 212–15.

[61]Santmire, "Healing," 57, 61–65.

[62]Knierim, *The Task*, 225–43.

[63]See, for example, Heil, 8–12, 17. The heightened attention to Jesus and Jesus' power over the forces of the sea is visible also in the biblical accounts, particularly in Matthew's sea-walking story in which Peter's failed attempt to walk on the sea turns attention more strongly to Jesus' power *over* the sea. Such interpretations, both inside the texts and outside them, emphasize what Paul Santmire identifies as the dominant spiritual motif in Christian theology, based on a metaphor of ascent. The alternative interpretations offered here have potential to highlight what Santmire calls the ecological motif, based on metaphors of fecundity and migration to a good land (See: Santmire, "Healing," 67–68).

[64]Clarence J. Glacken, *Traces on the Rhodian Shore: Nature and Culture in Western Thought from Ancient Times to the End of the Eighteenth Century* (Berkeley: University of California, 1967), 338–39, cf: 330–41; cited partially in Rasmussen, "Returning to our Senses," 40.

[65]Piero Bargellini, *The Little Flowers of Saint Clare*, trans. Edmund O'Gorman (Padua, Italy: Messaggero Editions, 1993), 74, cf: 70–74. St. Clare was foundress of the Poor Ladies of St. Damiens, also called Order of Poor Clares, the second Franciscan Order, in Assisi, Italy, 1211 C.E. A similar story is told of Clare and an empty vessel that was filled with oil (74). See also: Chiara Augusta Lainati, *Saint Clare of Assisi*, trans. Jane Frances (Assisi: Edizioni Porziuncola, 1994), 43–44.

[66]Blaiklock and Keys, *The Little Flowers of St. Francis*, 82, cf: 81–83.

[67]Jace Weaver, "Visions of Eloh': Reflections on a Cherokee Worldview," paper presented in Ecology and Native American Worldviews conference, cosponsored by the National United Methodist Native American Center and the Center for Process Studies, 1 June 1993, 4.

[68]Ibid.

[69]Jay McDaniel, "Green Grace: Four Ways to Find God through the Earth," *Creative Transformation*, vol. 3, no. 1 (Autumn 1993), 2, cf: 1–2, 6–8.

[70]See Tissa Balasuriya, *The Eucharist and Human Liberation* (Maryknoll, N.Y.: Orbis, 1979); Monika Hellwig, *The Eucharist and the Hunger of the World* (New York: Paulist, 1976). Balasuriya wrote from Sri Lanka, and Monika Hellwig from the United States, but their emphases are similar. Balasuriya sees the mass as "a bulwark of social conservatism" (8) and urges that it be understood and celebrated in relation to personal and social liberation. For Hellwig the eucharist represents, most fundamentally, the sharing of food, which is the ritualistic and covenantal blessing through which people, in turn, can become a blessing for others (57–82). This includes responding to the many hungers of the world (83–88). Both Balasuriya and Hellwig see the power of eucharist for human liberation, but neither focuses on the rest of creation as either gift or recipient in the sacraments.

⁷¹Alexander Schmemann, *For the Life of the World: Sacraments and Orthodoxy* (New York: St. Vladimir's Seminary, 1973), esp. 11–46. Schmemann describes the liturgy of the eucharist as "the journey of the Church into the dimension of the Kingdom" (26).

⁷²Gregory Cajete, *Look to the Mountain: An Ecology of Indigenous Education* (Durango, Co.: Kivaki Press, 1994), 19–24, 74–114. See also: Larry K. Brendtro, Martin Brokenleg, and Steven Van Bockern, *Reclaiming Youth at Risk: Our Hope for the Future* (Bloomington, Ind.: National Educational Service, 1990).

⁷³Others express similar views. See, for example Rasmussen, "Returning to our Senses," 56; Douglas John Hall, *Imaging God: Dominion as Stewardship* (Grand Rapids, Mich.: William B. Eerdmans, 1986); Jurgen Moltmann, *God in Creation: An Ecological Doctrine of Creation*, trans. Margaret Kohl (London: SCM, 1985), 1–19, 215–43.

⁷⁴Thomas Merton, *Spiritual Direction and Meditation* and *What Is Contemplation?* (Wheathampstead, Hertfordshire, England: Anthony Clark Books, 1975, 1950), 95–98. With a similar view, Marjorie Hewitt Suchocki proposes that our praying can actually make a difference in what God is able to do; Suchocki, *In God's Presence: Theological Reflections on Prayer* (St. Louis, Mo.: Chalice Press, 1996).

⁷⁵This quote is a reconstruction of Chief Seattle's protest to the President of the United States when his people were removed to a reservation. Chief Seattle made a speech between 1853 and 1855 regarding the Port Elliott Treaty, but the exact words of that speech were not recorded. The words quoted here were actually written by screenwriter Ted Perry for the film "Home." See *Environmental Ethics*, 11, 196.

CHAPTER THREE

¹See, for example, Vandana Shiva, ed., *Close to Home: Women Reconnect Ecology, Health and Development* (London: Earthscan Publications, Ltd., 1994); Maria Mies and Vandana Shiva, *Ecofeminism* (Halifax, Nova Scotia: Fernwood, 1993); Carol Johnston, "Economics, Eco-Justice, and the Doctrine of God," in Dieter T. Hessel, ed., *After Nature's Revolt: Eco-Justice and Theology* (Minneapolis: Fortress, 1992), 154–170.

²See, for example: Delores S. Williams, *Sisters in the Wilderness: The Challenge of Womanist God-Talk* (Maryknoll, N.Y.: Orbis, 1993); Katie G. Cannon, *Black Womanist Ethics* (Atlanta: Scholars Press, 1988); Jacqueline Grant, *White Women's Christ and Black Women's Jesus: Feminist Christology and Womanist Response* (Atlanta: Scholars Press, 1989); Emilie M. Townes, *Womanist Justice, Womanist Hope* (Atlanta: Scholars Press, 1993). Consider, also, the writing of women in Africa, such as: Mercy Amba Oduyoye, *Hearing and Knowing: Theological Reflections on Christianity in Africa* (Maryknoll, N.Y.: Orbis, 1986).

³See, for example, Ada María Isasi-Díaz and Yolanda Tarango, *Hispanic Women: Prophetic Voice in the Church* (New York: Harper & Row, 1988); Elsa Tamez, ed., *Through Her Eyes: Women's Theology from Latin America* (Maryknoll, N.Y.: Orbis, 1989); Gloria Anzaldua, ed., *Making Face, Making Soul (Haciendo Caras): Creative and Critical Perspectives by Women of Color* (San Francisco: An Aunt Lute Foundation Book, 1990); Hyun Kyung Chung, *The Struggle to Be Sun Again* (Maryknoll, N.Y.: Orbis, 1990); Virginia Fabella and Sun Ai Park, eds., *We Dare to Dream: Doing Theology as Asian Women* (Hong Kong: Asian Women's Resource Center for Culture and Theology, 1988); Virginia and Dolorita Martinez, *The Oaxtepec Encounter: Third World Women Doing Theology* (Port Harcourt, Nigeria: Ecumenical Association of Third World Theologians, 1989); Elizabeth Tapia, *The Contribution of Philippine Christian Women to Asian Women's Theology*, (Ph. D. Diss., Claremont Graduate University, 1989; Pui Lan Kwok, *Chinese Women and Christianity*, 1860–1927 (Atlanta: Scholars Press, 1992); Young Ae Kim, *Han: From Brokenness to Wholeness: A Theoretical Analysis of Korean Women's Han and a Contextualized Healing Methodology*, (Ph. D. Diss., Claremont School of Theology, 1991).

⁴Susan Griffin, "Split Culture," in Judith Plant, ed., *Healing the Wounds: The Promise of Ecofeminism* (Toronto: Between the Lines, 1989), 11; cf: Vandana Shiva, "Development, Ecology, and Women," in *Healing the Wounds*, 80–90. Both Griffin and Shiva demonstrate ways in which development has contributed to fragmenting or homogenizing thought patterns and actions. Shiva demonstrates further that development has continued a kind of economic colonialism that

replaces local economies, ecosystems, and cultural practices with production economies that actually create more real poverty.

[5]Iris Marion Young, *Justice and the Politics of Difference* (Princeton: Princeton University, 1990), esp. 39–65; Val Plumwood, *Feminism and the Mastery of Nature* (London: Routledge, 1993), 1; cf: 24–26. Plumwood attributes these changes and resulting tremors to the meeting of "four tectonic plates of liberation—those concerned with the oppressions of gender, race, class and nature." Plumwood critiques the reductionism that sometimes appears in liberation movements, as in Marxism, when they focus on one form of domination and reduce other forms to subsidiary status (5).

[6]Jay B. McDaniel, *With Roots and Wings: Christianity in an Age of Ecology and Dialogue* (Maryknoll, N.Y.: Orbis, 1995); Carol Johnston, "Economics, Eco-Justice, and the Doctrine of God"; Charles Birch and John B. Cobb, Jr., *The Liberation of Life: From the Cell to the Community* (Cambridge: Cambridge University, 1981); David Ray Griffin, "Whitehead's Deeply Ecological Worldview," in Mary Evelyn Tucker and John A. Grim, eds., *Worldviews and Ecology* (Maryknoll, N.Y.: Orbis, 1994), 190–206.

[7]David T. Suzuki and Peter Knudtson, *Genethics: The Ethics of Engineering Life* (Cambridge, Mass.: Harvard University, 1990); Suzuki, with Barbara Hehner, *Looking at the Environment* (New York: Wiley, 1992). Val Plumwood notes that Suzuki's message meets resistance because the dominant Western traditions have so long denied these relationships and have argued for a human identity that is little connected to the earth. See Plumwood, 6.

[8]See, for example, Yaakov Jerome Garb, "Perspective or Escape? Ecofeminist Musing on Contemporary Earth Imagery," in Irene Diamond and Gloria Feman Orenstein, eds., *Reweaving the World: The Emergence of Ecofeminism* (San Francisco: Sierra Club, 1990), 264–78; Maria Mies and Vandana Shiva, 8–13. A striking example of the complex relationship is also offered by sociologist Amos H. Hawley, who argues for certain correspondences and differences between human ecology and plant and animal ecology; Hawley, *Human Ecology: A Theoretical Essay* (Chicago: University of Chicago, 1986).

[9]Others share this view; see, for example, Val Plumwood, 5–6, 174. Plumwood says: "Respect for others involves acknowledging their distinctness and difference, and not trying to reduce or assimilate them to the human sphere. We need to acknowledge difference as well as continuity to overcome dualism and to establish non-instrumentalising relationships with nature, where both connection and otherness are the basis of interaction" (174). Plumwood is concerned, for example, that major forms of deep ecology have failed to keep the balance between difference and continuity by emphasizing "identification, interconnectedness, sameness and the overcoming of separation" (ibid.).

Similar ideas are asserted by Maria Mies and Vandana Shiva, for whom diversity and interconnectedness offer a way to ground our work in the particular, especially in the struggle for subsistence, while avoiding fragmentation, atomization and cultural relativism. See Mies and Shiva, 10–13; Vandana Shiva, *Monocultures of the Mind: Perspectives on Biodiversity and Biotechnology* (London: Zed Books, 1994).

[10]Robert Jay Lifton and Richard Falk describe this human quest for relationship with the past and future, identifying it as "'the ecology of infinity.'" See Lifton and Falk, *Indefensible Weapons: The Political and Psychological Case against Nuclearism* (New York: Basic Books, 1982), 64–65.

[11]Cornel West, *Race Matters* (Boston: Beacon, 1993); cf: West, *Prophesy Deliverance: An Afro-American Revolutionary Christianity* (Philadelphia: Westminster, 1982).

[12]James Cone, *God of the Oppressed* (New York: Seabury, 1975); cf: Cone, *Black Theology and Black Power* (New York: Seabury, 1969).

[13]Elizabeth A. Johnson, *She Who Is: The Mystery of God in Feminist Theological Discourse* (New York: Crossroad, 1994), 4.

[14]Elsa Tamez, *The Bible of the Oppressed* (Maryknoll, N.Y.: Orbis, 1979).

[15]Lifton and Falk, 100–106.

[16]Ibid., 105–6. These symbols, forms, and roots are vital for human life because they have power to evoke feeling and sustained responses, rather than spasmodic and unconnected reactions.

[17]Erazim Kohák, *The Embers and the Stars: A Philosophical Inquiry into the Moral Sense of Nature* (Chicago: University of Chicago, 1984), 89–130, esp. 122–23, 127–30. Kohák sees this as a larger

philosophy than humanism, which might be understood more as a special theory of humans within the more comprehensive philosophy of personalism (122–3).

[18]Ibid., 122–3, 89–90. The emphasis on respectful relationships is akin to Paul Santmire's theological proposal of I–Thou relationships among humans and I–Ens (rather than I–It) relationships between humans and the rest of the world. See Santmire, "Healing the Protestant Mind: Beyond the Theology of Human Dominion," in *After Nature's Revolt*, 74–77. Santmire, like Kohák, argues against an overemphasis on human uniqueness and human dominion; he argues instead for a vision of humanity as *homo cooperans*. The I–Ens relationship points to "a relationship of contemplation and cooperation with nature" (75). Kohák describes the I-Thou relationship with very similar ideas.

[19]Ibid., 127–30. Kohák has radicalized the position by extending Edgar Sheffield Brightman's view of personhood, arguing that personhood is grounded in the dignity of the natural world, rather than in a being's possession of certain characteristics which other beings do not have (128–29).

[20]Brian J. Walsh, Marianne B. Karsh, and Nik Ansell, "Trees, Forestry, and the Responsiveness of Creation," *Cross Currents*, vol. 44, no. 2 (Summer 1994), 150, quoted from: Martin Buber, *I and Thou*, trans. Walter Kaufman (New York: Charles Scribner's Sons, 1970). Walsh, Karsh and Ansell develop these ideas in relation to a view of creation as active and responsive (149–62).

[21]Thomas D. Parker, "Covenant," in Donald W. Musser and Joseph L. Price, eds., *A New Handbook of Christian Theology* (Nashville: Abingdon, 1992), 106; cf: 105–7, emphases mine.

[22]David Brown, *Invitation to Theology* (Oxford: Basil Blackwell Ltd., 1989), 50.

[23]Ibid.

[24]Ibid., 53.

[25]Aracely de Rocchietti, "Women and the People of God," in Elsa Tamez, ed., *Through Her Eyes: Women's Theology from Latin America* (Maryknoll, N.Y.: Orbis, 1989), 97.

[26]Ibid., 99.

[27]Ibid., 101; cf: 96–117.

[28]David Napier, "Renewed Humanity for a Renewed Earth," unpublished paper delivered in Forum on Church and Land, Proceedings, vol. 1, (Claremont, Calif., November 1986,) 31–33.

[29]Sean McDonagh, *The Greening of the Church* (Maryknoll, N.Y.: Orbis, 1990), 129. McDonagh uses these two examples of how the covenant tradition extends to animals.

[30]Lewis S. Mudge, *The Sense of a People: Toward a Church for the Human Future* (Philadelphia: Trinity Press International, 1992), 17, emphasis original.

[31]See, for example, C. Dean Freudenberger, "The Ecology of Human Existence: Living within the Natural Order," in Allen J. Moore, ed., *Religious Education as Social Transformation* (Birmingham: Religious Education, 1989), 177–200.

[32]James A. Nash, *Loving Nature: Ecological Integrity and Christian Responsibility* (Nashville: Abingdon, in cooperation with The Churches' Center for Theology and Public Policy, 1991), 164.

[33]Ibid.; cf: Maria Harris, *Proclaim Jubilee! A Spirituality for the Twenty-First Century* (Louisville: Westminster/John Knox Press, 1996); Bruce C. Birch and Larry L. Rasmussen, *The Predicament of the Prosperous* (Philadelphia: Westminster, 1978), 87–88.

[34]Nash, 101. Nash discusses the ambiguity regarding God's motivation in the flood and the clarity of an ecological covenant that "requires caring and careful responses from humans"; he concludes that acts of environmental destruction are "a violation of the Rainbow Covenant and the ecological covenant that it symbolizes" (Ibid.; cf: 100–102).

[35]Bernhard W. Anderson, "Creation and the Noachic Covenant," in Philip N. Joranson and Ken Butigan, eds., *Cry of the Environment* (Santa Fe, N.Mex.: Bear and Co., 1984), 50–51.

[36]Padraic O'Hare, *The Enduring Covenant: The Education of Christians and the End of Antisemitism* (Valley Forge, Pa.: Trinity, 1997), 4.

[37]Ibid.

[38]Heather Ackley Bean, *Fly, Pretty Bird: An Appalachian Woman's Theodicy*, (Ph.d. Diss., Claremont Graduate University, 1996); cf: Heather Ann Ackley, "A Process of Survival: A Feminist Theodicy of Sexual Abuse," *Creative Transformation*, vol. 3, no. 1 (Autumn 1993), 3–4. See some examples of lament in Albert J. Fritsch, *Appalachia: A Meditation* (Chicago: Loyola University, 1986).

[39]Tereza Cavalcanti, "The Prophetic Ministry of Women in the Hebrew Bible," in Elsa Tainez, ed., *Through Her Eyes: Women's Theology from Latin America* (Maryknoll, N.Y.: Orbis, 1989), 131.

[40]Ibid., 132.

[41]Ibid.

[42]Ibid., 132–34.

[43]Ibid., 128.

[44]Ibid.

[45]Ibid., 131.

[46]Mary E. Hunt, "How a Garden Grows," *WATER-wheel*, vol. 10, no. 3 (Fall 1997), 1.

[47]Ivone Gebara, "Brazilian Women's Movements and Feminist Theologies," *WATER-wheel*, 3.

[48]Chieng Leh Hii, Sstory included in "STM Retreat 1994," *Berita STM*, vol. 10, no. 1 (April 1994), 2.

[49]Larry L. Rasmussen, *Moral Fragments and Moral Community: A Proposal for Church in Society* (Minneapolis: Fortress, 1993), 148–69; cf: Rasmussen, "A People of the Way, Part II," *Auburn Views*, vol. 1, no. 1 (Fall 1994), 8–11.

[50]Rasmussen, *Moral Fragments*, 163.

[51]Ibid., 164.

[52]Ibid.

[53]Ibid., 165.

[54]I changed Rasmussen's word "membership" to "participation" so as not to assume a United States democratic ideal as the primary guide for community. Ecumenical and egalitarian participation would often include ecumenical and egalitarian membership, but it might not always, as in a group of African Americans who have good reason to limit a particular group's membership to African Americans.

CHAPTER FOUR

[1]Matthew Fox, *Original Blessing: A Primer in Creation Spirituality* (Santa Fe: Bear and Co., 1983); Fox, *The Coming of the Cosmic Christ* (San Francisco: Harper and Row, 1988); Fox, *Creation Spirituality: Liberating Gifts for the Peoples of the Earth* (San Francisco: Harper, 1991).

[2]Christopher Lewis, "Setting the Scene," in Dan Cohn-Sherbok, ed., *Many Mansions: Interfaith and Religious Intolerance* (London: Bellew Publishing, 1992), ix–xv. Organizing was done by the WWF Network on Conservation and Religion; arrangements were made by the International Consultancy of Religion, Education and Culture (x). The purpose was to bring people together around ecological issues.

[3]Ibid., xi.

[4]Ibid. Lewis acknowledges that the concert—the other event held in the Cathedral building—did include "some words which would not have been suitable for Christian worship." He noted, however, that the concert was "unambiguously not worship and was seen by most people as equivalent to the many other concerts and events which take place in Canterbury, as in other cathedrals" (ibid.).

[5]Ibid., xi–xii. Lewis adds, "From there it was a short step to associate the festival with occult practices" (xii).

[6]Ibid., xii.

[7]See, for example: Cohn-Sherbok, ed., *Many Mansions*. This book is a collection of responses to the Open Letter, and it exemplifies the seriousness with which the interfaith discussions are being addressed.

[8]John B. Cobb, Jr., *Is It Too Late? A Theology of Ecology*, rev. ed. (Denton, Tex.: Environmental Ethics Books, 1995, 1972), 83–85. One example of change is the movement away from anthropocentrism in the World Council of Churches of Christ.

[9]Ibid., 85.

[10]Ibid., 11–13.

[11]See Val Plumwood, *Feminism and the Mastery of Nature* (London: Routledge, 1993), 7–18; cf: 19–68, 165–89. Val Plumwood offers an extensive philosophical version of my critique; she argues that dualistic thinking perpetuates abuse of the earth. Even ecofeminists, deep ecologists, and social ecologists frame issues dualistically in order to level their critiques and offer alternatives.

Ecological feminists identify problems with men and dominant male perspectives; social ecologists establish a hierarchy of oppressions; and deep ecologists argue for a religious or personal view of transformation without crediting other views of human oppression as relevant. The result is elitism and fragmentation.

[12]See Vandana Shiva, *Monocultures of the Mind: Perspectives on Biodiversity and Biotechnology* (London: Zed Books, 1994); Mary Evelyn Tucker and John A. Grim, eds., *Worldviews and Ecology: Religion, Philosophy, and the Environment* (Maryknoll, N.Y.: Orbis, 1994), 11–13. Shiva argues that, just as biodiversity is a key to ecological stability and survival, so the ability to think in alternatives (including local and indigenous knowledge) is a key to the survival and enhancement of life on earth. Tucker and Grim argue that *"no one religious tradition or philosophical perspective has the ideal solution to the environmental crisis"* (11). They emphasize plurality, urging people "to recognize that diversity in life forms, in sustained bioregional habitats, and in cosmological thinking is necessary" (11–12).

[13]Peter Bellwood, "The Origins of Pacific Peoples," in Max Quanchi and Ron Adams, eds., *Culture Contact in the Pacific: Essays on Contact, Encounter and Response* (Cambridge: Cambridge University, 1993), 11. Bellwood offers examples of prehistoric degradation of the land (periodic ravaging), but he argues that early people had far more positive achievements in living harmoniously with nature.

[14]Steve Charleston, "The Old Testament of Native America," in Susan Brooks Thistlethwaite and Mary Potter Engel, eds., *Lift Every Voice: Constructing Christian Theologies from the Underside* (San Franciso: Harper and Row, 1990), 49.

[15]Ibid.

[16]Ibid., 54.

[17]Ibid., 55.

[18]Ibid., 59.

[19]Ibid., 60.

[20]George E. Tinker, "Native Americans and the Land: 'The End of Living, and the Beginning of Survival,'" in *Lift Every Voice*, 141–142.

[21]Ibid., 143–150. The Native American accent on sacred relationships between Native people and their homelands is increasingly recognized. See, for example, Joseph Epes Brown, *The Spiritual Legacy of the American Indian* (New York: Crossroad, 1991); John A. Grim, "Native North American Worldviews and Ecology," in *Worldviews and Ecology*, 41–54. Grim underscores the pathos in such traditions when circles of life are broken (42–3), and their power to inspire humans to respect the earth and cultivate goodness (43–51). The traditions involve both understanding and practice, so they are embodied in narratives, rituals, and prohibitions. Note similarities with Judaism; both teach relationships with the earth via particularized narrative, ritual and practice. See the discussion of Psalms in chapter 1, and the exposition of Eric Katz in: Katz, "Judaism and the Ecological Crisis," in *Worldviews and Ecology*, 55–70.

[22]Tinker, 143.

[23]Ibid., 144, as told in and quoted from Frank Waters and Oswald White Bear Fredericks, *The Book of the Hopi* (New York: Viking, 1963), 5, 12.

[24]Tinker, 144.

[25]Ibid., 147. See also Tinker, *Missionary Conquest: The Gospel and Native American Cultural Genocide* (Minneapolis: Fortress, 1993).

[26]Tinker, "Native Americans and the Land," 151, quoted from Seathl's letter to President Franklin Pierce in Peter Nabokov, ed., *Native American Testimony* (New York: Harper and Row, 1978), 108.

[27]George E. Tinker, "Creation as Kin: An American Indian View," in Dieter T. Hessel, ed., *After Nature's Revolt: Eco-Justice and Theology* (Minneapolis: Fortress, 1992), 144–53.

[28]Ibid., 152.

[29]Ivone Gebara, "El Gemido de la Creacion y Nuestros Gemidos," *La Revista de Interpretación Bíbilica Latinoamericana*, no. 21 (1996); Vitor Westhelle, "Creation Motifs in the Search for a Vital Space: A Latin American Perspective," in *Lift Every Voice*, 128–40. Westhelle worries about people who are displaced from the land; he argues for an eschatological approach to creation, hoping that displacement can be overcome in the continuing creation.

[30]Nora Chadwick, *The Celts* (London: Penguin Books, 1991, 1971), 193–212; Ian Bradley, *The Celtic Way* (London: Darton, Longman and Todd, 1993), 8–11, 60–61. Philip Sheldrake warns against oversimplifying distinctions between Celtic and Roman traditions; both were diverse and complex. See Sheldrake, *Living Between Worlds: Place and Journey in Celtic Spirituality* (Boston: Cowley Publications, 1996), 1–8.

[31]Bradley, 6–7, 54, 75; Christopher Bamford, "Ecology and Holiness: The Heritage of Celtic Christianity," in Christopher Bamford and William Parker Marsh, eds., *Celtic Christianity: Ecology and Holiness* (Edinburgh: Floris Books, 1986, 1982), 18–21.

[32]Ibid.; David Adam, *The Cry of the Deer* (London: Triangle/SPCK, 1987), 28.

[33]Roger Sherman Loomis, *The Grail: From Celtic Myth to Christian Symbol* (London: Constable, 1992, 1963); Anna Ritchie, *Picts* (Edinburgh: HMSO, 1989), 29–37; Chadwick, 220–54, esp. 237–54 (regarding Celtic art); Chadwick, 181 (regarding the tradition of Saint Brigid); Bradley, 15; cf: 23, 35, 43, 57, 86. See also Bamford, 20–21; Robin Flower, *The Irish Tradition* (Oxford: Clarendon, 1947).

[34]Bradley, 8–11, 60–61; Chadwick, 186–219, esp. 194–95, 210–11.

[35]Bradley, 77; Esther De Waal, *A World Made Whole: Discovering the Celtic Tradition* (London: Fount/HarperCollins, 1991), 53–54.

[36]Bradley, 19–23, 76–83; De Waal, 53–64.

[37]Nelle Morton, *The Journey Is Home* (Boston: Beacon, 1985). Morton's own religious roots were Scottish Presbyterian, though she does not make explicit Celtic connections in her writing.

[38]Bamford, 12–13; DeWaal, 67–80; 117–37; Bradley, 31–50; Mary Low, *Celtic Christianity and Nature: Early Irish and Hebridean Traditions* (Edinburgh: Edinburgh University, 1996), esp. 180–90; Sheldrake, 70–82.

[39]William Parker Marsh with Christopher Bamford, "An Anthology of Celtic Christianity," in Bamford and Marsh, eds., *Celtic Christianity*, 82.

[40]Bamford, 15–16.

[41]Ibid., 92, as quoted from the Lives of the Saints from the "Book of Lismore."

[42]Bradley, 55–56; Ester De Waal, *A World Made Whole*, 81–88. De Waal says, "Bears and wolves, animals that in most cultures would be hunted down without pity, are here shown warmth and gentleness by these men of prayer, and the animals respond in kind" (82). Tales of animals and monks are found throughout the lore of the Celts; they have traditionally been prominent in inspirational literature.

[43]Marsh with Bamford, 47, 49, as quoted from Patrick's "The Deer Cry."

[44]Ibid., 48.

[45]Ibid., 122, as quoted from the writings of Columbanus.

[46]Stephen R. L. Clark, *How to Think about the Earth: Philosophical and Theological Models for Ecology* (London: Mowbray, 1993), esp. 2, 38–40. Clark does not make a strong distinction between pantheism (identifying God with the world) and pan*en*theism (understanding God as being *in* the world). He includes many views under the rubric of pantheism. See also Stephen R. L. Clark, *God's World and the Great Awakening: Limits and Renewals 3* (Oxford: Clarendon, 1991). In this book, also, Clark critiques pantheism, holistic and teleological philosophies (including Teilhard de Chardin and process philosophies), and nihilism; he advocates what he calls more traditional formulations (esp. 1–15, 169–87).

[47]Clark, *How to Think*, 2.

[48]Ibid., 10, 13, 15–18.

[49]Ibid., 2; cf: 147–62.

[50]Ibid., 162.

[51]Ibid.

[52]Colin E. Gunton, *Christ and Creation* (Grand Rapids, Mich.: William B. Eerdmans, 1992), 101.

[53]Ibid., 102; cf: 98, 102–3, 121–22.

[54]Ibid., 117–18. Gunton sees the former as more important for our humanity, but both as important to the human calling.

[55]Ibid., 100–1; cf: 11–98.

[56]Ibid., 103.

[57]Ibid., 104–5.

[58]Ibid., 124.

[59]Ibid., 126.

[60]Ibid., 108; cf: 109–16.

[61]Charlene Spretnak, "Ecofeminism: Our Roots and Flowering," in Irene Diamond and Gloria Feman Orenstein, eds., *Reweaving the World: The Emergence of Ecofeminism* (San Francisco: Sierra Club Books, 1990), 5–6. See also Judith Plant, ed., *Healing the Wounds: The Promise of Ecofeminism* (Toronto: Between the Lines, 1989).

[62]Maria Mies and Vandana Shiva, *Ecofeminism* (Halifax, Nova Scotia: Fernwood, 1993), 13–16. Mies and Shiva emphasize the particularity of incidents, issues, and groups of women who have gathered together to deal with focused issues, only to discover interconnections in their issues of feminism, militarization, genetic engineering, reproductive technology, and ecology. Ecofeminist reflection often begins with particulars and looks for connections.

[63]Riane Eisler, "The Gaia Tradition and the Partnership Future: An Ecofeminist Manifesto," in *Reweaving the World*, 23.

[64]Ibid., 23–34, esp. 26.

[65]Rosemary Radford Ruether, *Gaia and God: An Ecofeminist Theology of Earth Healing* (San Francisco: HarperSan Francisco, 1992), 4; cf: 205–74.

[66]See, for example, Sally Abbott, "The Origins of God in the Blood of the Lamb," in *Reweaving the Creation*, 35–40; Paula Gunn Allen, "The Woman I Love Is a Planet; The Planet I Love Is a Tree," ibid., 52–7; Allen, *The Sacred Hoop: Recovering the Feminine in American Indian Traditions* (Boston: Beacon, 1986); Mara Lynn Keller, "The Eleusinian Mysteries: Ancient Nature Religion of Demeter and Persephone," in *Reweaving the Creation*, 41–51; Carolyn Merchant, "Ecofemism and Feminist Theory," ibid., 100–105; Merchant, *The Death of Nature: Women, Ecology and the Scientific Revolution* (San Francisco: Harper & Row, 1980).

[67]Lee Quinby, "Ecofeminism and the Politics of Resistance" in *Reweaving the Creation*, 123; cf: 122–27. Quinby cites "ecofeminism as an example of theory and practice that has combated ecological destruction and patriarchal domination without succumbing to the totalizing impulses of masculinist politics" (123).

[68]Ibid., 124.

[69]Carolyn Merchant, "Ecofeminism and Feminist Theory," 100–5; Ynestra King, "Healing the Wounds: Feminism, Ecology, and the Nature/Culture Dualism," 109–15; Judith Plant, ed., *Healing the Wounds.*

[70]Marti Kheel, "Ecofeminism and Deep Ecology: Reflections on Identity and Difference," in *Reweaving the Creation*, 128–37, esp. 129; Michael E. Zimmerman, "Deep Ecology and Ecofeminism: The Emerging Dialogue," ibid., 138–54.

[71]Warwick Fox, *Toward a Transpersonal Ecology: Developing New Foundations for Environmentalism* (Albany, N.Y.: State University of New York, 1995, 1990), 197–247; Val Plumwood, 5, 27. As a deep ecologist, or transpersonal ecologist, Fox places more emphasis on personal consciousness, and as a feminist, Plumwood accents cultural analysis. From Plumwood's perspective, the cultural acceptance of a dominating master is related to class, race, and human species, as well as to gender. She critiques the limitation of ecofeminism when the focus is placed more narrowly on maleness; she argues that issues cannot be neatly divided into homogeneous gender orientations. Deep ecologists would agree; they differ more in emphasis. See Warwick Fox, "The Deep Ecology Ecofeminism Debate and Its Parallels," in George Sessions, ed., *Deep Ecology for the Twenty-First Century* (Boston: Shambhala, 1995), 269–89.

[72]Merchant, "Ecofeminism and Feminist Theory," 103; King, 113–15. Striking parallels exist with the deep ecologists' descriptions of relationships between people and the rest of nature (characterized by anthropocentricism and selfish personal attachment), and with the social ecologists' descriptions of problematic social and economic hierarchies among humans (Plumwood, 14–26). See also Warwick Fox, *Toward a Transpersonal Ecology*, 262–3; Murray Bookchin, *Remaking Society* (New York: Black Rose Books, 1989), 41–46. The similarities are real, even though Fox's analysis is transpersonal, and Bookchin is focused on social analysis and libertarian ethics.

[73]Rosemary Radford Ruether, *New Woman/New Earth: Sexist Ideologies and Human Liberation* (New York: Seabury, 1975); Ruether, *Sexism and God-Talk: Toward a Feminist Theology* (Boston: Bea-

con, 1983); Ruether, *Gaia and God*; Susan Griffin, *Pornography and Silence: Culture's Revenge against Nature* (New York: Harper and Row, 1981); Griffin, "Split Culture," in Judith Plant, ed., *Healing the Wounds*, 7–17; Val Plumwood, 31–68, cf: 69–88.

[74]Plumwood, *Feminism and the Mastery of Nature*, 31. Plumwood sees ecological feminism as offering an alternative and integrative project (36–40). She argues that some aspects of the environmental movement, including some aspects of ecological feminism, actually reinforce dualisms, such as male-female, or they deny difference altogether (5–11, 173–6). Plumwood's critique of dualisms, including a critique of the Hegelian and Marxist dialectical concept of history, is shared by other ecofeminists as well. See: Mies and Shiva, 5–8.

[75]King, 120.

[76]Plumwood, 21. Note that Plumwood is not speaking of stewardship but of being *with* the rest of the natural world; she believes that all of nature has agency and intentionality (5).

[77]Ibid., 185–6. Plumwood speaks of these not as private virtues, but as ways to resist destructive social patterns (186–7). She explains: "With nature, as with the human sphere, the capacity to care, to experience sympathy, understanding and sensitivity to the situation and fate of particular others is an index of our moral being" (185).

[78]Dorothee Soelle speaks eloquently about God's vulnerability in Christ; Soelle, *The Window of Vulnerability: A Political Spirituality*, trans. Linda M. Maloney (Minneapolis: Fortress, 1990), xi–xii.

[79]Larry Rasmussen, "Returning to Our Senses," in Dieter T. Hessel, ed., *After Nature's Revolt*, 47–48.

[80]Ibid., 49.

[81]Keith Ward, *Religion and Creation* (Oxford: Clarendon, 1996), 45, cf: 51–2.

[82]Ward, 53, cf: 19–24.

[83]Ward, 44. He says: "For the main Christian tradition, through the life of Jesus, God enters the world in grace, to reorient human wills, to destroy selfish desire and unite humans to the divine life. Such inner transformations are often expressed, in mystical Jewish thought, in the form of cosmic occurrences connected with the 'end of all things,' the final goal of divine creation."

[84]Jay McDaniel, "The Garden of Eden, the Fall, and Life in Christ: A Christian Approach to Ecology," in *Worldviews and Ecology*, 78–81.

[85]Ibid., 79–80. In the latter view, McDaniel explains that "life in Christ" can be "conceived as "a contribution to the very history of creation" (79). God offers new possibilities, and human beings are called into new life. By accepting lost innocence, God's limitless love, and God's healing, humans can become vehicles for God's love, nourished by a "living Christ who is our deepest center" (80).

[86]Burton L. Mack argues that this story gives rationale for diversity among the early Jesus people; Mack, *A Myth of Innocence: Mark and Christian Origins* (Philadelphia: Fortress, 1988), 197.

[87]Some of the difficulties and varieties of interpretation are noted by D. E. Nineham, *St. Mark* (Philadelphia: Westminster, 1977, 1963), 198–201; David Bruce Taylor, *Mark's Gospel as Literature and History* (London: SCM, 1992), 184–85; Hugh Anderson, *The Gospel of Mark* (London: Marshall, Morgan, and Scott, 1976), 188–92.

[88]John Paul Heil, *Jesus Walking on the Sea: Meaning and Gospel Functions of Matthew 14:22–33, Mark 6:45–52 and John 6:15b–21* (Rome: Biblical Institute, 1981), 137–38.

[89]Many commentators emphasize Jesus' healing act; the words actually describe an action by the woman, which is acknowledged by Jesus. See the emphasis on Jesus' action in Nineham, 199; Taylor, 185.

[90]Various interpretations are given for the words "as a little child," and whether the act of blessing refers to infant baptism, an issue for the early church. See Anderson, 244–47; Nineham, 267–69; John Bowman, *The Gospel of Mark: The New Christian Jewish Passover Haggadah* (Leiden: E. J. Brill, 1965), 211–22.

[91]Anabel Colman Proffitt approaches religious education with wonder at the center. She also looks to children to deepen her understandings. See Proffitt, "The Importance of Wonder in Religious Education" (Paper presented to the International Seminar on Religious Education and Values [ISREV], Banff, Canada, August 1992, publication forthcoming in *Religious Education)*; Proffitt, "Mystery, Metaphor and Religious Education: The Challenge of Teaching in a Postmodern World," (Paper presented to ISREV, Goslar, Germany, August 1994).

[92]Charles R. Foster, *Teaching in the Community of Faith* (Nashville: Abingdon, 1982); James Newton Poling, *The Abuse of Power: A Theological Problem* (Nashville: Abingdon, 1991); Herbert Anderson and Susan Johnson, *Regarding Children: A New Respect for Childhood and Families* (Louisville: Westminster/John Knox Press, 1994).

[93]Burton Mack explains how issues in Mark's community shaped his choices for content, organization and style; the Gospel is a myth of origins for the community; Mack, *A Myth of Innocence*, 9–24; cf: Mack, *The Lost Gospel: The Book of Q and Christian Origins* (San Francisco: HarperSanFrancisco, 1993).

[94]Edward C. Martin, "Deny Yourself and Live!" Sermon preached at Newport Center United Methodist Church, Corona del Mar, Calif., 14 September 1997.

CHAPTER FIVE

[1]H. Paul Santmire, "Healing the Protestant Mind: Beyond the Theology of Human Dominion," in Dieter T. Hessel, ed., *After Nature's Revolt: Eco-Justice and Theology* (Minneapolis: Augsburg Fortress, 1992), 67–68.

[2]Ibid., 68.

[3]Ibid., 67–70. Santmire's analysis is profound; the critique here is to shift the accent, not to undermine his basic argument. The ascent metaphor is also given careful critique by Margaret Miles, who presents some of the assets and limitations of traditional conceptualities; cf: Margaret R. Miles, *Practicing Christianity: Critical Perspectives for an Embodied Spirituality* (New York: Crossroad, 1990), 63–85.

[4]Martin Ravndal Hauge, *Between Sheol and Temple: Motif Structure and Function in the I-Psalms* (Sheffield, England: Sheffield Academic Press, 1995), 95–101; cf: 75–118, 131–43. Hauge sees an ideological character in the topographical references and concludes that the topography gives a religious description of human beings as being "located somewhere in a sacred landscape of temple, contrast locality, and way" (95). In such a landscape, the I of the I-Psalms moves in this "sacred landscape of Temple, Sheol, and Way" and undergoes continual transformation (96). Thus, the journey motif is described dynamically as a journey in relation to the Temple (and the presence of God represented there) and Sheol (and the contrast and negativity represented there).

[5]Claus Westermann, *Praise and Lament in the Psalms* (Atlanta: John Knox Press, 1981); Patrick D. Miller, Jr., *Interpreting the Psalms* (Philadelphia: Fortress, 1986), esp. 3–11, 48–78. Miller identifies the plea for help and praise for God's glory as "primal forms of speech and faith" (65).

[6]Walter Brueggemann, *Abiding Astonishment: Psalms, Modernity, and the Making of History* (Louisville: Westminster/John Knox Press, 1991), esp. 29–35, 54–61.

[7]Walter Brueggemann, *The Message of the Psalms: A Theological Commentary* (Minneapolis: Augsburg, 1984); Brueggemann, "Psalms and the Life of Faith: A Suggested Typology of Function," *Journal for the Study of the Old Testament* 17 (1980) 3–32.

[8]Miller, 48–78.

[9]Brueggemann, *Abiding Astonishment*, 21. Brueggemann explains that "the Psalms attest to Yahweh's sovereign faithfulness and to Israel's need to come to terms with that sovereign fidelity" (21). He adds that they "invite Israel in every generation to participate in the drama of fidelity with Yahweh" (ibid.).

[10]Ibid., 21, 21–8.

[11]Ibid., 28.

[12]Ibid., 37–46. Patrick Miller makes a similar point, adding that such approaches deny the poetry of the psalms; Miller, 3–17, 29–47.

[13]Brueggemann, *Abiding Astonishment*, 47–53.

[14]Ibid., 54–61.

[15]Thomas Merton, *Bread in the Wilderness* (Collegeville, Minn.: Liturgical Press, 1986, 1953), 36–37.

[16]Ibid., 68–72.

[17]Ibid., 58, 67. One finds similar themes in the personal asides of biblical scholars as well. See, for example: Miller, *Interpreting the Psalms* (vii). Miller expresses the conviction "that the

psalms belong both at the center of the life and worship of Christian congregations and in the midst of the personal pilgrimage that each of us makes under the shadow of the Almighty" (vii).

18Merton, 71. Merton expands that the psalms portray God as above all the heavens and yet near to those who call upon God, above all and in all (71–72).

19Ibid., 72.

20Ibid., 76; cf: 76–81. The cosmic symbolism points to God but has become fallen, along with humans, and thus longs for regeneration (78–79). Merton also speaks of typological symbolism, such as the deluge that represents God's purification of the world and destruction of sin (83; cf: 81–4).

21Ibid., 74. Merton develops this idea with a critique of pantheism and a sense that the "mute creation" is not able in itself to offer praise to its God (74, cf: 74–80).

22Miller, *Interpreting the Psalms*, 22–28. Miller recognizes that the psalms are, in some places and ways, time-bound; he also notes that their history and content are not time-bound on the whole.

23Larry Rasmussen, "Returning to Our Senses: The Theology of the Cross as a Theology for Eco-Justice," in Dieter T. Hessel, ed., *After Nature's Revolt*, 51.

24Ibid., 50–54.

25Ibid., 54.

26John Muir, "The Story of My Boyhood and Youth," in *John Muir: The Eight Wilderness Discovery Books*, intro. Terry Gifford (Seattle: The Mountaineers, 1992), 111.

27Muir, "A Thousand-Mile Walk to the Gulf," in *John Muir*, 113–83.

28Muir, "My First Summer in the Sierra" in *John Muir*, 253.

29Muir, "A Thousand-Mile Walk," 182.

30Muir, "Travels in Alaska," in *John Muir*, 752.

31Muir, as quoted by Terry Gifford, "Introduction," in *John Muir*, 19.

32Muir, "Travels in Alaska," 742.

33Muir, "The Mountains of California," in *John Muir*, 404, cf: 402–7.

34Muir, "A Thousand-Mile Walk," 171.

35Muir, "Our National Parks," in *John Muir*, 535. The sentiment here is also accented in Anabel Proffit's proposals for ministry; see "The Importance of Wonder in Educational Ministry," *Religious Education* 93, No. 1 (Winter 1998), 102–113.

36The stories and interpretations of Abraham, Sarah, and Hagar vary in Judaism, Christianity, and Islam, and interreligious dialogue is needed to understand the ancient texts as well as contemporary relations among peoples of the three religions. Some commentary on this subject can be found in: Hans Küng, *Judaism*, trans. John Bowden (London: SCM, 1992), 6–18; Küng, *Global Responsibility: In Search of a New World Ethic*, trans. John Bowden (New York: Crossroad, 1991).

37Delores S. Williams, *Sisters in the Wilderness: The Challenge of Womanist God-Talk* (Maryknoll, N.Y.: Orbis, 1993), 15–33.

38Ibid., 3–6, 34–83.

39This idea of promise laid upon promise is one which Jürgen Moltmann recognizes as contributing to the radical future orientation of the Jewish and Christian traditions. See particularly: Jürgen Moltmann, *Theology of Hope* (San Francisco: Harper & Row, 1975, 1967).

40Philip Sheldrake, *Living Between Worlds: Place and Journey in Celtic Spirituality* (Boston: Cowley Publications, 1995), 92.

41Miles, 43–45.

42*Egeria's Travels*, trans. John Wilkinson (London: S.P.C.K., 1971); Augustine, *City of God*, ed. David Knowles, trans. Henry Bettenson (Middlesex, England: Penguin, 1972).

43Miles, 48–56.

44Gwen Kennedy Neville, *Kinship and Pilgrimage: Rituals of Reunion in American Protestant Culture* (New York: Oxford University Press, 1987).

45Larry L. Rasmussen, *Moral Fragments and Moral Community: A Proposal for Church in Society* (Minneapolis: Fortress, 1993), 136–69.

[46]James W. Fowler, *Faithful Change: The Personal and Public Challenges of Postmodern Life* (Nashville: Abingdon, 1996).

[47]Marcus J. Borg, *Meeting Jesus Again for the First Time: The Historical Jesus and the Heart of Contemporary Faith* (San Francisco: HarperCollins, 1995).

[48]Mary Elizabeth Moore, "Mono Lake: Remembrance, Repentance, Regeneration," July 1996.

[49]Marjorie Hewitt Suchocki, *The Fall to Violence: Original Sin in Relational Theology* (New York: Continuum, 1994), 48; cf: 48–64.

[50]Ibid., 75–80.

[51]Ibid., 78. Truth is "God's absolute knowledge of every entity in the fullness of what it has become"; love is "God's absolute acceptance of every entity in the fullness of what it can be"; and beauty is "God's ability to integrate every entity not only with all others in a 'reconciliation of all things' within God's own nature, but also with the infinite resources of the divine harmony."

[52]Gayle Carlton Felton, Letter in "Open Forum," *Circuit Rider*, September 1997, 24.

[53]Ibid.

[54]Dorothee Soelle, *The Window of Vulnerability: A Political Spirituality*, trans. Linda M. Maloney (Minneapolis: Fortress, 1990), 24.

[55]Sheldrake, 30–2; cf: 46–57.

[56]Ibid., 58–61. Sheldrake says, "Celtic spirituality offers a tension between attachment to place (and inheritance) and ascetical detachment by means of journey" (59).

[57]J. Wilson, *Life of Columba* (Dublin: Clonmore & Reynolds, 1954), 15; as quoted in Christopher Bamford and William Parker Marsh, eds., *Celtic Christianity: Ecology and Holiness* (Edinburgh: Floris Classics, Lindisfarne Press, 1986, 1982), 26.

[58]Sheldrake, 66; cf: 58–69.

[59]Ibid., 76.

[60]Christopher Bamford, "Ecology and Holiness: The Heritage of Celtic Christianity," in Bamford and Marsh, *Celtic Christianity*, 26. Bamford elaborates on the wisdom of these wanderers and the delight with which they were received. He says, "The kings and chieftains of Europe loved these *peregrini*; they were as welcome at court as at church or in the monastery. Their habits of thought in science, music, literature, as well as theology, were to have far-reaching and profound effects" (34). He even attributes to these *peregrini* the "transformation of European culture" through monasteries, cathedrals, and universities (ibid.).

[61]E. M. Blaiklock and A. C. Keys, trans., *The Little Flowers of St. Francis: The Acts of St. Francis and his Companions* (London: Hodder and Stoughton, 1985), 81. Francis had written into the Rule "that all his brethren should serve the Lord as pilgrims and strangers in this world." The healing of leprosy is given as one example of living in this pilgrim way as Christ (81–83). See also: Salvator Butler, trans., *We Were with St. Francis* (Assisi: Edizioni Porziuncola, 1997, 1967), 92–6.

[62]Blaiklock and Keys, 35–41; 69–72.

[63]Ibid., 70–71.

[64]Nora Chadwick, *The Celts* (Harmondsworth, England: Penguin Books, 1991, 1971), 189.

[65]Virgilio Elizondo, *The Future is Mestizo: Life Where Cultures Meet* (Bloomington, Ind.: Meyer-Stone, 1988).

[66]Miles, 61.

[67]Ibid., 62.

[68]Williams, 110–11.

[69]Henry D. Thoreau, *Walden, or Life in the Woods* (Boston: Ticknor and Fields, 1854); Mary Jo Churchwell, *The Cabin on Sawmill Creek: A Western Walden* (Caldwell, Idaho: Caxton Printers, Ltd., 1997).

[70]Rebecca A. Reynolds, *Bring Me the Ocean: Nature as Teacher, Messenger, and Intermediary* (Acton, Mass.: VanderWyk and Burnham, 1995), xi.

[71]Ibid., xii.

[72]Howard Clinebell, *Ecotherapy: Healing Ourselves, Healing the Earth* (Minneapolis: Fortress, 1996), 3–9, 188–211.

[73]Theodore Roszak, Mary E. Gomes, and Allen D. Kanner, eds., *Ecopsychology: Restoring the Earth, Healing the Mind* (San Francisco: Sierra Club Books, 1995); Ellen Cole, Eve Erdman, and

Esther D. Rothblum, eds., *Wilderness Therapy for Women: The Power of Adventure* (New York: Harrington Park, 1994).

[74]Robert Greenway, "The Wilderness Effect and Ecopsychology," in Roszak, Gomes, and Kanner, eds., *Ecopsychology*, 122–35; Steven Harper, "The Way of Wilderness," in *Ecopsychology*, 183–200.

[75]Gwen Kennedy Neville, *Kinship and Pilgrimage*; Neville, *The Mother Town: Civic Ritual, Symbol, and Experience in the Borders of Scotland* (New York: Oxford University, 1994).

[76]Neville, *Kinship and Pilgrimage*, 15.

[77]Ibid., 4, 16–17.

[78]Victor Turner's basic understanding of *communitas* is described in: Victor W. Turner, *The Ritual Process: Structure and Anti-Structure* (Harmondsworth, England: Penguin Books, 1974, 1969), esp. 82, 112–18. Here Turner draws connections between *communitas* and periods of liminality, such as initiation rituals. Elsewhere Turner associates *communitas* with religious movements that diverge from the established social order, such as Saint Francis's movement of poverty (Ibid., 128–43). The Franciscan movement itself, as any instance of communitas, moved increasingly away from spontaneous communitas and toward more structure.

[79]Miles, 51.

[80]Neville, *Kinship and Pilgrimage*, 27.

[81]Committee on Outdoor Ministries, "Statement of Church Camping and Outdoor Ministries," National Council of Churches of Christ in the U.S.A., 1981, 1.

[82]See, for example: Barbara A. Babcock, ed., *The Reversible World: Symbolic Inversion in Art and Society* (Ithaca, N.Y.: Cornell University Press, 1978).

[83]Neville, *Kinship and Pilgrimage*, 25.

[84]Sheldrake, 66.

[85]Greenway, 124–28.

[86]Neville, *Kinship and Pilgrimage*, 31–32; cf: Neville, "Outdoor Worship as a Liturgical Form" in Gwen Kennedy Neville & John H. Westerhoff, III, *Learning Through Liturgy* (New York: Seabury, 1978).

[87]Neville, *Kinship and Pilgrimage*, 28–35, 41.

[88]Ibid., 106. Neville also deals with the role of sacred places in a highly mobile society (79–104).

[89]Sheldrake, 70–94.

[90]See, for example, Neville, *Kinship and Pilgrimage*, 98, 116.

[91]Robert Frost, "The Road Not Taken," in Edward Connery Lathem, ed., *The Poetry of Robert Frost: The Collected Poems, Complete and Unabridged* (New York: Henry Holt and Company, 1979, 1969), 105.

[92]Rachel Carson, *Silent Spring* (Boston: Houghton Mifflin, 1987, 1962), 277.

[93]Ibid., xiii.

[94]W. E. B. Du Bois, *The Souls of Black Folk* (New York: Bantam Books, 1989, 1903), 187.

[95]Ibid., 187–88.

[96]Robert D. Bullard, ed., *Confronting Environmental Racism: Voices from the Grassroots* (Boston: South End, 1993); Richard Hofrichter, ed., *Toxic Struggles: The Theory and Practice of Environmental Justice* (Philadelphia: New Society Publishers, 1993); Toinette M. Eugene, "Womanist Justice, Ecology, and Education: 'Now You Have Struck a Rock!,'" Paper presented in Ministers Convocation, Claremont School of Theology, November 1997; Laura Westra and Peter S. Wenz, eds., *Faces of Environmental Racism: Confronting Issues of Global Justice* (Lanham, Md.: Rowman and Littlefield Publishers, 1995).

CHAPTER SIX

[1]Paulo Freire, *Pedagogy in Process* (New York: Seabury, 1978), 20–22.

[2]Similar ideas are developed in: Mary Elizabeth Mullino Moore, "Listening to Silent Voices," *Professional Approaches for Christian Educators*, vol. 22 (December 1992), 6–9; "Ministering with Forgotten Partners," *Professional Approaches for Christian Educators*, vol. 22 (April 1993), 15–17;

"Institutional Leadership and Social Transformation," *Creative Transformation*, vol. 5, no. 2 (Winter 1996), 4–5, 20–23.

³Leonardo Boff, *Ecology and Liberation: A New Paradigm*, trans. John Cumming (Maryknoll, N.Y.: Orbis, 1995), 7. According to Boff, all beings are interrelated in natural, human, and social ecologies.

⁴Ibid., 11. See also: Jürgen Moltmann, *God in Creation: An Ecological Doctrine of Creation*, trans. Margaret Kohl (London: SCM, 1985), esp. 94–103.

⁵For full development of these issues, see: Kathy Black, *A Healing Homiletic: Preaching and Disability* (Nashville: Abingdon, 1996). Carol J. Adams and Marjorie Procter-Smith also discuss the limits of word-oriented theology in relation to animals and other beings of creation that communicate without words; Adams and Procter-Smith, "Taking Life or 'Taking on Life,'" in Carol J. Adams, ed., *Ecofeminism and the Sacred* (New York: Continuum, 1994), 301–2. Adams and Procter-Smith note that humans have less capacity to hear than many other animals; yet, they deny the subjectivity of the voiceless (303–4).

⁶George Sessions, "Ecocentrism, Wilderness, and Global Ecosystem Protection," in George Sessions, ed., *Deep Ecology for the Twenty-First Century* (Boston: Shambhala,1995),356–75.

⁷Ursula K. LeGuin, "Women/Wilderness," in Judith Plant, ed., *Healing the Wounds: The Promise of Ecofeminism* (Philadelphia: New Society, 1989), 45–7. LeGuin adds that women are often identified as "having nothing to say" (46). She describes a positive identification of women with nature, saying: "They [women] speak for themselves and for the other people, the others who have been silent, or silenced, or unheard, the animals, the trees, the rivers, the rocks. And what they say is: We are sacred" (Ibid.). Though LeGuin's statement over-idealizes women, it offers an inspiring vision for listening to wilderness.

⁸Robert D. Bullard, "Anatomy of Environmental Racism and the Environmental Justice Movement," in Bullard, ed., *Confronting Environmental Racism: Voices from the Grassroots* (Boston: South End, 1993), 22, cf: 7–39.

⁹See particularly: Robert D. Bullard, "Anatomy of Environmental Racism," in Richard Hofrichter, ed., *Toxic Struggles: The Theory and Practice of Environmental Justice* (Philadelphia: New Society, 1993), 25–35; Marianne Lavelle and Marcia A. Coyle, "Unequal Protection: The Racial Divide in Environmental Law," ibid., 136–43; Beverly Hendrix Wright and Robert D. Bullard, "The Effects of Occupational Injury, Illness, and Disease on the Health Status of Black Americans: A Review," ibid., 153–62; Cesar Chavez, "Farm Workers at Risk," ibid., 163–70; Robert D. Bullard, "Anatomy of Environmental Racism and the Environmental Justice Movement," in Bullard, ed., *Confronting Environmental Racism*, 15–39.

¹⁰Carl Anthony, "Ecopsychology and the Deconstruction of Whiteness," in Theodore Roszak, Mary E. Gomes, and Allen D. Kanner, eds., *Ecopsychology: Restoring the Earth: Healing the Mind* (San Francisco: Sierra Club, 1995), 273, cf: 263–78.

¹¹Cited in: Penny Newman, "Killing Legally with Toxic Waste: Women and the Environment in the United States," in Vandana Shiva, ed., *Close to Home: Women Reconnect Ecology, Health and Development* (London: Earthscan Publications, Ltd., 1994), 51.

¹²Cited in: Charles Lee, "Beyond Toxic Wastes and Race," in Bullard, ed., *Confronting Environmental Racism*, 49. These figures are part of an extensive report entitled *Toxic Wastes and Race*.

¹³Ibid., 48. See also: Robert D. Bullard, *Dumping in Dixie: Race, Class, and Environmental Quality* (Boulder, Col.: Westview, 1990).

¹⁴This and other examples are cited by: Dana Alston and Nicole Brown, "Global Threats to People of Color," in Bullard, ed., *Confronting Environmental Racism*, 180, cf: 179–94.

¹⁵Heather Eaton, "Rwanda: Survival of the Dominant," *Theology and Public Policy*, vol. viii, nos. 1 & 2 (Summer and Winter, 1996), 80–94.

¹⁶James Martin-Schramm, with Kirsten Hoffstedt, "Consuela's Dilemma: Ethics, Refugees, and Immigration Policy—The Case," *Theology and Public Policy*, 57–62; James A. Nash, "Consuela's Dilemma: Ethics, Refugees, and Immigration Policy—Commentary," ibid., 62–69.

¹⁷Bullard, "Anatomy of Environmental Racism and the Environmental Justice Movement," 30–31; Bullard, "Conclusion: Environmentalism with Justice," in Bullard, ed., *Confronting Environmental Racism*, 195–206; Newman, "Killing Legally with Toxic Waste" in Vandana Shiva, ed., *Close to Home*, 52–53.

[18]Mary Field Belenky, Blythe McVicker Clinchy, Nancy Rule Goldberger, & Jill Mattuck Tarule, *Women's Ways of Knowing* (New York: Basic Books, Inc., 1986).

[19]Nelle Morton, *The Journey Is Home* (Boston: Beacon Press, 1985), 54–56, 127–29.

[20]Ibid., pp. 127–30.

[21]Ibid., p. 55; cf: 128–29.

[22] Carol Gilligan, Nona Lyons, and Trudy Hanmer, eds., *Making Connections: The Relational Worlds of Adolescent Girls at Emma Willard School* (Cambridge, Mass.: Harvard University, 1989).

[23]See, for example: Tillie Olson, *Silences* (New York: Delta/Seymour Lawrence, 1978); Rita L. Irwin, *A Circle of Empowerment: Women, Education, and Leadership* (Albany, N.Y.: State University of New York, 1995); Marilyn Loden, *Feminine Leadership* (New York: Random House, 1985).

[24]Gloria Anzaldua, ed., *Making Face, Making Soul (Haciendo Caras): Creative and Critical Perspectives by Women of Color* (San Francisco: Aunt Lute Foundation, 1990); Karen Baker-Fletcher, *A Singing Something: Womanist Reflections on Anna Julia Cooper* (New York: Crossroad, 1994); Katie G. Cannon, *Black Womanist Ethics* (Atlanta: Scholars Press, 1988); Hyun Kyung Chung, *The Struggle to Be Sun Again: Introducing Asian Women's Theology* (Maryknoll, N.Y.: Orbis, 1991); Ada María Isasi-Díaz, *En la Lucha: In the Struggle: A Hispanic Women's Liberation Theology* (Minneapolis: Fortress, 1993); Virginia and Dolorita Martinez, *The Oaxtepec Encounter: Third World Women Doing Theology* (Port Harcourt, Nigeria: Ecumenical Association of Third World Theologians, 1989); Shamara Shantu Riley, "Ecology Is a Sistah's Issue Too: The Politics of Emergent Afrocentric Ecowomanism," in Carol J. Adams, ed., *Ecofeminism and the Sacred* (New York: Continuum, 1994), 191–204; Elsa Tamez, ed., *Through Her Eyes: Women's Theology from Latin America* (Maryknoll, N.Y.: Orbis, 1989); Emilie M. Townes, *Womanist Justice, Womanist Hope* (Atlanta: Scholars Press, 1993); Delores S. Williams, *Sisters in the Wilderness: The Challenge of Womanist God-Talk* (Maryknoll, N.Y.: Orbis, 1993); Williams, "Sin, Nature, and Black Women's Bodies," in Adams, ed., *Ecofeminism and the Sacred*, 24–29.

[25]Ada María Isasi-Díaz and Yolanda Tarango, *Hispanic Women: Prophetic Voice in the Church* (New York: Harper & Row, 1988); Isasi-Díaz, *En la Lucha: In the Struggle*.

[26]Baker-Fletcher, 16, cf: 13–21. Cooper imaged God as a "*Singing* Something."

[27]Rita Sebastian, "Ethnic Conflict in Sri Lanka: Its Ecological and Political Consequences," in Shiva, ed., *Close to Home*, esp. 124–27.

[28]Caroline Allison, *It's Like Holding the Key to Your Own Jail: Women in Namibia* (Geneva: World Council of Churches, 1986), 34.

[29]Riet Bons-Storm, *The Incredible Woman: Listening to Women's Silences in Pastoral Care and Counseling* (Nashville: Abingdon, 1996).

[30]Sally Sontheimer, ed., *Women and the Environment: A Reader—Crisis and Development in the Third World* (London: Earthscan, 1991); Irene Diamond, *Fertile Ground: Women, Earth, and the Limits of Control* (Boston: Beacon, 1994); Alternative Women in Development, *Women's Agenda for Action: From UN Conferences to U.S. Priorities* (Washington, D.C.: Alt-WID, 1996); The Center for Development and Population Activities, *Interfaith Reflections on Women, Poverty and Population* (Washington, D.C.: CEDPA, 1996); Carolyn Merchant, *Earthcare: Women and the Environment* (New York: Routledge, 1996).

[31]Gustavo Gutiérrez, *The God of Life* (Maryknoll, N.Y.: Orbis, 1996), xi, cf: xi–xiii.

[32]Loreta B. Ayupan and Teresita G. Oliveros, "Filipino Peasant Women in Defence of Life," in Shiva, ed., *Close to Home*, 113–20; David Pena and Joseph Gallegos, "Nature and Chicanos in Southern Colorado," in Bullard, ed., *Confronting Environmental Racism*, 141–60; Marion Moses, Farmworkers and Pesticides," ibid., 161–78.

[33]Paulo Freire, Address to Religious Education Association, November 1982; Freire's story is also recorded in: Alice Frazer Evans, Robert A. Evans, and William Bean Kennedy, *Pedagogy for the Non-Poor* (Maryknoll, N.Y.: Orbis, 1987), 227–29.

[34]Robert Coles, *The Moral Life of Children* (Boston: Atlantic Monthly, 1986), 208–9.

[35]Marian Wright Edelman, *Guide My Feet: Prayers and Meditations on Loving and Working for Children* (Boston: Beacon, 1995).

[36]Kathryn Spink, *Mother Teresa: A Complete Authorized Biography* (San Francisco: HarperSanFrancisco, 1997); Lucinda Vardey, comp., *Mother Teresa: A Simple Path* (New York: Ballantine, 1995).

[37]Some people raise these issues on behalf of children. See: Janet Phoenix, "Getting the Lead Out of the Community," in Bullard, ed., *Confronting Environmental Racism*, 77–92; Marion Moses, "Farmworkers and Pesticides," ibid., 161–78; Penny Newman, "Killing Legally with Toxic Waste," ibid., 43–59.

[38]Vandana Shiva, *Monocultures of the Mind: Perspectives on Biodiversity and Biotechnology* (London: Zed Books, 1994). Shiva shows how local knowledge systems, built upon the natural capacities of tropical forests, are replaced by dominant knowledge, based on the commercial value of timber (14–5, cf: 9–39).

[39]Ibid., 22–7. Shiva describes the process by which the chaos and weed phenomena work.

[40]Gwaganad, "Speaking for the Earth the Haida Way," in Plant, ed., *Healing the Wounds*, 76.

[41]Ibid., 77.

[42]Ibid., 78.

[43]Ibid., 79. She adds, "Without that land, I fear very much for the future of the Haida nation."

[44]Alice Miller, *For Your Own Good*, trans. Hildegarde and Hunter Hannum (New York: Farrar, Straus, Giroux, 1984, 1983).

[45]Adams and Procter-Smith, 304; quoted from: Susan B. Anthony and Ida Husted Harper, *The History of Woman Suffrage*, vol. 4 (1883–1900), reprint (New York: Arno, 1969, 1902). Adams and Procter-Smith suggest that this kind of listening is important if we are to release our control relationships with animals. This includes reflection on Christian symbolism, such as the lamb symbolism in the eucharist (295–310).

[46]Zoe Weil, "Ecofeminist Education: Adolescence, Activism, and Spirituality," in Adams, ed., *Ecofeminism and the Sacred*, 313. See also: Carol J. Adams, *The Sexual Politics of Meat: A Feminist-Vegetarian Critical Theory* (New York: Continuum, 1990).

[47]Alicia Suskin Ostriker, *Feminist Revision and the Bible* (Oxford: Blackwell, 1993), 41–2; J. Cheryl Exum, *Fragmented Women: Feminist (Sub)Versions of Biblical Narratives* (Valley Forge, Pa.: Trinity, 1993), 99.

[48]Gregory Cajete, *Look to the Mountain: An Ecology of Indigenous Education* (Durango, CO: Kivaki, 1994), 35. Cajete develops the idea that in indigenous cultures, relationship is cultivated with the land and with other people (78, cf: 78–91, 172–78). People are encouraged to be unique and diverse, but "they can realize themselves by being of service to their community, their people" (172).

[49]C. A. Bowers and David J. Flinders, *Responsive Teaching: An Ecological Approach to Classroom Patterns of Language, Culture, and Thought* (New York: Teachers College, 1990), 233–50. They argue that the common purposes identified for education—technocratic, academic-rationalist, and critical-pedagogy—"share a core set of Cartesian/liberal assumptions" and are "totally silent" about the interdependence between culture and nature (241). See also: Bowers, *Educating for an Ecologically Sustainable Culture: Rethinking Moral Education, Creativity, Intelligence, and Other Modern Orthodoxies* (Albany, N.Y.: State University of New York, 1995).

[50]See particularly: Letty Russell, *The Future of Partnership* (Philadelphia: Westminster, 1979); Russell, *Growth in Partnership* (Philadelphia: Westminster, 1981); Lynn N. Rhodes, *Co-Creating: A Feminist Vision of Ministry* (Philadelphia: Westminster, 1987).

[51]See particularly: Rosemary Radford Ruether, *New Woman New Earth* (New York: Seabury, 1975), 80–81; Ruether, "The Call of Women in the Church Today," in Virginia Ramey Mollenkott, ed., *Women of Faith in Dialogue* (New York: Crossroad, 1987), 79; Ruether, *Women-Church: The Theology and Practice of Feminist Liturgical Communities* (New York: Harper & Row, 1986).

[52]Dorceta E. Taylor, "Environmentalism and the Politics of Inclusion," in Bullard, ed., *Confronting Environmental Racism*, 53–57.

[53]Ibid., 59.

[54]Conner Bailey, Charles E. Faupel, and James H. Gundlach, "Environmental Politics in Alabama's Blackbelt," in Bullard, ed., *Confronting Environmental Racism*, 107–22.

[55]Vernice D. Miller, "Building on Our Past, Planning for Our Future: Communities of Color and the Quest for Environmental Justice," in Hofrichter, ed., *Toxic Struggles*, 128–35; Maria Mies and Vandana Shiva, *Ecofeminism* (Halifax, Nova Scotia: Fernwood, 1993).

[56]Loreta B. Ayupan and Teresita G. Oliveros, "Filipino Peasant Women in Defence of Life," in Shiva, ed., *Close to Home*, 113–20.

[57]Miller, 129–31.

[58]Sunday bulletin, Lahaina United Methodist Church, July 1994.

[59]Ibid.

[60]Ibid.

[61]See a fuller development of this case study in: Mary Elizabeth Mullino Moore, *Book of Readings: Curriculum Design and Pedagogical Theory*, unpublished book of library research and case materials, September 1994.

[62]See particularly: *A New Zealand Prayer Book: He Karakia Mihinare o Aotearoa* (Auckland: William Collins Publishers, Ltd., 1989). The prayer book is both multilingual and multicultural, representing historical liturgies from the Anglican worldwide communion (reshaped in some cases by the Church of New Zealand), and also representing liturgies and prayers from the Maori, Fijian, and Tongan peoples.

[63]The Anglican Church has organized its church structures into three parts—Maori, Pakeha (white immigrants from Europe), and Polynesian (people from other Pacific Islands). The Methodist Church has organized into two parts—a Maori division and another division—largely Pakeha and Polynesian. In both cases, the decision is based on culture and justice for all peoples rather than on the numbers. For example, the Maori population of these churches is much smaller than one-third or one-half respectively, but the need for Maori participation in the political process is addressed in the political structure.

[64]Interviews conducted August 1995 and October 1997.

[65]Lloyd Saatjian, Pastor of First United Methodist Church, Santa Barbara, California. Interview conducted 6 September 1989.

[66]Jerome W. Berryman, *Godly Play: An Imaginative Approach to Religious Education* (Minneapolis: Augsburg, 1995, 1991), 7. Berryman makes connections between Godly play and worship as well, recognizing the role of worship in stimulating symbolic activity and openness to God (17–23; 103–5). He also recognizes that worship can function as mere performance or stimulus for defensive regression. The community-based worship of the staff retreats described here seems to be more like Godly play.

[67]Gail Bernice Holland, "The Garden Project," *Connections*, September 1997, 4.

[68]Ibid., 5.

[69]Timothy Fry, *The Rule of St. Benedict in English* (Collegeville, Minn.: Liturgical Press, 1982); Columba Cary-Elwes, ed. and commentary, *Work and Prayer: The Rule of St. Benedict for Lay People*, trans. Catherine Wybourne (Tunbridge Wells, Kent: Burns and Oates, 1992).

[70]Boff, *Ecology and Liberation*, 158–62.

[71]This idea builds upon the work of Maura O'Neill. She has studied ways by which interreligious dialogue is enriched by personal sharing. She draws from research in communications and from observations of women in interreligious dialogue. See: O'Neill, *Women Speaking, Women Listening: Women in Interreligious Dialogue* (Maryknoll, N.Y.: Orbis, 1990).

[72]Boff, 158–62. See also: Gustavo Gut2iérrez, *On Job: God-Talk and the Suffering of the Innocent*, trans. Matthew J. O'Connell (Maryknoll, N.Y.: Orbis, 1993), xiii–xiv.

[73]Vardey, comp., *Mother Teresa*, 7.

[74]Mies and Shiva, 2.

[75]Ibid., 3, cf: 1–5.

[76]Peter M. Senge, *The Fifth Discipline: The Art and Practice of the Learning Organization* (New York: Currency, Doubleday, 1990), 9.

[77]Senge, 3–16. Senge sees the continuing need for the other disciplines as well, namely personal mastery, mental models, building shared vision, and team learning (6–12).

[78]Ibid., 12–13.

[79]Barbara R. Hauser, "Cinderella Can Be Tough, John Wayne Can Cry," in John Renesch, ed., *Leadership in a New Era: Visionary Approaches to the Biggest Crisis of Our Time* (San Francisco: New Leaders, 1994), 39–50.

[80]See, for example Senge, 10.

[81]Vincent Wimbush, *Paul, the Worldly Ascetic: Response to the World and Self-Understanding to I Corinthians 7* (Macon, Ga.: Mercer University, 1987); Cain Hope Felder, *Troubling Biblical Waters: Race, Class, and Family* (Maryknoll, N.Y.: Orbis, 1991); Phyllis Trible, *God and the Rhetoric of Sexuality* (Philadelphia: Fortress, 1980); Trible, *Feminist Approaches to the Bible: Symposium at the Smithsonian Institute* (Washington, D.C.: Biblical Archaeology Society, 1995); Elisabeth Schüssler Fiorenza, *Jesus: Miriam's Child, Sophia's Prophet: Critical Issues in Feminist Christology* (New York: Continuum, 1994).

[82]One collection of liturgies engaging with neglected people and traditions is: Miriam Therese Winter, *Woman Prayer Woman Song: Resources for Ritual* (New York: Crossroad, 1991).

[83]One good example of a written and artistic resource is Philip and Sally Scharper, *The Gospel in Art by the Peasants of Solentiname* (Maryknoll, N.Y.: Orbis, 1982).

[84]Such conversations have taken place in Hawaii for some time. One consequence is a public apology to the indigenous people: Richard J. Scudder, intro., *The Apology to Native Hawaiians: On Behalf of the United States for the Overthrow of the Kingdom of Hawaii* (Kapolei, Hawaii: Ka'imi Pono, 1994).

[85]Boff, 155.

[86]Marilyn Loden, *Feminine Leadership*, 84. Loden found that women leaders are often quite concerned with the empowerment of others, which is in itself a prophetic act (118).

CHAPTER SEVEN

[1]Mary Elizabeth Moore, "Called to Live in Hope," 1989.

[2]Erazim Kohák, *The Embers and the Stars: A Philosophical Inquiry into the Moral Sense of Nature* (Chicago: University of Chicago, 1984), 73; Jürgen Moltmann, *God in Creation: An Ecological Doctrine of Creation*, trans., Margaret Kohl (London: SCM, 1985), 276–96; Catharina J. M. Halkes, *New Creation: Christian Feminism and the Renewal of the Earth,* trans., Catherine Romanik (Louisville: Westminster, 1991, 1989), 83–86; Stephen R. L. Clark, *God's World and the Great Awakening: Limits and Renewals 3* (Oxford: Clarendon, 1991), 219.

[3]Larry Rasmussen, "Returning to our Senses: The Theology of the Cross as a Theology for Eco-Justice," in Dieter T. Hessel, ed., *After Nature's Revolt: Eco-Justice and Theology* (Minnesota: Fortress, 1992), 44.

[4]Maria Harris, *Proclaim Jubilee: A Spirituality for the Twenty-First Century* (Louisville: Westminster/ John Knox Press, 1996), 16. In Hebrew tradition, the Year of Jubilee is to be celebrated every fiftieth year—at the close of the 49th year, or "seven weeks of years" (Leviticus 25:8). It is a time of forgiving debts and restoring justice and harmony with people and the land. The futuristic dimensions of Jubilee are central to many interpreters. See Sharon H. Ringe, *Jesus, Liberation and the Biblical Jubilee* (Philadelphia: Fortress, 1985); Mortimer Arias, "The Jubilee: A Paradigm for Mission Today," *International Review of Mission* (Geneva: Commission on World Mission and Evangelism of the World Council of Churches, Jan. 1984), 33–48; Emilio Castro, *Your Kingdom Come* (Geneva: World Council of Churches, 1980); James A. Sanders, "From Isaiah 61 to Luke 4," in Jacob Neusner, ed., *Christianity, Judaism and Other Greco-Roman Cults: Studies for Morton Smith at Sixty*, 4 vols. (Leiden, the Netherlands: E. J. Brill, 1975).

[5]Harris, 18–19, 96–99. Harris cites many examples of Jubilee celebrations in the recent past and near future.

[6]Hong-ki Kim, "The Theology of Jubilee Examined in the Thought of John Wesley and its Application to the Reunification Movement of North and South Korea," paper presented in Oxford Institute in Methodist Theological Studies, August 1997; Hoo-Jung Lee, "Jubilee and Spirituality in John Wesley," paper presented in Oxford Institute.

[7]Salvator Butler, ed. and trans., *We Were with St. Francis* (Milan: Edizioni Porziuncola, 1997, 1976), 123–24.

[8]Jerry Mander, *In the Absence of the Sacred: The Failure of Technology and the Survival of the Indian Nations* (San Francisco: Sierra Club, 1991), 246–62. Among other sources, Mander draws extensively upon: Marshall Sahlins, *Stone Age Economics* (Chicago: Aldine-Atherton, 1972).

[9]Mander, 250–61.

[10]Eric Katz, "Judaism and the Ecological Crisis," in Mary Evelyn Tucker and John A. Grim, eds., *Worldviews and Ecology: Religion, Philosophy and the Environment* (Maryknoll, N.Y.: Orbis,

1994), 57–60. Katz cites direct texts such as Leviticus 25:23, indirect texts such as commands to give blessings over food, and several scholars who communicate that creation is God's, and human beings are to enjoy, be thankful, conserve, respect, and care for the well-being of creation. To practice Sabbath is to remember these relationships and to practice restraint in one's stewardship (59).

[11]Cited in Katz, 59.

[12]Ibid.

[13]Tilden Edwards, *Sabbath Time* (Nashville: Upper Room, 1992), 15. Edwards sees Sabbath time as offering a structure and symbol that resist the works-righteousness of contemporary culture, while still valuing work. He describes the relationship between Sabbath and ministry as dialectical, inviting people into a rhythmic movement between Sabbath qualities and actions (such as relaxation and being) and ministry qualities and actions (such as seeking and doing) (50–51). See also Denham Grierson, *Work and Leisure Revisited: Work—Blessing and Curse, Leisure—Promise and Threat* (Melbourne: Victorian Council of Christian Education, 1993).

[14]Ibid., 23.

[15]Maria Harris, *Proclaim Jubilee!*, 26–35.

[16]Edwards, 52–85. The practice of community, for Edwards, involves the whole creation, including "the pesky, poisonous, dangerous kinds of beings with whom we share this planet" (84).

[17]Ibid., 140–47; Harris, *Proclaim Jubilee!*; Harris, *Jubilee Time: Celebrating Women, Spirit, and the Advent of Age* (New York: Bantam Books, 1995). Both Edwards and Harris give specific suggestions regarding the practice of Sabbath and Jubilee in different moments of a week or year, as well as in dramatic moments of one's life, such as a fiftieth birthday or the death of a spouse.

[18]Harris, *Proclaim Jubilee!* 18–111.

[19]Ibid., 9–16.

[20]Kohák, *The Embers and the Stars*, 81.

[21]Unknown Celtic hermit, quoted in: De Waal, *A World Made Whole*, 81. De Waal's source is Peter O'Dwyer, *Celi De: Spiritual Reform in Ireland 750–900* (Dublin: Editions Tailliura, 1981), 140.

[22]Nora Chadwick, *The Celts* (London: Penguin, 1991, 1971), 218–19. Chadwick's appreciation of Celtic Christianity can also be seen in her earlier work: Chadwick, *The Age of the Saints in the Early Celtic Church* (Oxford: Oxford University, 1961). One significant contrast between the Celts and even their Roman Christian contemporaries of the fourth and fifth centuries was a contrast between their strong sense of religious location, which made them more locally minded than universally minded. See Philip Sheldrake, *Living Between Worlds: Place and Journey in Celtic Spirituality* (Cambridge: Cowley Publications, 1995), 15–16.

[23]Kwang–Shik Kim, "Harmony and Unfolding versus Analysis and Synthesis," *Yonsei Journal of Theology*, vol. 1 (1996): 97–106.

[24]Mary Elizabeth Mullino Moore "Meditation: For My Husband in the Year of His Retirement," November 1993.

[25]Ruth Ziedonis, "Portfolio for Education and Spiritual Formation in a Pluralistic World," May 1996, 51. Ruth wrote this as part of a class assignment, which included weekly meditations. The particular assignment for this week was: "Spend some time during the week meditating in the natural world. Enter the silence, and experience whatever is being communicated to you through the creation."

[26]Katz, 60; cf: Jonathan I. Helfand, "The Earth Is the Lord's: Judaism and Environmental Ethics," in Eugene C. Hargrove, ed., *Religion and Environmental Crisis* (Athens: University of Georgia, 1986), 46.

[27]Katz, 61–2.

[28]Katz, 62–7.

[29]Katz, 61; cf: 62–67. Katz's interpretation is influenced by Helfand, 45.

[30]Rasmussen, "Returning to Our Senses," 45–46. See also Douglas John Hall, *Imaging God: Dominion as Stewardship* (New York: Friendship, 1986), 98–112.

[31]Howard Clinebell, *Ecotherapy: Healing Ourselves, Healing the Earth* (Minneapolis: Fortress, 1996); Linda Filippi, "Place, Feminism, and Healing: An Ecology of Pastoral Counseling," *The*

Journal of Pastoral Care, vol. 45, no. 3 (Fall 1991), 231–42; Filippi, *Of Sweet Grapes, Wheat Berries, and Simple Meeting: Feminist Theology, Gestalt Therapy, Pastoral Counseling and The Earth*, (Ph.D. Diss., Claremont School of Theology, 1990); Peter Mwiti Rukungah, *The Cosmocentric Model of Pastoral Psychotherapy: A Contextualized Holistic Model from a Bantu African Worldview*, (Ph.D. Diss., Claremont School of Theology, 1994).

[32]Gregory Cajete, *Look to the Mountain: An Ecology of Indigenous Education* (Durango, Colo.: Kivaki, 1994), 36–41.

[33]Ibid., 41.

[34]Ibid.

[35]Steven C. Rockefeller, "The Earth Charter Process," *Earth Ethics: Evolving Values for an Earth Community*, vol. 8, nos. 2 & 3 (Winter/Spring 1997), 3–8. The Earth Charter Commission builds upon earlier work of the United Nations and the 1992 U. N. Conference on Environment and Development (UNCED), known as the Rio Earth Summit. When the Commission completes its global consultations and presents a final draft in June 1998, efforts will begin to get full support in the U.N. General Assembly.

[36]"The Earth Charter," *Earth Ethics*, 1.

[37]Ibid.

[38]Leonardo Boff, *Ecology and Liberation: A New Paradigm*, trans. John Cumming (Maryknoll, N.Y.: Orbis, 1995), 5. Boff explains further that hope is realized in these efforts. He concludes his wordplay with: "Truly, truly I say unto you: you will be truly happy because in this way you will bring happiness to my sons and daughters, and you will already be travelling along the road to the kingdom you are helping to build" (ibid.).

[39] Gustavo Gutiérrez, *On Job: God-Talk and the Suffering of the Innocent* (Maryknoll, N.Y.: Orbis, 1993), xiii, emphasis original.

[40]Ibid., 30; cf: 27–30.

[41]Robert Jay Lifton and Richard Falk, *Indefensible Weapons: The Political and Psychological Case against Nuclearism* (New York: Basic Books, 1982), 227–37. Lifton and Falk focus on this crisis because the policies and actions in that moment of history led very close to the edge of nuclear war (228–30). See also, Lifton, *Hiroshima in America: A Half Century of Denial* (New York: Avon Books, 1996).

[42]Lifton and Falk, *Indefensible Weapons*, 234. Lifton and Falk are concerned that the fear of changing frameworks prevents real transformation and contributes to disillusionment (234–38; 244–46). Among the abiding frameworks is what they call the Machiavellian world picture, which still dominates political assumptions and activities. Though they recognize that Niccolo Machiavelli's motives for writing *The Prince* in 1512 are disputed, they critique the amoral view of politics that bears his name, the view that is grounded in competition for power and ceaseless struggle for ascendancy (240; cf: 239–43).

[43]Ibid., 263; cf: 244–65.

[44]Peter F. Drucker, "The Age of Social Transformation," *The Atlantic Monthly*, Nov. 1994, 53.

[45]Ibid., 54.

[46]Ibid.

[47]Rebecca Chopp, "Anointed to Preach: Speaking of Sin in the Midst of Grace," Plenary Address, Oxford Institute in Methodist Theological Studies, July 1992, 12.

[48]Chopp, 9–13. Chopp speaks of the desire for flourishing as a critical contributor to human liberation.

[49]John Tillman Lyle, *Regenerative Design for Sustainable Development* (New York: John Wiley and Sons, Inc., 1994). Some of the early planning and rationale are communicated in this book.

[50]Taylor McConnell and June McConnell, "Cross-Cultural Ministry with Church and Family: The Final Report of a Research Project," *Religious Education*, vol. 86 (Fall 1991), 581–96; McConnell and McConnell, "Strategies of Christian Education in Multicultural Situations," *Quarterly Review*, vol. 12 (Fall 1992), 39–50.

[51]Gustavo Gutiérrez, *The God of Life*, trans. Matthew J. O'Connell (Maryknoll, N.Y.: Orbis, 1996), xi–xvii. See references, also, in chapter 6.

[52]Ivone Gebara, "Women Doing Theology in Latin America," in Elsa Tamez, ed., *Through Her Eyes: Women's Theology from Latin America* (Maryknoll, N.Y.: Orbis, 1989), 39.

[53]H. Paul Santmire, "Healing the Protestant Mind: Beyond the Theology of Human Dominion," in Hessel, ed., *After Nature's Revolt*, 74–77; cf: 57, 61–65.

[54]Katz, 56–60; Dieter Hessel, "Eco-Justice Theology after Nature's Revolt," in Hessel, ed., *After Nature's Revolt*, 12; Sean McDonagh, *The Greening of the Church* (Maryknoll, N.Y.: Orbis, 1990), esp. 119–20; McDaniel, "The Garden of Eden, the Fall, and Life in Christ: A Christian Approach to Ecology," in Tucker and Grim, eds., *Worldviews and Ecology*, 73–5; Hall, *Imaging God*, 183–205.

[55]McDaniel, 74–75. Katz argues that the Jewish theocentric tradition of dominion is particularly helpful in mediating the debates between anthropocentric (or human-centered) and non-anthropocentric approaches to the environment. To hold a theocentric view is to reject the idea that nature exists purely for human benefit, but it is also to reject "worshipful noninterference" with nature and the idea that natural beings are sacred (66–67; cf: 57). According to Katz's interpretation of theocentrism, the natural world belongs to God and needs to be cared for accordingly.

[56]Quoted in: C. A. Bowers, *Educating for an Ecologically Sustainable Culture: Rethinking Moral Education, Creativity, Intelligence, and Other Modern Orthodoxies* (Albany: State University of New York, 1995), 4. The statement was made to the General Assembly of the U.N.

[57]Bruce Babbitt, "A Sacred Covenant: Between the Flood and the Rainbow," *Earth Light*, vol. 22 (Summer 1996), 8–9, 24.

[58]Kenneth Kraft, "The Greening of Buddhist Practice," *Cross Currents*, vol. 44, no. 2 (Summer 1994), 163–79.

[59]Peter Bellwood, "The Origins of Pacific Peoples," in Max Quanchi and Ron Adams, eds., *Culture Contact in the Pacific: Essays on Contact, Encounter and Response* (Cambridge: Cambridge University, 1993), 11.

[60]Roger E. Timm, "The Ecological Fallout of Islamic Creation Theology," in Tucker and Grim, eds., *Worldviews and Ecology*, 88; cf: 83–95.

[61]Ibid., 86–7.

[62]Ibid., 88. The accent here is on the role of all creation to show signs of Allah's sovereignty and grace *and* to worship; thus, people are encouraged to respect the natural world, which both signifies and worships God (89–90).

[63]Ibid., 90–2.

[64]Thomas Merton, *New Seeds of Contemplation* (New York: New Directions Book, 1972, 1961), 29.

[65]Ibid., 30.

[66]Ibid., 32.

[67]Mary Elizabeth Moore, "Called to Live in Hope," 1989.

APPENDIX

[1]The design evolved from retreats led by the author and has been revised for use by others.

[2] For the Ignatian form of this spiritual exercise see: Ignatius of Loyola, *The Spiritual Exercises of Saint Ignatius of Loyola*, trans. W. H. Longridge (London: A. R. Mowbray & Co., Ltd., 1955, 1919), 52–60.

[3]Mary Elizabeth Mullino Moore, "Gathering Prayer," Hawaii, April 1997.

[4]Mary Elizabeth Mullino Moore, "The Gift of Time," Hawaii, April 1997.

[5]Gustavo Gutiérrez, *We Drink from Our Own Wells* (Maryknoll, N.Y.: Orbis, 1984).

[6]Mary Elizabeth Mullino Moore, "I Know a Woman, I Know a Man," February 1997.

[7]Mary Elizabeth Mullino Moore, "Five Powerful Women," February 1997.

[8]Mary Elizabeth Mullino Moore, "Be Still," Summer 1983, revised 1997.

[9]Mary Elizabeth Mullino Moore, "Passing by the Sea," Lobos Point, Monterey, California, 13 July 1979.

[10]Mary Elizabeth Mullino Moore, "Hiddenness," Massachusetts, 14 July 1979.

[11]Mary Elizabeth Mullino Moore, "A River's Journey," Yosemite, California, Summer 1983.

[12]Mary Elizabeth Mullino Moore, "Desert Mountains," New Mexico, December 1985.

[13]Mary Elizabeth Mullino Moore, "Spirit," December 1986.

[14]Mary Elizabeth Mullino Moore, "Gathering the Fabrics of My Life," Julian, California, March 1996.

[15]Howard Thurman, *With Head and Heart: The Autobiography of Howard Thurman* (New York: Harcourt Brace Jovanovich, 1979), 5.

[16]Ibid., 6.

[17]Ibid., 11–12.

[18]Ibid., 18–19.

[19]Ibid., 24.

[20]Ibid., 24–25, dedication

[21]Ibid., 8.

[22]Ibid.

[23]Ibid., 8–9.

[24]Ibid., 143.

[25]Ibid., 146.

[26]Ibid.

[27]Ibid., 146–55.

[28]Julian of Norwich, *Showings*, trans. Edmund Colledge and James Walsh (New York: Paulist, 1978), 298.

[29]Ibid., 183.

[30]Ibid., 135.

[31]Ibid., 183.

[32]Pat Sims, "Kihei Woman Puts Heart and Soul into Creation of Hawaiian Quilts," *The Maui News*, Sunday, 13 April 1997, E1.

[33]Ibid.

[34]Ibid., E1–E2.

[35]Esther De Waal, comp. and ed., *The Celtic Vision* (London: Darton, Longman & Todd, 1988), 79.

[36]Ibid., 87–88.

[37]Ibid., 95.

[38]Filimone Havili Mone, "Tin-Can Coconut," in Janet W. Parachin and Mary Elizabeth Mullino Moore, eds., *Resources for Sacred Teaching, Vol. 2* (Claremont, Calif.: Moore Multicultural Resource and Research Center, 1997), 70–1.

[39]Jim Strathdee, "Jubilee," in Jim and Jean Strathdee, *Jubilee* (Ridgecrest, Calif.: Caliche Records, 1988), 2–3; also quoted and discussed in Maria Harris, *Proclaim Jubilee!: A Spirituality for the Twenty-first Century* (Louisville: John Knox Press 1996), 94.

[40]Dan Wakefield, "Spiritual Impact: Encounters with Henri Nouwen," *Christian Century*, 19–26 March 1997, 303.

[41]Ibid.

[42]Chris Glaser, "Nouwen's Journey," *Christian Century*, 19–26 March 1997, 305.